AF893822

Kira Schumacher

Public acceptance of renewable energies – an empirical investigation across countries and technologies

PRODUKTION UND ENERGIE

Karlsruher Institut für Technologie (KIT)
Institut für Industriebetriebslehre und Industrielle Produktion
Deutsch-Französisches Institut für Umweltforschung

Band 34

Eine Übersicht aller bisher in dieser Schriftenreihe erschienenen Bände finden Sie am Ende des Buches.

Public acceptance of renewable energies – an empirical investigation across countries and technologies

by
Kira Schumacher

Scientific
Publishing

Dissertation, Karlsruher Institut für Technologie
KIT-Fakultät für Wirtschaftswissenschaften

Tag der mündlichen Prüfung: 7. Juni 2019
Erster Gutachter: Prof. Dr. Frank Schultmann
Zweiter Gutachter: Prof. Dr. Valentin Bertsch

Impressum

KIT Scientific Publishing

Karlsruher Institut für Technologie (KIT)
KIT Scientific Publishing
Straße am Forum 2
D-76131 Karlsruhe

KIT Scientific Publishing is a registered trademark
of Karlsruhe Institute of Technology.
Reprint using the book cover is not allowed.

www.ksp.kit.edu

This document – excluding the cover, pictures and graphs – is licensed under a Creative Commons Attribution-Share Alike 4.0 International License (CC BY-SA 4.0): https://creativecommons.org/licenses/by-sa/4.0/deed.en

The cover page is licensed under a Creative Commons Attribution-No Derivatives 4.0 International License (CC BY-ND 4.0): https://creativecommons.org/licenses/by-nd/4.0/deed.en

Print on Demand 2019 – Gedruckt auf FSC-zertifiziertem Papier

ISSN 2194-2404
ISBN 978-3-7315-0948-6
DOI 10.5445/KSP/1000097148

Public acceptance of renewable energies – an empirical investigation across countries and technologies

zur Erlangung des akademischen Grades eines

Doktors der Wirtschaftswissenschaften
(Dr. rer. pol.)

von der KIT-Fakultät für Wirtschaftswissenschaften
des Karlsruher Instituts für Technologie (KIT)

genehmigte
Dissertation

von
Kira Schumacher
M.A., Dipl. Betriebswirtin (FH)

Tag der mündlichen Prüfung: 7. Juni 2019
Erster Gutachter: Prof. Dr. Frank Schultmann
Zweiter Gutachter: Prof. Dr. Valentin Bertsch

“If men define situations as real, they are real in their consequences.”

Thomas Theorem by Thomas and Swaine Thomas (1928)

Abstract

In the context of the so-called "energy transition", national energy systems are currently undergoing fundamental structural changes. This involves a rapid development of renewable energies, which means that new facilities are built or existing ones expanded. Moreover, the transformation of predominantly large-scale, mainly centralized electricity systems into smaller, at least partly decentralized generation units changes the geographic energy landscape and increases the number of contact points between society and plants. Consequently, it is more important than ever that new energy projects meet the acceptance of the general public. Otherwise, citizens' initiatives are capable to delay or stop projects which in consequence leads to cost increase or the collapse of the whole project.

Against this background, public acceptance of renewable energy innovations has become an important topic in energy research. Many studies address public acceptance through a case-based empirical lens with rather specific conclusions for individual technologies and in a given context. Comparison between studies is often difficult because of non-representative data and differences in the research designs. This compromises the generalizability of results and therefore the ability to provide meaningful guidance for the practice.

This thesis goes beyond existing studies by applying the same rigorous research design in four countries, which allows for comparative testing of various hypotheses from the research field across countries and technologies. The comparison adds significant explanatory power to the results, which can be assessed regarding their generalizability for other contexts. Based on this, recommendations for policy makers and project developers can be derived, which are applicable in different countries, including best practices and lessons learned which can be transferred from one country to another.

A noteworthy contribution of this thesis to the research field consists in the quality and comprehensiveness of the collected data. Applying a mixed-methods research design, roughly 100 semi-structured interviews with bioenergy experts, three representative questionnaire-based surveys with more than 3,300 participants and 6 stakeholder workshops were carried out in Chile, France, Germany, and Switzerland. The three surveys cover around 70 variables on personal attitudes, beliefs, perceptions, and evaluations with respect to some of the most prominently discussed hypotheses in the area of acceptance research on renewable energy innovations. The hypotheses refer to acceptance levels, dispositions to act, acceptance dimensions, spatial proximity, previous experiences with renewable energies, explanatory factors for public acceptance, as well as the link between public acceptance, community energy, and energy autonomy. Moreover, the surveys focus on those renewable energy technologies which potentially evoke interactions with the general public due to their high degree of decentralization and potential local impacts which include large-scale ground-installed photovoltaic (PV) systems, small-scale PV rooftop systems, onshore wind energy plants, and bioenergy systems.

The major findings of the thesis include:

- General acceptance of energy projects is higher than acceptance of plants in the neighborhood.
- Disposition to act towards local renewable energy plants depends on the quality of former experience with the respective technology. Positive experience is likely to result in higher support, and negative experience in higher resistance.
- Public acceptance increases with larger distance of the plant to the respondent's home. However, neither is distance a remedy for lacking public acceptance nor is proximity an exclusion criterion. Instead, contextual factors and (expected) local impacts of the technology moderate the role of proximity.
- Respondents without previous experience with renewable energy plants in their vicinity tend to overestimate local impacts and therefore desire a larger distance to their home.

- Perceived benefits are by far the most important predictors for public acceptance of bioenergy plants.
- Predictors for public acceptance vary according to the acceptance dimension. For concrete projects rather abstract attitudes of general support are superposed by factors, which directly exert an impact on the community level, such as perceived costs or odor emissions.

Regarding the comparison between the countries, results show significant differences in preferences for the various technologies as well as in both acceptance levels and dispositions to act. However, also similarities between the countries are revealed, such as the wish to get more deeply involved in the energy turnaround, including planning and decision-making with respect to local plants. It is concluded that the political and cultural context in which renewable energy projects are embedded are important determinants for public acceptance. Hence, policy makers and project developers need to include considerations on public acceptance into the design of policy frameworks and projects to anticipate public conflicts and create a truly sustainable energy system. Such a system also needs to account for social concerns, not just as minor side effect, but as important success factor of renewable energy projects.

Acknowledgements

I would like to express my sincere gratitude towards all persons, who have supported me in the process of writing this thesis. Especially, I thank my supervisor Prof. Dr. Frank Schultmann for his constant guidance, feedback, and confidence. Moreover, I thank Dr. Carsten Sauer and Anna Bruk for their scientific support as well as Caspar Groß, Christoph Semperowitsch, Wojciech Kata, Natalie Lanzrath, and Felix Krones for supporting my work as research assistants. I also would like to thank the interviewers, the interviewees, and participants of the surveys.

I gratefully acknowledge the funding of this work by two major research projects: the project "OUI Biomasse - Innovations for a Sustainable Biomass Utilization in the Upper Rhine Region", financed by the European Regional Development Fund (ERDF) in collaboration with the cooperation program INTERREG "Oberrhein – Rhin Supérieur" and other national co-financiers, and the project "SeMoBioEnergy" (Semi-Mobile Bioenergy from Agricultural and Forest Residues in Chile and Beyond) financed by the German Federal Ministry of Education and Research (BMBF). Moreover, I am grateful to Dr. Alex Berg from Universidad de Concepción (UdeC) and Prof. Dr. Patricio Carey from Universidad Austral de Chile (UACH) for hosting me for three months during my research stay in Chile, which was funded by the Karlsruhe House of Young Scientists (KHYS).

I sincerely thank all my colleagues at the Institute of Industrial Production (IIP) at the Karlsruhe Institute of Technology (KIT) for their support, constructive discussions, feedback, and motivation. Especially, I thank those, who have supported me editing this thesis: Dr. Sonja Babrowski, Dr. Simon Glöser-Chahoud, Dr. Marina Maier, Hanns-Maximilian Schmidt, Dr. Natalie Schmidt, Sabrina Ried, Dr. Rebekka Volk, and Tobias Zimmer. Personally, I thank my friends and family, who have supported me in various ways over the last years. Most of all I thank my parents for their constant support and love.

Karlsruhe, April 2019 *Kira Schumacher*

Contents

List of Figures

List of Tables

List of Abbreviations and Symbols

Abbreviations

EEG	Erneuerbare-Energien-Gesetz (German renewable energy law)
CHP	Combined heat and power
FIT	Feed-in tariff
GIS	Geographical Information System
H	Hypothesis
HDI	Human Development Index
km/ km^2	Kilometer/ square kilometer
kW_{el}	Kilowatt electric
MW	Megawatt
NIMBY	Not In My Backyard
NGO	Non-governmental organization
PV	Photovoltaic
pp	Percentage point
RE	Renewable energy
RES	Renewable energy source
URR	Upper Rhine region

Statistical Symbols and Abbreviations

adjusted R^2	Adjusted coefficient of determination
ANOVA	Analysis of variance
α	(1) Cronbach's index of internal consistency
	(2) Significance level (the probability of making a type I error)
B	Unstandardized regression coefficient
β	Standardized regression coefficient
d	Cohen's measure of effect size for comparing two sample means
df	Degrees of freedom
F	F-Statistic
M	Arithmetic mean
n	Number of observations
η^2	Eta-squared (measure of strength of relationship)
p	Error probability
R^2	Coefficient of determination
r_p	Pearson correlation coefficient
SD	Standard deviation
VIF	Variance inflation factor
Δ	Increment of change

1 Introduction

1.1 Problem Description

Energy is the lifeblood of our modern society. The access to sustainable, reliable, and affordable energy is directly connected to the well-being of the society, the economy, and the industry (UN, 2019). At the same time, the energy sector accounts for 25% of global greenhouse gas emissions (Statista, 2014), which are responsible for anthropogenic climate change. International efforts to mitigate climate change have led to a social discourse on the future direction of energy policy. It is generally agreed that the current way energy is generated and consumed is not sustainable. In addition, the disaster in Fukushima once again showed that nuclear power bears many risks, too. (UBA, 2015) In consequence, many countries have decided to fundamentally transform their energy systems towards renewable energies.

Energy policy is an emotionally charged field as it touches upon many issues which are important for the whole society, such as the cost of energy, the aesthetics of the landscape, the protection of biodiversity and the climate, to name only a few. Consequently, it is vital that energy projects meet the acceptance of the general public. Otherwise, citizens' initiatives are capable to delay or stop projects which in consequence leads to cost increases or the collapse of the whole project. For energy policy, this means that the traditional "energy policy target triangle", which forms the balance between the goals of economic efficiency, environmental and climate compatibility, as well as security of supply, must be extended by the dimension of public acceptance (cf. Figure 1-1). Hence, public acceptance has become the "social license to operate" and a necessary precondition for energy policy to achieve the other three targets. (Hauff et al., 2011)

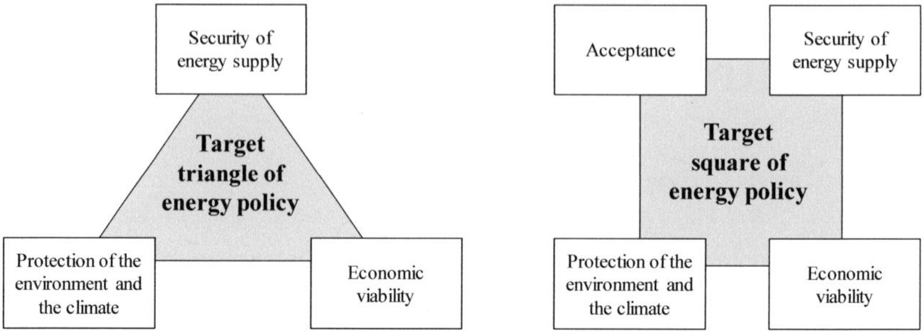

Figure 1-1: Change of the target geometry of energy policy from triangle to square (Hauff et al., 2011)

In the context of the so-called "energy transition", national energy systems are currently undergoing fundamental structural changes. In particular, this involves a rapid development of renewable energies, which means that new facilities are built or existing ones expanded. Moreover, the transformation from predominantly large-scale, mainly centralized electricity systems into smaller, mostly decentralized generation units changes the geographic energy landscape (Fast, 2013; McKenna, 2018; Wolsink, 2018a) and increases the number of contact points between society and plants for energy generation (Kortsch et al., 2015).

Most of the renewable energy technologies are in principle hardly controversial, but if planning and construction take concrete shape, conflicting goals become visible. Hence, despite the wide support of renewable energies by the general public, local renewable energy projects frequently lack social acceptance and must contend with opposition (Hauff et al., 2011; Wüstenhagen et al., 2007; Zoellner et al., 2008). The reasons of opposition are mostly rooted in perceived injustice regarding the decision-making process and the sharing of burdens and benefits (Rau et al., 2012; Soland et al., 2013). Local residents in particular have to cope with changes in their living environment because of direct impacts induced by the renewable energy plant (Kortsch et al., 2015).

However, renewable energy projects also offer opportunities for both the society as a whole and for local communities. Smartly designed projects can create various benefits through the stimulation of the local economy, such as the creation of jobs in rural areas (Jenssen et al., 2014; Wüste and Schmuck, 2012). Moreover, decentralization provides the population with opportunities to actively shape the transition to renewable energy concepts tailored to the local needs (Hildebrand et al., 2012; Kortsch et al., 2015). There is also growing public support and engagement for renewable energies, especially in the context of community energy. In these projects, local stakeholders are involved along the value chain and stand to reap the benefits (Walker, 2008; Walker et al., 2010). Precisely this direct engagement can be a key influencing factor for the level of public acceptance (Aitken, 2010) and is arguably equally if not even more important than the technologies themselves.

Finally, the importance of public acceptance of renewable energy as key factor for the success of the energy transition has been reflected by a growing body of scientific literature (Upham et al., 2015). Existing studies predominantly examine public acceptance of specific actors towards a concrete renewable energy project in a single country, hence, adopting a case-based point of view. Comparison between studies is often difficult because of non-representative data on the one hand, and differences in research designs (such as measurement instruments, sample characteristics, and timeframes) on the other. This compromises the generalizability of results and therefore the ability to provide meaningful guidance for policymakers and project developers. Several authors have highlighted the lack of comparative research (cf. e.g., Aas et al., 2014; Sovacool, 2014), as well as the missing implementation of findings from research into the practice (Rand and Hoen, 2017; Sovacool, 2014; Wolsink, 2018b).

1.2 Aim and Approach

The aim of this work is to provide meaningful insights into the formation of public acceptance of renewable energies. From a methods perspective, this work goes beyond existing studies by comparing different countries, technologies, and acceptance dimensions. The conduction of research in several countries is motivated by the fact that very few studies have analyzed public acceptance of renewable energies in different national contexts in a systematic way (see section 2.1.2). Thus, it is still not clear whether public acceptance is shared across countries and institutional settings or a country or project specific phenomena. A systematic comparison of public acceptance phenomena between countries, technologies, and acceptance dimensions allows to draw more generalizable conclusions than could be obtained from an investigation of single case studies (cf. Eisenhardt and Graebner, 2007). Moreover, cross-country comparisons provide insights into practices, which positively influence public acceptance of renewable energies, and which might potentially be transferred to other countries (c.f. Mignon and Rüdinger, 2016). Hence, the adoption of a comparative approach generates important information for project developers and policymakers to anticipate public conflicts and create a truly sustainable energy system which also accounts for social concerns.

This work adopts a cross-national research approach to comparatively test several hypotheses (H) from the public acceptance literature are comparatively tested across countries and technologies. The author decided to focus on some of the most often discussed topics of social acceptance, including acceptance levels and dispositions to act (cf. e.g., Bertsch et al., 2016; Schweizer-Ries, 2008; Zoellner et al., 2008), public acceptance regarding different acceptance dimensions, namely socio-political and community acceptance (cf. e.g., Petrova, 2016; Sonnberger and Ruddat, 2017; Wüstenhagen et al., 2007), the relevance of spatial proximity of renewable energy plants to residential areas (cf. e.g., Bertsch et al., 2016; Betakova et al., 2015; Kontogianni et al., 2014) and the role of previous experiences with renewable energy projects for public acceptance (cf. e.g., Kontogianni et al., 2014; Warren et al., 2005).

In addition to testing the hypotheses on the acceptance of renewable energies, two focus topics are investigated using the same comparative, cross-country research approach as described above.

Focus topic "Bioenergy": In this focus topic, factors influencing public acceptance of one specific renewable energy technology, namely bioenergy, are exemplarily explored in detail. The public acceptance of bioenergy plants is particularly interesting due to strong differences in political frameworks in the four countries and comparatively low acceptance levels for the technology (cf. e.g., Soland et al., 2013; Schumacher and Schultmann, 2017). In this thesis, case study 1 (section 4.3) and case study 3 (section 4.5) have dedicated sections to investigate public acceptance of bioenergy in more detail. Case study 2 (section 4.4) focuses exclusively on community public acceptance of biogas plants in the French, German, and Swiss Upper Rhine region (URR).

Focus topic "Community Energy and Energy Autonomy": This work further complements the existing literature by examining the public acceptance of renewable energies, community energy, and energy autonomy in conjunction and in different national contexts. So far, scholars have mostly focused on explaining the phenomena of non-acceptance or rejection, without a deeper analysis of the different facets of positive acceptance and support (Batel et al., 2016; for a review, see Fast, 2013). This lacking attention on support, risks neglecting the active engagement of the public for the transition towards renewable energy. Therefore, the relation between public acceptance, community energy and energy autonomy, if any, is assessed in more detail in case study 1.

1.3 Structure

After this introduction into the topic and the presentation of the aims and the approach of this thesis (section 1), the remainder of this work is structured as follows:

Section 2 provides an introduction to the theoretical background of social acceptance research of renewable energy innovations. The purpose of this section is to define the scope of this thesis and show how it contributes to close persisting research gaps in the literature. To this end, important underlying theoretical concepts from social acceptance research are presented (cf. section 2.1), the state of the art of the research field is described (cf. section 2.2), and relevant empirical studies on public acceptance (cf. section 2.3) as well as explanatory factors for public acceptance (cf. section 2.4) are reviewed.

Section 3 presents the methodological approach of this thesis. Section 3.1 highlights the steps of the mixed-methods research design and describes the advantages of combining quantitative and qualitative methods. Then the most important steps of the research approach are described in detail, including the conduction of expert interviews, the questionnaire development, the statistical methods applied, and the validation of results. Section 3.2 then adds methodological considerations regarding the selection of countries, renewable energy technologies, and hypotheses on public acceptance for the empirical case studies.

Section 4 presents the three empirical, survey-based case studies. Firstly, section 4.1 provides a brief overview of the three cases with regard to their geographical scope, the covered technologies and dimensions of acceptance, as well as the characteristics of the samples. Section 4.2 provides a more detailed description of the study regions including their geography, their current state of development of renewable energies and relevant political frameworks for renewable energies. Sections 4.3, 4.4, and 4.5 present each of the three case studies in detail including the materials and methods used as well as the obtained results. The survey results are presented along the raised hypotheses and tested across countries and renewable energy technologies. Section 4.6 closes with a discussion of the results of the case studies and a comparison of findings with related work from the literature.

Section 5 summarizes and concludes the findings of this thesis and offers recommendations for project developers and policy makers. Section 5.1 starts with a summary of findings of the empirical case studies of this thesis and the literature for each of the 13 hypotheses and discusses them with respect to their generalizability for other contexts. Section 5.2 translates the findings into recommendations for action to effectively inform the policy debate and to create practical knowledge for project developers. Section 5.3 concludes with a summary of the main contributions of this thesis to the research field.

Subsequently, section 6 discusses the transferability of results, critically reflects the presented approach, and derives suggestions for future research. Section 6.1 provides a critical discussion of limitations of this thesis regarding the study scope, the used theoretical concepts, challenges of cross-national studies, data collection, as well as inherent characteristics of opinion surveys. Then section 6.2 discusses in how far the developed research approach, the measurement instruments, and gained insights from this thesis are transferable to other studies and contexts. Section 6.3 proposes avenues for future research to improve existing research practices and add depth and relevance to the wider research field of social acceptance of renewable energy innovations.

2 Theoretical Background of Social Acceptance Research on Renewable Energy Innovations

Due to the increasing recognition of social acceptance as a key success factor for the transition to renewable energies (Hauff et al., 2011), a growing body of literature is dedicated to investigate levels of public acceptance as well as the associated drivers. Scholars look at social acceptance phenomena from various disciplinary angles, using multiple methods and theoretical frameworks (Upham et al., 2015). In particular, sociology, environmental–psychology, political science, geography, economics, and innovation studies have contributed to this field of research. The following section provides an overview of the theoretical foundations of the research field of social acceptance of renewable energy innovations. The purpose of this section is

(i) to define some important concepts
(ii) to describe the scope of the empirical investigations conducted in this thesis and
(iii) to show the gap in the current literature and demonstrate how this thesis corresponds to the identified research needs.

Section 2.1 starts with an introduction of important theoretical concepts from social acceptance and based on this introduces the scope of this thesis. Section 2.2 subsequently reviews the state of the art in social acceptance research and highlights the need for more comprehensive and comparative research. After the overview of the literature on social acceptance in general, the specific field of public acceptance is described in more detail. Section 2.3 provides a brief review of empirical studies on public acceptance and presents the contribution of this thesis to the body of literature. Section 2.4 analyzes the literature on explanatory variables for public acceptance and discusses relevant factors for public acceptance of bioenergy.

2.1 Concepts and Definitions[1]

Due to the abstract nature of social acceptance, there are various theoretical concepts and definitions suggested by the literature (Busse and Siebert, 2018). To undertake investigations of this subject, it is therefore vitally important to define what is meant by acceptance in this thesis. Therefore, this section presents the following three relevant and highly cited concepts from the social acceptance literature according to which the scope of this thesis is precisely defined:

(i) the acceptance dimension
(ii) the acceptance subject, object, and context, as well as
(iii) the used definition for the term acceptance.

(i) Acceptance dimension: A highly cited paper by Wüstenhagen et al. (2007) introduced a concept distinguishing between three dimensions of social acceptance, which are socio-political, community, and market acceptance. Whereas socio-political acceptance deals with the acceptance of institutional settings of renewable energies by key stakeholders as well as the acceptance of renewable energies by the larger public; community acceptance refers to specific renewable energy plants and the reactions of the local stakeholders which are directly affected, such as residents and local authorities. Market acceptance refers to the diffusion of renewable energy technologies within the market and the extent to which its participants, such as consumers and companies, accept them (cf. also Sovacool and Lakshmi Ratan, 2012; Wolsink, 2017b). Wolsink (2018a) has further supplemented the model of Wüstenhagen et al. (2007) by emphasizing the non-hierarchical and multi-level character of the three social acceptance dimensions. He suggests that the socio-political dimension should be seen as the basis for social acceptance as the conditions set in this dimension (e.g., legislation for energy markets and local actors) can be seen as the "rules of the game" and strongly affect the acceptance processes in the other two dimensions (Wolsink, 2018a, p. 289). Moreover,

[1] Parts of this section have previously been published in Schumacher et al. (2019b) and Schumacher and Schultmann (2017).

he introduces the prosumer as additional dimension to the concept where community and market-acceptance overlap. The concept is graphically displayed by Figure 2-1.

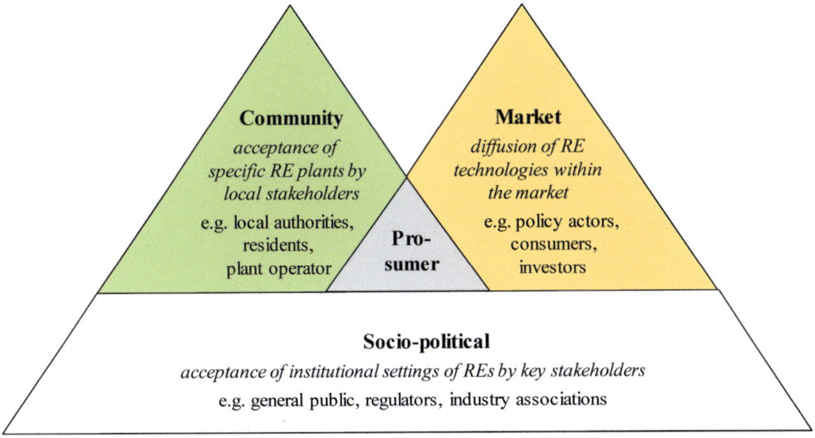

Figure 2-1: Dimensions of social acceptance (own depiction based on Wolsink, 2018a; Wüstenhagen et al., 2007)

In each of the three dimensions, different stakeholder groups are present and influence social acceptance of renewable energies through their interplay. Table 2-1 provides examples of stakeholders participating in each of the three interdependent and non-hierarchical dimensions (cf. Wolsink, 2017b, 2018a; Wüstenhagen et al., 2007).

Table 2-1: Examples of stakeholder roles by social acceptance dimension (own depiction based on Fast, 2013; Upham et al., 2015)

Stakeholder	Acceptance dimension		
	Socio-political	Community	Market
Public	Citizen, general public	Resident	Consumer, prosumer, investor
Government	Regulator, policy actor, legislative authority	Local authority	Regulator, policy actor, taxing and subsidizing authorities
Companies	Industry association, lobbying group, focal company	Focal company, investor, operator, supplier	Producer, distributor, investor, network operator, intra-firm adopter
Other	Non-governmental organizations (NGO), media	Local interest groups, local clubs, local media	Consumer interest groups

(ii) Acceptance subject, object, and context: According to Lucke (1995), it is further necessary to carefully define what is accepted (or not), by whom, in which society, situation, and at which point in time, due to which reasons and motives. Lucke (1995) highlights the relational and transitive nature of acceptance, claiming that acceptance is highly dependent on the subject, the object, and the context of acceptance. The acceptance *subject*, i.e. the person, institution or company supposed to accept, may assume different roles (cf. Table 2-1). With regard to public acceptance, a person can evaluate renewable energy technologies from a general point of view, e.g., as a citizen, from a specific point of view, e.g., as a resident living next to a renewable energy plant, or from the market perspective, e.g., as a consumer. The *object* of acceptance, i.e. the policy, technology, infrastructure to be accepted by the acceptance subject, can range from renewable energy projects with their specific characteristics (e.g., a community owned wind park), framework conditions for renewable energies (e.g., subsidies or tariffs), or renewable energy related infrastructure (e.g., high voltage power lines). The acceptance *context* varies according to the acceptance situation. For example, the national

context is supposed to be a relevant factor, even though few studies have addressed this issue in depth so far (Sovacool, 2014).

(iii) Acceptance definition: An often cited concept by Schweizer-Ries (2008) defines the term "acceptance" in the context of renewable energies by an attitudinal- and an action-level. More precisely, the definition differentiates between the following four levels of (non)-acceptance: passive acceptance, called "approval", and active acceptance, called "support", passive non-acceptance, called "rejection", and active non-acceptance, called "resistance" (cf. also Rau et al., 2012). Hence, according to this concept, a positive appraisal of the object is a necessary condition for acceptance. Figure 2-2 displays the concept graphically.

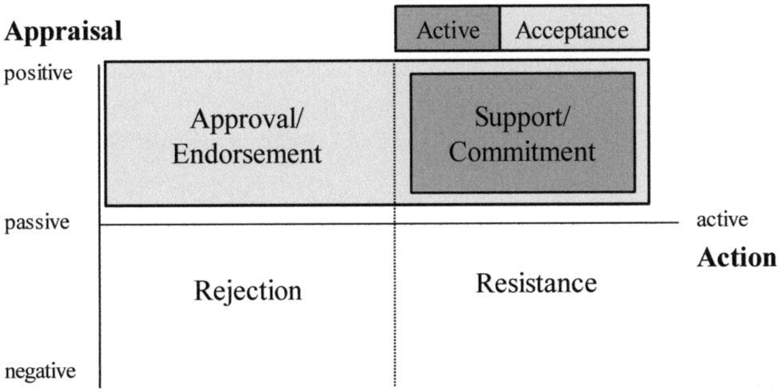

Figure 2-2: Four levels of public acceptance (Rau et al., 2012; Schweizer-Ries, 2008)

Based on the three afore presented theoretical concepts, the scope of this thesis is defined as follows: Based on representative population data (subjects), public acceptance of a set of renewable energy technologies (objects) in the URR and Chile (contexts) are examined. Public acceptance is investigated with regard to the socio-political and the community dimension requesting attitudes towards different renewable energy technologies in general and towards specific renewable energy plants in the neighborhood. Concerning the study scope, the results of this thesis are limited to the point of view of the public. It is important to acknowledge, that the market dimension is omitted in this thesis as because it requires a distinct point of view: Whereas the socio-political and community dimension mainly address public attitudes towards renewable energy technologies and local renewable energy plants, the market dimension focusses on preferences for renewable energy-related products (e.g., green energy tariffs, renewable energy technologies on the household level).

2.2 State of the Art of Social Acceptance Research

Social acceptance of renewable energies has been approached from various disciplinary angles and theoretical backgrounds. As the research field matures, an increasing number of publications offer overarching conceptual frameworks (Devine-Wright et al., 2017; Sovacool and Lakshmi Ratan, 2012; Wüstenhagen et al., 2007), consolidating different viewpoints (Batel et al., 2013), reviewing existing literature (Busse and Siebert, 2018; Fast, 2013; Gaede and Rowlands, 2018; Sovacool, 2014; Upham et al., 2015), proposing new approaches (Dermont et al., 2017), and questioning the assumptions of the research field (Aitken, 2010; Wolsink, 2017b, 2018a, 2018b).

Several recent review articles aim at consolidating topics, concepts, and theories by proposing frameworks and definitions or highlighting avenues for future research. For example, Fast (2013) reviews the research field to identify trends in the literature with regard to the coverage of acceptance dimensions, roles of the public, and geographical concepts. Sovacool (2014) identifies future research needs and proposes research methods, topics, and questions to deepen the contribution of social sciences to energy research. Upham (2015) proposes a "framework for thinking about energy technology 'acceptance'" (p. 100), and Busse and Siebert (2018) reveal the lack of a common understanding of the term "acceptance" and the unclear theoretical foundations of the research field. Another recent review by Gaede and Rowlands (2018) identified basic trends and characteristics in the literature by mapping research fronts to their respective intellectual roots. The number of reviews and their findings demonstrate that there is still a lot of dissent regarding the conceptualization of social acceptance. A good example is Wolsink's (2018a) critique of the review article by Gaede and Rowlands (2018) concerning its methodology and assumptions and the subsequent response by Gaede and Rowlands (2019). To sum up, the research field is interdisciplinary, growing, and consolidating in a dynamic manner. However, many scholars critique the lacking *comprehensiveness* and *comparability* of the empirical evidence obtained so far on social acceptance (cf. e.g., Batel et al., 2013; Sovacool, 2014).

With respect to *comprehensiveness*, most studies limit their scope to only one specific dimension of social acceptance (Sovacool, 2014), even though there is consensus that social acceptance is a multidimensional construct (Wolsink, 2018a; Wüstenhagen et al., 2007). The often-voiced critique concerns the lack of studies which combine socio-political, community, and market acceptance or investigate the interrelations between them (Devine-Wright et al., 2017; Sovacool, 2014; Wolsink, 2018a). Another issue raised with regard to comprehensiveness concerns the initial focus on local opposition rather than exploring the many facets of acceptance and support (Dermont et al., 2017; Devine-Wright and Batel, 2017). Scholars argue that non-opposition does not equal acceptance (Rau et al., 2012) and that a sustainable transition to renewable energies cannot be imposed by top down decisions but requires positive appraisal as well as active involvement of the population (Batel et al., 2013). For example, the various forms of community energy demonstrate much more than non-opposition, but rather an approval and active support of local (renewable) energy.

Regarding *comparability*, there is a lack of methodologies to measure social acceptance and the associated constructs (Batel et al., 2013; Rand and Hoen, 2017). In combination with an often qualitative, case-based view, comparability between studies is difficult. The lack of comparative, cross-cultural research is addressed by Sovacool (2014) pointing out that testing hypotheses across different contexts results in stronger evidence and broader applicability of findings. Similarly, Aas et al. (2014) state that comparative studies are rare and public acceptance has mostly been investigated for single projects and single national contexts. From a methodological point of view, the investigation of several cases significantly increases the quality of knowledge gained (Eisenhardt and Graebner, 2007). Moreover, comparisons between countries allow for a broader perspective on governance (Devine-Wright et al., 2017) and the role of national energy policies (Sonnberger and Ruddat, 2017).

The few existing studies in the field of social acceptance research, which employ comparative approaches can be classified into three main stands:

(i) Studies examining the effectiveness of policy incentives for the diffusion of renewable energy technologies (cf. e.g., Avril et al., 2012; Deshmukh et al., 2012),
(ii) Studies analyzing the institutional settings for social acceptance e.g., through indicators (cf. e.g., Sovacool and Lakshmi Ratan, 2012; Toke et al., 2008), and
(iii) Studies collecting empirical data to compare acceptance phenomena between cases, regions or countries.

The third group of empirical studies, to which this thesis belongs, is small in numbers and addresses public acceptance either at the community dimension through comparative, cross-country case studies (cf. e.g., Jobert et al., 2007; Schumacher and Schultmann, 2017; Warren et al., 2005) or at the national level through representative opinion polls (cf. e.g., Aas et al., 2014; Harold et al., 2018).

This thesis takes the above described shortcomings in the literature as a starting point. With respect to *comprehensiveness*, public acceptance of a set of renewable energy technologies is explored comparing public attitudes at the socio-political and the community dimension. Regarding *comparability*, this thesis applies a comparative research approach to investigate public acceptance with respect to various acceptance objects (renewable energy technologies) in different acceptance contexts (the URR and Chile) within the same study design. This contributes to a better understanding of the complex relationship between subject, object and context of acceptance. Moreover, this thesis contributes more universal insights into public acceptance phenomena by testing hypotheses from the acceptance literature across countries and renewable energy technologies. It further complements the existing literature by examining the link between public acceptance of renewable energies, community energy, and energy autonomy in several national contexts.

2.3 Review of Empirical Studies on Public Acceptance

Having provided an overview of the literature on social acceptance of renewable energy innovations in section 2.2, this chapter exclusively presents those studies, which correspond to the research focus of this thesis. The selection of studies is based on an evaluation of existing reviews, followed by an own literature screening, and finally the identification of the subsequently presented studies as the most relevant to this thesis. More precisely, the literature is narrowed down to (i) empirical, (ii) peer-reviewed studies investigating (iii) public acceptance phenomena on the (v) socio-political and community dimension with regard to (iv) renewable energies. Table 2-2 presents an overview of the studies classified by the following criteria:

- The country covered by the empirical analysis.
- The level(s) of observation covered, differentiating between the local, regional, and national level.
- The methodology employed for the collection of empirical data.
- The acceptance dimension(s) covered, differentiating between socio-political, community, and market acceptance according to the concept by Wüstenhagen et al. (2007) (cf. section 2.1).
- The renewable energy technology or set of technologies covered.

Table 2-2 reveals several communalities of the reviewed studies. Regarding the country coverage, all studies either refer to Europe, Switzerland, or the USA. Similarly, Sovacool (2014) and Busse and Siebert (2018) find a strong research focus on Europe and the United States in their reviews, whereas research data from Africa, Latin America, the Middle East, and Australia is rare. Looking at the acceptance dimensions covered, twelve of the reviewed studies examine community and four socio-political acceptance. Only three of them jointly investigate both acceptance dimensions at once.

Table 2-2: Review of empirical studies on public acceptance

Authors	Country	Acceptance dimension	Level of observation	Technology	Methodology
Betakova et al. (2015)	Czech Republic	Socio-political	Local	Wind turbines	Survey
Bertsch et al. (2016)	Germany	Socio-political	National	Set of RE technologies and infrastructure	Survey
Kortsch et al. (2015)	Germany	Socio-political, community	Regional	Biogas plants	Interviews and survey
Musall and Kuik (2011)	Germany	Community	Local	Wind turbines	Survey
Sonnberger and Ruddat (2017)	Germany	Socio-political, community	National	Wind turbines	Survey
Zoellner et al. (2008)	Germany	Socio-political	Regional	Set of RE technologies	Interviews and survey
Kontogianni et al.(2014)	Greece	Community	Regional	Wind energy	Survey
Wolsink (2000)	Netherlands	Community	National	Wind energy	Survey
Soland et. al. (2013)	Switzerland	Community	Local	Biogas	Survey
Sütterlin and Siegrist (2017)	Switzerland	Socio-political	National	Hydroelectric, wind and solar power	Survey
Upreti (2004)	United Kingdom	Community	Local	Biomass plant	Interviews, document research, content analysis, focus groups, survey

Authors	Country	Acceptance dimension	Level of observation	Technology	Methodology
Upreti and van der Horst (2004)	United Kingdom	Community	Local	Biomass plant	Interviews, content analysis, survey, focus groups, participatory appraisal methods
Upham and Shackley (2006)	United Kingdom	Community	Local	Bioenergy plant	Survey, focus groups, interviews
Upham and Shackley (2007)	United Kingdom	Community	Local	Bioenergy plant	Survey
Upham (2009)	United Kingdom	Community	Local	Bioenergy plant	Survey
Petrova (2016)	USA	Community	Local	Wind turbines	Survey
Jobert et al. (2007)	France and Germany	Community	Local	Wind energy	Interviews
Warren et al. (2005)	Ireland & Scotland	Community	Local	Wind energy	Interviews and survey
Aas et al. (2014)	Norway, Sweden & UK	Community, socio-political	National	High voltage power lines	Survey
This thesis	France, Germany, Switzerland, Chile	Community, socio-political	National, regional and local	Set of RE technologies	Interviews, surveys, and workshops

As a result of the focus on community acceptance, the predominant level of observation is the local level with eleven studies, followed by five studies looking at the national level, and three studies conducting research on the regional level. With respect to technologies, eight studies look at wind energy, seven at bioenergy, three at a set of several renewable energies and infrastructure, and one at high voltage power lines. Here again, most of the studies focus on one specific technology and only few take comparative approaches comparing the public acceptance of several technologies. Concerning the employed research methods, the large majority of studies relies on survey data (twelve out of nineteen reviewed articles) and only few use mixed methods, combining qualitative and quantitative data. The findings in terms of the focus, trends and coverage of the reviewed studies fits very well the findings of more comprehensive literature reviews (cf. Busse and Siebert, 2018; Sovacool, 2014). It is therefore concluded that the limited sample of reviewed literature still provides a good representation of empirical studies in the field.

Table 2-3 lists the reviewed empirical studies on public acceptance in more detail and assesses them in terms of the critiques elaborated in section 2.2. More precisely, it is examined in how far the reviewed studies contribute to improve *comprehensiveness* and *comparability* of the research field by applying the following criteria:

- The study covers more than one country.
- The study assesses more than one acceptance dimension according to the concept by Wüstenhagen et al. (2007) (cf. section 2.1).
- The study considers more than one technology.
- The study is conducted on more than one level of observation.
- The study takes a comparative approach, meaning comparisons either between countries, regions, communities, or otherwise defined cases.
- The study uses representative data for the chosen level of observation.

The conducted review confirms the critiques expressed in the literature (cf. section 2.2). While many articles present case studies or take a deeper look into the public acceptance in a specific country, comparative studies are rare (meaning that more than one country, region, or community is investigated in the same study). Moreover, the large majority of reviewed studies focus on one dimension of acceptance and one specific technology. Only three out of the nineteen reviewed studies examine public acceptance in more than one country, cover more than one acceptance dimension, or consider more than one technology. In this context, the study by Ass et al. (2014) merits special emphasis regarding its contribution to comparability. For their survey on public acceptance of high voltage power lines, representative data in three countries was collected, which refer to the community and socio-political dimensions of public acceptance at the same time. The other few existing empirical studies which compare public acceptance in different countries point to the need for more systematic cross-cultural comparisons as they unanimously find empirical evidence for substantial differences between the investigated countries. Aas et al. (2014) for example report significantly lower acceptance levels and lower trust in the UK than in Norway and Sweden towards high-voltage power lines. Jobert et al. (2007) reveal that visibility of wind turbines is more important in the French sample communities than in the German. Despite the reported differences, similarities have been equally stated by the authors, such as a low involvement of residents in decision making procedures in the study by Aas et al. (2014).

Table 2-3: Review of empirical studies on public acceptance regarding comprehensiveness and comparability

Author	> One country	> One dimension	> One technology	Comparative	Representative
Betakova et al. (2015)	–	–	–	–	–
Bertsch et al. (2016)	–	–	✓	–	✓
Kortsch et al. (2015)	–	✓	–	–	–
Musall and Kuik (2011)	–	–	–	✓	N.A.
Sonnberger and Ruddat (2017)	–	✓	–	–	✓
Zoellner et al. (2008)	–	–	✓	–	–
Kontogianni et al. (2014)	–	–	–	–	✓
Wolsink (2000)	–	–	–	–	N.A.
Soland et. al. (2013)	–	–	–	–	✓
Sütterlin and Siegrist (2017)	–	–	✓	–	N.A.
Upreti (2004)	–	–	–	✓	–
Upreti and van der Horst (2004)	–	–	–	–	–
Upham and Shackley (2006)	–	–	–	–	N.A.
Upham and Shackley (2007)	–	–	–	–	N.A.
Upham (2009)	–	–	–	–	N.A.
Petrova (2016)	–	–	–	✓	N.A.
Jobert et al. (2007)	✓	–	–	✓	N.A.
Warren et al. (2005)	✓	–	–	✓	✓
Aas et al. (2014)	✓	✓	–	✓	✓
This thesis	✓	✓	✓	✓	✓

Notes: ✓: the study fulfills the criteria, – : the study does not fulfil the criteria.
N.A.: not sufficient information available with regard to representativeness of the data.

2.4 Explanatory Factors for Public Acceptance[2]

A substantial part of the acceptance literature aims at identifying variables which explain public acceptance of both planned and existing renewable energy projects. It is assumed that understanding the influencing factors helps to draw conclusions on how public acceptance of specific projects can be enhanced. The diversity of studies is especially large as the variables depend to a big extent on the acceptance dimension and technology in question. The following section is therefore divided into two parts: firstly, a brief overview of studies, which offer comprehensive information about explanatory variables for public acceptance is provided. Secondly, those variables, which are relevant for the empirical investigation of public acceptance in this thesis, are presented in detail.

There are few studies proposing generic frameworks for explanatory variables. One example is Huijts et al. (2012), who introduce a set of psychological factors based on a review of empirical studies on technology acceptance and theories from psychology. In addition, there are few studies assessing explanatory variables of several renewable energy technologies at once. One example is the study by Zoellner et al. (2008), which uses an approach from environmental psychology to assess explanatory variables for the public acceptance of large PV (photovoltaic) ground-installed systems, wind turbines, and biomass plants in one study design. The majority of studies, however, concentrate on the identification of explanatory variables for one specific renewable energy technology. For example, a comprehensive literature review on wind energy acceptance in North America is provided by Rand and Hoen (2017). Other empirical investigations of influencing factors of wind energy acceptance are conducted by Petrova (2016), Sonnberger and Ruddat (2017), and Jobert et al. (2007). Whereas Petrova (2016) stresses the visual impact of wind turbines and the perceived degradation of the landscape, Sonnberger and Ruddat (2017) compare explanatory variables for wind energy acceptance on

[2] Parts of this section have previously been published in Schumacher and Schultmann (2017).

the community and the socio-political dimension. Jobert et al. (2007) qualitatively examine success factors of five wind energy case studies in Germany and France to understand how community acceptance is influenced by different policy frameworks. Soland et al. (2013) and Kortsch et al. (2015) use different methodological approaches to assess technology-specific factors influencing public acceptance of bioenergy plants. Soland et al. (2013) use structural equation modelling to analyze influencing factors for the public acceptance of residents living near nineteen biogas plants in Switzerland. Kortsch et al. (2015) conduct a longitudinal study with three points of measurement to assess public acceptance and the corresponding explanatory factors of biomass plants over time in a "bioenergy-region" in Germany. To conclude, the body of literature which aims at detecting explanatory variables for public acceptance is vast. Therefore, the subsequent section focusses in those explanatory variables only, which are relevant for the empirical investigations of this thesis (cf. section 4). More precisely, the following sections provide an overview of the theoretical concepts used in this thesis and describes how the identified factors are translated into the context of public acceptance of bioenergy plants.

2.4.1 NIMBYism and General Advocacy

A noticeable amount of studies discusses the discrepancy between general support of renewable energy technologies and rejection of energy projects on a local level, often labeled as "not in my back yard", or NIMBY effect (cf. e.g., Devine-Wright, 2005; Upreti, 2004; van der Horst, 2007). The NIMBY theory is based on rational choice theory and basically assumes that self-interests lead to opportunistic behavior of local residents, who support the transition to renewable energies but refuse to be confronted with the associated impacts of those technologies in their own "back yard" (Soland et al., 2013). However, there is empirical evidence of this assumption being insufficient to explain social acceptance of specific local renewable energy projects (cf. e.g., Rau et al., 2012; Soland et al., 2013; Zoellner et al., 2008). Therefore, the NIMBY concept has been widely critiqued for oversimplification (cf. e.g., Devine-Wright, 2009; Rand and Hoen, 2017) as general attitudes are inadequate to explain attitudes towards local renewable energy projects (Hübner, 2012). Moreover, NIMBYism attributes all responsibility for non-acceptance to the local community instead of aiming at a deeper analysis of the claims and arguments of the conflicting parties. It consequently prevents possible reasons associated with the behavior of other involved parties, such as plant operators, project planers, or public authorities from being examined in further detail. (Hübner, 2012) The author of this thesis therefore refrains from using the NIMBY effect as the sole explanation of non-acceptance. Nevertheless, it is argued that advocacy of renewable energies is still one (of several) important attitudinal factor which determines public acceptance. This assumption is backed by findings by other studies, according to which general support of renewable energies is a predictor of public acceptance (cf. Kortsch et al., 2015; Zoellner et al., 2008).

2.4.2 Procedural and Distributive Justice

Procedural and distributive justice are two key concepts of equity theory (cf. e.g., Adams, 1965), on which the assumptions of various studies in the field of public acceptance research are based on (cf. e.g., Goedkoop and Devine-Wright, 2016; Gross, 2007; Soland et al., 2013).

Distributive justice refers to the distribution of costs, benefits, and risks between the parties involved. Perceived costs and perceived benefits are assumed to enter into a subjective cost-benefit ratio, which, inter alia, determines the perceived fairness of the outcome (Soland et al., 2013). In the acceptance context, the meaning of costs and benefits is not limited to monetary outcomes but includes a wide range of factors. In the case of biogas plants, perceived benefits comprise regional value creation (e.g., through jobs in rural areas), individual financial benefits (e.g., through the use of waste heat for local district heating), and the contribution of renewable energies to climate protection compared to fossil energy (cf. e.g., Devine-Wright, 2007; Hildebrand et al., 2012; Kortsch et al., 2015; Upham and Shackley, 2007). Perceived costs refer to the direct local impacts of biogas plants (e.g., emissions into air and water), the visual impact of the plant and connected activities (e.g., landscape modification), as well as to other financial costs for local residents (e.g., value losses of neighboring houses or properties) (cf. e.g., Bertsch et al., 2016; Schweizer-Ries, 2008; Soland et al., 2013; Zoellner et al., 2008). With respect to biogas plants, relevance of odor emissions to public acceptance was highlighted by the literature (cf. e.g., Bertsch et al., 2016; Kortsch et al., 2015; Soland et al., 2013; Upham, 2009; Upham and Shackley, 2006; Upham and Shackley, 2007; Upreti, 2004; Upreti and van der Horst, 2004; Wüste, 2013; Wüste and Schmuck, 2013) and hence receives special attention in this thesis.

The concept of procedural justice refers to the fairness and transparency of the decision-making process through appropriate information and participation possibilities for local stakeholders (Rau et al., 2012; Soland et al., 2013; Zoellner et al., 2008). To analyze procedural justice of renewable energy projects, this thesis refers to the participation pyramid by Rau et al. (2012) (see Figure 2-3), which is based on Arnstein's ladder of participation (Arnstein, 1969). According to the pyramid, information and participation processes of renewable energy projects can take place on four levels of involvement: reception of information, consultation, cooperation, and citizens' control. The higher the level of involvement, the more responsibility is assumed by the participants and the greater the citizens' active contribution to the process.

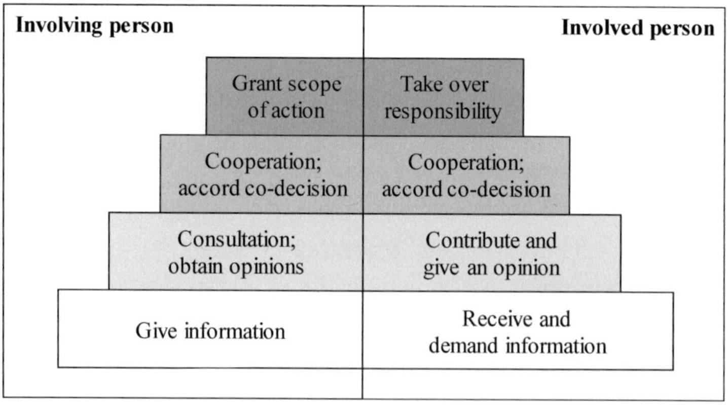

Figure 2-3: Participation pyramid (adapted from Rau et al., 2012)

2.4.3 Trust in Authorities

Trust in relevant authorities is another frequently cited factor for public acceptance. In the renewable energy context, a number of studies highlight the importance of citizens' trust in the competence, neutrality, and fairness of project planners, plant operators, or other local authorities (cf. e.g., Soland et al., 2013; Upreti, 2004; Upreti and van der Horst, 2004; Zoellner et al., 2008). Trust is closely linked to the concepts of procedural justice as trust enables cooperation and participation, with the latter helping to create trustful relationships. Walker et al. (2010, p. 2657) describe trust as a self-reinforcing concept which is "both a necessary characteristic and a potential outcome of cooperative behaviours." Upreti (2004) describes mistrust as a major barrier to promoting biomass energy and emphasizes the importance of an open dialog to build trust in the early project stage. In this thesis, trust in the plant operator is assessed in terms of his/her perceived competence, accuracy of information offers, and fairness with respect to the consideration of local residents' concerns.

2.4.4 Summary of Relevant Explanatory Factors

The review of the literature on factors influencing public acceptance of renewable energy projects in section 2.4 reveals a controversial discussion on the NIMBY concept and the role of general advocacy of renewable energies as explanatory factor. A broad consensus, however, exists regarding the importance of creating an environment of procedural and distributive justice. Procedural justice can be achieved by offering appropriate information and participation options for local residents, which in turn helps establish trustful relationships between the parties. Distributive justice can be achieved by a perceived positive cost-benefit ratio, through a fair distribution of local benefits and costs. Trust is also without controversy an important factor for public acceptance and closely linked to the concepts of procedural justice as trust enables cooperation and participation.

3 Development of a Mixed-Methods Research Approach to Assess Public Acceptance of Renewable Energies

This section provides an overview of the methods applied in the research process of this thesis. Section 3.1 highlights the steps of the mixed-methods research approach and describes the advantages of combining quantitative and qualitative data. The most important steps of the research approach are described in detail, including the conduction of expert interviews, the questionnaire development, the statistical methods applied and the validation of results. Section 3.2 subsequently presents methodological considerations regarding the selection of case studies, renewable energy technologies, and hypotheses for the empirical case studies. In addition to the rather broad methodological considerations presented in this section, more detailed information about the survey methodology of each case study is provided in section 1.

3.1 Mixed-Methods Research Design

Mixed-methods generally means combining qualitative and quantitative research methods (Kuckartz, 2014). How and in which sequence these methods are combined in this thesis is illustrated by Figure 3-1. Each of the steps of the research process is briefly described in the following paragraphs.

- Firstly, a *literature review* of the field of social acceptance of renewable energies is conducted and the scope of this work is defined. Moreover, suitable theories are identified and measurement instruments developed in other studies to assess public acceptance of renewable energies are selected. The literature review is described in section 2.

- Secondly, semi-structured *expert interviews* are carried out in the URR and in Chile with participants of the biomass value chain. The interviews provide information on factors influencing public acceptance of biomass plants and help to familiarize with the context of renewable energies in the four countries. The process of conducting the expert interviews is described in detail in section 3.1.1.
- The development of the *questionnaire* is based on the combined insights from the *literature review* and the *expert interviews*. Measurement instruments are taken as far as available from existing studies and are supplemented through the insights from the interviews. Four language versions of the questionnaire are developed and pretested in the respective countries under investigation. The development of the questionnaire is described in section 3.1.2.
- The *data collection* is carried out using several sampling criteria and survey modes depending on the case study's specific target group. The modes include personal, paper-pencil, and online interviews. As the method of data collection differs between the individual case studies, a detailed description is provided for each of them in section 4.
- The data is subsequently processed and prepared for *statistical analysis*. The analysis of the survey data is carried out with the statistics Software SPSS (Version 21). For the statistical analysis both descriptive and inferential statistics are applied. More information regarding the statistical methods is provided in section 3.1.3. Additional information regarding the process of data processing is provided in section 4 for the individual case studies.
- The final step consists in the *validation of results* through several workshops with stakeholders from the biomass value chain and experts in the area of renewable energy from the four countries. During four workshops the results are presented and put up for discussion, which enables the interpretation of results at the background of the specific national context. The insights are incorporated in the conclusions of the individual case studies presented in section 4.

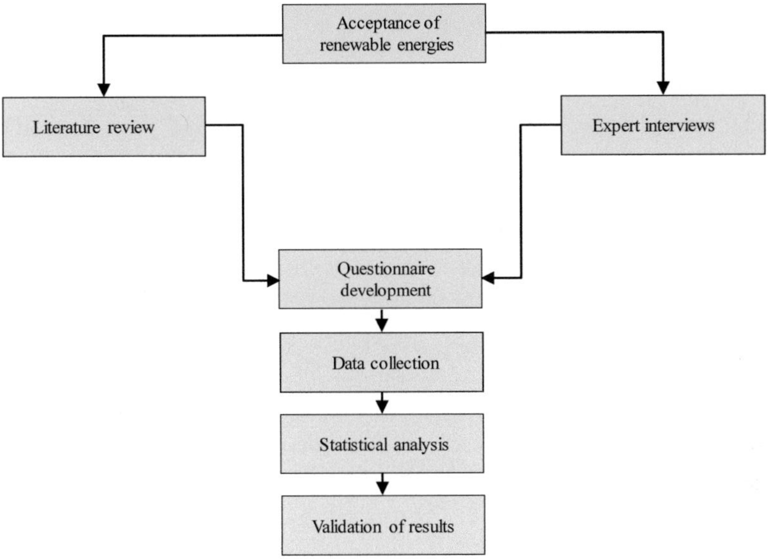

Figure 3-1: Research process of this thesis

According to Greene et al. (2016) there are five potential purposes for using a mixed-methods research design, which are triangulation, complementarity, development, initiation, and expansion. The purpose of implementing the above presented mixed-methods design in this thesis is twofold:

- *Development:* The expert interviews are used in combination with the literature research to develop the survey design and the measurement scales of the questionnaire.
- *Complementarity:* The stakeholder workshops complement the interpretation of the quantitative data from the questionnaire survey against the background of the national context.

Hence, the mixed-methods design of this study combines the advantages of qualitative and quantitative methods with another. The combination of expert interviews, questionnaire based surveys, and stakeholder workshops uses the strengths of the individual methods and thus increases the validity of the measurement instruments and the results (cf. Greene et al., 2016).

3.1.1 Expert Interviews[3]

This section presents the results of an extensive interview study, which was conducted by a team of researches as part of two research projects (OUI Biomasse and SeMoBioEnergy). The author of this thesis performed a major part of the interviews by herself and contributed substantially to the research design, but also relies on the results of other researchers. The subsequently presented analysis of the interview data with regard to public acceptance, however, is a genuine work of the author of this thesis. Other parts of the interview analysis have previously been published in Daniel and Bailly (2015), Steiger et al. (2015), and Siems and Seuring (2018). Due to the project context, the interviews took place in a larger setting and also covered aspects beyond public acceptance. Moreover, the scope of the interviews was limited to the biomass sector and only marginally addressed public acceptance of other renewable energies. Despite these limitations, the interviews yielded interesting insights into factors influencing public acceptance of bioenergy and were useful for the author to familiarize with the characteristics of the national energy sectors as well as the cultural background in the four countries under investigation.

The major purpose of the interviews was to use the insights on public acceptance of bioenergy to develop the survey design and the measurement scales of the questionnaire, particularly with regard to the focus topic on bioenergy. Therefore, this section is assigned to the methodology section of this thesis, even though it contains results itself. In the following, the method of data collection is presented and relevant results of the interviews for public acceptance of biomass plants are highlighted.

3.1.1.1 Materials and Methods of the Interviews

Sampling

Given the diversity of biomass value chains depending on the conversion pathway (e.g., biogas, wood combustion, bio-ethanol) and of actors comprising

[3] Parts of this section have previously been published in Steiger et al. (2015)

these chains, the interviews are limited to key individuals with an overarching view of the subject. These people, who can be called "informants", were chosen so that a maximum of existing biomass value chains in the respective countries were covered, while leaving leeway to re-orientate the composition of the sample as the survey and the interviews progressed. Moreover, the sampling aimed at meeting a variety of different actors from the biomass supply chains, starting with the biomass supplier, to the energy industry, the plant operator, as well as the technology provider. In addition, external stakeholders were interviewed to get a holistic picture of the value chain comprising governmental actors, such as policy makers and administrative staff, associations and NGOs, key individuals from research as well as local consumers of bioenergy. The categorization of stakeholders is based on the framework by Gold (2011) and Gold and Seuring (2011) presented in Table 3-1.

Table 3-1: Stakeholders of the bioenergy value chain (based on Gold, 2011)

Main category	Sub category	Stakeholder
Supply chain actors		Energy industry/ plant operators Biomass suppliers/ farmers Landowners/ forest owners Project developers Forest managers Technology providers Biorefinery
External stakeholders	Governmental bodies	Policy-makers Government in general Planners and technicians Administration
	NGOs and associations	NGOs and associations Universities
	Residents, consumers, citizens	Residents and local communities Society and public in general Consumers

Data Collection

In total 98 experts were interviewed, thereof 15 from the French, 25 from the German URR, and 16 from the Swiss URR as well as 42 experts from Chile. Table 3-2 presents the interview partners by category and country.

Table 3-2: Interview partners by category and country

Stakeholder category	France	Germany	Switzer-land	Chile	Total
Supply chain actors					
Energy industry/ plant operators	6	8	5	13	32
Biomass suppliers/ farmers	-	7	3	6	16
Technology providers	-	1	-	-	1
External stakeholders					
Governmental bodies	5	2	3	4	13
Associations and NGOs	3	2	3	2	10
Universities	-	-	1	10	9
Consulting	-	4	-	4	8
Residents and local communities	1	1	1	3	6
Total	15	25	16	42	98

Even though not all types of actors identified by Gold (2011) (cf. Table 3-1) have been interviewed, there is still a large variety and good coverage of the main stakeholder groups by the interviewees. The interviews were conducted during two separate field phases. The first field phase took place over several months in 2014 in the three sub-regions of the URR, the second field phase took place from November 2016 to July 2017 in Chile. The team of researchers, who carried out the face-to-face interviews, were native speakers from the respective countries, with exception for the Chilean field work, which was carried out by a team of German researchers, which spoke fluently Spanish. Interview partners were informed that their participation was voluntary and that all information shared was treaded anonymously.

Interview Guidelines

To account for the diversity of actors in the different bioenergy value chains, several stakeholder-specific, semi-structured interview guidelines were developed. The aim was to structure the interviews as little as possible so that the interviewees would talk freely about their activities and were able to set the focus of the interview on topics they considered as important. While having the interviews, not all questions were asked in the same sequence as presented in the questionnaire, and when discovering new aspects during the interviews, subsequent questions were adapted. The interview guidelines were translated from English into the three languages (German, French, Spanish) and pretested in the respective countries. As afore mentioned, the topic of public acceptance of bioenergy was only one out of several topics of the interviews. Therefore Table 3-3 and Table 3-4 display only the relevant excerpts of the full interview guidelines, which refer to the topic of public acceptance.

Table 3-3: Questions on public acceptance of the interview guideline for the URR

Topic	Guideline questions
Public acceptance problems	Have you encountered public acceptance problems? If yes, what were the reasons? How did you deal with the conflict? What did you learn from it?
Influencing factors of public acceptance	Which factors favor public acceptance of bioenergy projects (on a general/ community level)?
Social impacts of bioenergy projects	What impact does bioenergy projects have on the society (e.g., with regard to rural development, local value creation, energy costs)?
Participation	In which project phase did you involve the local community in the project? How did you involve the local community (e.g., discussion rounds, working groups, local citizen survey)?

Table 3-4: Questions on public acceptance of the interview guideline for Chile

Topic	Guideline questions
Social perception	How is bioenergy perceived by the population? In how far is bioenergy publicly accepted?
Impact of bioenergy on social groups	Which social groups profit from bioenergy projects? Which social groups are negatively affected by bioenergy projects?
Social impacts, benefits and environmental challenges of bioenergy	Which social impacts does bioenergy have (e.g., with regard to distribution of wealth, land use)? Which social benefits does bioenergy create (e.g., with regard to employment, protection of non-renewable resources, rural development, local value creation)? Which environmental challenges does bioenergy create (e.g., with regard to deforestation, pollution, water use)?

Data Analysis

All interviews were tape-recorded, transcribed and analyzed via qualitative content analysis (with only few exceptions in case that the interviewee did not agree with audiotaping the interview). To analyze the raw data, an explorative approach was adopted with categories and topics emerging from the data material, in contrast to theory driven analysis. As the interviewers differed between the countries, the categorization method differed as well. The interviews from the URR were analyzed by dividing the material into appropriate sections of sense to identify main arguments. These arguments were then discussed in the team of researchers from the three sub-regions of the URR and appropriate categories were identified reflecting the main arguments. The raw data from Chile was analyzed using classical content analysis according to Mayring (2010) including frequency analysis.

3.1.1.2 Results of the Interviews

In the following, the main categories identified regarding public acceptance are presented. As the interviews have been conducted in two field phases, the results for the URR and for Chile are presented in two separate sections. All quotes were translated to English by the author and grammatically revised if necessary. It needs to be mentioned that only those aspects related to the public perception of bioenergy are presented in this section. In addition, it is important to note that the categories and statements emerged from the empirical material and reflect the subjective view of the interviewees. Therefore, the categories presented might not be complete and cannot replace an objective description of the study regions, which is provided in section 4.2 for each of the three case studies.

Upper Rhine Region

The categories, which emerged from the raw data collected in the URR are briefly described, comparing between the three national sub-regions. Table 3-5 summarizes the categories and provides short illustrative quotes of the interviewees for each of the sub-categories.

Direct local impact: This category refers to impacts of bioenergy plants, which have been reported by the experts to potentially cause public acceptance problems on the community dimension. Because of differences between the impacts, experts differentiated between biogas and wood combustion plants.

- *Traffic:* The interviews revealed for all three sub-regions that a major reason for non-acceptance of both wood combustion and biogas plants is increased traffic in residential areas induced by the biomass supply and, in case of biogas plants, by the removal of digestates.

- *Odor nuisances:* Regarding biogas plants, experts from all three sub-regions reported public acceptance problems associated with odor nuisances, which even led to a discontinuation of projects. One Swiss plant operator faced the problem by implementing a weather station to operate his plant according to the weather conditions to avoid odor nuisances for local residents. In addition, weather data, in particular wind speed and wind direction, was used as evidence in case of complaints regarding odors, which were not caused by the plant but by other agricultural activities.

- *Landscape changes:* Changes of the rural landscape through the sight of the local bioenergy plant have been reported as an important factor influencing public acceptance in the French sub-region.

- *Perceived safety risks:* French experts stated that the local population perceived biogas plants as a potential source of danger with regard to explosions. The larger the plant, the more likely it would be labeled as gas plant ("usine à gaz") and the more dangerous it would be perceived.

Local value creation: This category contains statements of the experts regarding potential socio-economic benefits for communities in which bioenergy plants are erected.

- *Incomes for farmers and foresters:* The operation of local plants creates additional incomes for farmers and foresters. Unlike other renewable energies, such as wind or solar energy, biogas plants continue to create employment after the construction phase due to the fact that the plant requires a constant supply of feedstock, which needs to be produced locally on a continuous basis.

- *Employment in rural areas:* German plant operators stated that high-skilled jobs in the area of operating the plant are created, which strengthens rural development.

- *Development of the rural infrastructure:* The installation of biogas plants potentially contributes to the development of rural infrastructure through the extension of transport routes and local heating networks. Especially the connection of municipal or private houses to the local district heating network, which uses excess heat from the biogas plant, was mentioned by the experts as very favorable for public acceptance.

Environmental impact: This category comprises statements by the experts regarding the environmental impacts of bioenergy plants, which are perceived or assumed by the public.

- *Emissions into the air:* In all three sub-regions experts mentioned that air emissions from wood combustion plants are potentially causing local public resistance. In Switzerland experts stated that particularly small plants cannot economically afford filters which would be technically available. In consequence, the plants are struggling to comply with the allowed maximum levels of nitrogen oxides (NO_x) and particulate matter in the exhaust fumes.

- *Overexploitation of forests:* In all three sub-regions experts mentioned public concerns regarding deforestation. German experts from the forestry and wood processing industry stated that the public was worried regarding the overexploitation of forests and associated risks for soil quality and biodiversity. From the experts' point of view, however, these fears are unfounded and arise because of lacking knowledge regarding sustainable forest practices and standards, which prevent this type of adverse impacts. In France, experts expressed the risk of degrading soil fertility and biodiversity through an overuse of small diameter branches from the forests, the cutting of old trees and the widening of forest tracks. This argument was also supported by French institutional actors in the timber sector who fear long-term implications of a short-term forest management oriented towards a predominantly energetic use.

- *Use of energy crops:* The interviews revealed that the cultivation of energy crops is perceived highly critical by the public, mostly due to ecological concerns and changes of the rural landscape. Despite the marginal use of energy crops in France, experts expressed concerns regarding the intensification of mono-cropping practices and associated impacts on soil fertility and biodiversity. In Switzerland, no debate on energy crops exists as biogas plants exclusively process organic residues from households, agriculture, and industry.

- *"Food versus fuel" debate*: A prominent issue in the German sub-region was the "food versus fuel" debate, which is closely linked to the afore mentioned topic of energy crops. The debate refers to the use of edible crops, in particular corn, for energetic purposes instead of food and feed production. Many experts referred to the societal debate around this topic and pointed out that in addition to direct environmental impacts, indirect land use changes must be considered for a complete assessment of the impacts of augmenting the production of energy crops.

Information and participation: This category includes acceptance factors connected to information and participation options for local communities with regard to bioenergy projects.

- *Information:* Experts in all three sub-regions emphasized the importance of a close dialog with local authorities, communities, and residents as a prerequisite for public acceptance. In addition, information has to be accurate, precise, and reliable to create a relationship of trust between the parties. If promises made by the operator cannot be kept, there is the danger that acceptance collapses. If externalities from the project have already created negative impacts on the local community, it is usually harder to regain the trust of the local population. In consequence, it is recommended to implement a cautious communication strategy. Experts however, disagreed regarding the timing of communication activities. On the one hand, most of them recommended that the communication about the project must start at a very early project stage when potential adaptations to the initial planning are still possible. On the other hand, some experts mentioned challenges of communication in the early planning phase before economic feasibility of the project has been proven.

- *Financial participation:* French and German experts mentioned financial participation of the public in bioenergy projects as a possibility to increase the identification with the project and to promote public acceptance.

Trust: This category refers to statements of the experts with regard to the role of trust in key actors for public acceptance.

- *Trust in the capabilities of the plant operator:* German and French experts stated that a trustful relationship between the community and the plant operator is important for public acceptance. One expert mentioned a project in which local resistance to a proposed bioenergy plant had been triggered by the knowledge of another unsuccessful project run by the same plant operator. Hence, trust in the plant operator and his ability to run the plant efficiently was identified as important factor for public acceptance. Moreover, experts suggested to offer visits to plants, which are considered best practice to increase the acceptance of the population for local projects.

- *Trust in local key actors:* French and German experts emphasized that besides trust in the plant operator, there must also be trust in key actors, which should function as ambassadors for local bioenergy projects. In France, the experts further emphasized that bioenergy projects need to be embedded in the local context, for example through cooperation with local companies and farmers or through the support of the project by local (elected) representatives or other authorities.

Siting and plant design: This category refers to option with respect to siting and plant design which are relevant for public acceptance of bioenergy plants.

- *Siting under consideration of local impacts:* Experts in all three sub-regions stated that the choice of an appropriate site for the biomass plant is decisive for public acceptance. Besides technical factors such as access to an electricity or gas grid, a district heating network, or transport infrastructure, there are acceptance related issues, which need to be considered. For example, transport routes should be carefully chosen to avoid problems with increased traffic in residential areas due to the biomass supply. In addition, incorporating wind directions into siting decisions may prevent problems with odor nuisances for local residents.

- *Plant design to avoid local nuisances, especially odor:* Both German and Swiss experts mentioned the plant configuration as important determinant for public acceptance. For example, the storage and processing of the biomass feedstock can either be done in a closed storehouse or openly. The choice of the system directly influences the intensity of odor nuisances for the surroundings. Moreover, technologies such as air filters or sealed substrate and digestate storage help to reduce gaseous emissions. The installation of such technology, however, causes additional costs for the plant operator and therefore is often described as a trade-off between reducing local nuisances and increasing profitability. Beside the quantity and the type of feedstock, French experts further mentioned the size of the plant as important factor for its public acceptance, with higher acceptance for smaller plants.

Table 3-5: Category framework based on inductive content analysis of the interviews from the URR

Main category	Sub-category	Quote
Direct local impact	Traffic	Traffic can become a problem if the plant is built close to a residential area. (Energy industry/ plant operator, Switzerland)
	Odor nuisances	I know that we once had a project which had problems with odor nuisances. I think it was actually the reason why the project was stopped or at least one of the reasons. But it was definitely an essential one. (Energy industry/ plant operator, Germany)
	Landscape changes	The second aspect is the landscape aspect. [...] We try to do the best we can to make it [the plant] fit well, in quotation marks, into the landscape. So these are all very important aspects but they all have significant costs. (Energy industry/ plant operator, France)
	Perceived safety risks	We always hear the same prejudices, the same refrain. Here it is: "there will be flies", "there will be trucks every day", "it's disgusting", "it stinks", "it explodes, in Germany there have been deaths". (Energy industry/ plant operator, France)
Local value creation	Incomes for farmers and foresters	We set up a holistic concept in order to make sure that certain sources of income for the local farmers and the foresters are created. (Residents and local communities, Germany)
	Employment in rural areas	We thereby create some highly qualified jobs in the area of plant operation. (Energy industry/ plant operator, Germany)
	Development of rural infrastructure	As a result [of the local biogas plant], we have a district heating network, we have new water and power lines, a new DSL line, and a new district road on top. (Residents and local communities, Germany)

Main category	Sub-category	Quote
Environmental impact	Emissions into the air	The “air-hygienists” don't like wood energy that much because of the fine dust. (Governmental body , Switzerland)
	Overexploitation of forests	There was a certain fear of the people that the Basel region will soon no longer have a forest. (Energy industry/ plant operator, Switzerland)
	Use of energy crops	The broad population only sees the problem of corn. [...] If the operator can say that he does not only cultivate corn, but also has a field with mixed flowers where the bees hum, then this is good for the acceptance. (Association/ NGO, Germany)
	“Food versus fuel” debate	This means that today the use of bioenergy from renewable raw materials is in direct competition with food and feed production. (Association/ NGO, Germany)
Information and participation	Information	Very early on, we prepared a brochure for the general public to communicate in a very general way on the advantages of biogas. We don’t hide the impacts. If we are asked about the trucks, we have to be very precise. It’s not telling them “my plant treats 8000 tons”. No, you need to tell them exactly how many trucks there are because there are supply trucks and digestate trucks. We must play the transparency card. (Energy industry/ plant operator, France)
	Participation	If you say, I’m going to build a biogas plant and I’d like you [the population] to put money into my project, it has a whole other meaning. People will become interested. It would be their project as well. (Governmental body, France)

Main category	Sub-category	Quote
Trust	Trust in the plant operator	It turned out that the operator already has a biogas plant which is an absolute disaster. Then of course they [the population] said, if he operates the other plant, everything will go down the drain. So, the project would be good in itself, but not with this operator. (Association/ NGO, Germany)
	Trust in local key actors	You have to win trust. That is very, very important. One [the mayor] must provide support here from a neutral position. (Resident/ local community, Germany)
Siting and plant design	Siting considering local impacts	The locations are now selected in such a way that there are no problems. Of course, transport can be an issue for surrounding communities. But in the end, we do not cause much more traffic now than before, because before there were also agricultural movements. Also we do not drive around at night and we mostly take larger roads. (Energy industry/ plant operator, Germany)
	Plant design to avoid local nuisances, especially odor	In the beginning, everyone was afraid that it stinks. […] That's why we had to make such a large reception hall with a lock system. No gate opens inside if there is an open gate outside. In the beginning I fought against it, because it costs one additional million euros. Now it is worth a lot: we have no discussions, no complaints. (Energy industry/ plant operator, Switzerland).

Chile

The following section presents the categories, which emerged from the analysis of the interview data collected in Chile. Table 3-6 provides an overview of the categories as well as short illustrative quotes of the interviewees. The statements of the interviewees refer exclusively to wood combustion plants, which are concentrated in south-central Chile and constitute the predominant conversion pathway of bioenergy in Chile.

Societal aspects: This category refers to societal issues connected to the use of bioenergy in Chile.

- *Firewood as low-cost energy source for households:* Many households in south-central Chile use firewood for heating and cooking purposes. Firewood is by far the cheapest energy source and many households from the lower and middle social classes strongly rely on it because of their limited financial resources. Consequently, an increased demand for wood by industrial biomass combustion plants might potentially create social conflicts if it is associated with an increase in firewood prices.

- *Knowledge:* It was a common view amongst interviewees that the population rejects bioenergy projects because of a limited understanding of the technology, the associated impacts, and the potential benefits. Moreover, many interviewees addressed the lack of knowledge and awareness of the population with regard to the health and environmental impacts of the combustion of humid firewood by households for heating purposes. As afore mentioned, the use of firewood for cooking and heating purposes is still very common in south-central Chile and especially the unclean combustion of humid firewood causes severe air pollution in south-central cities.

- *Critical public:* Many interviewees mentioned a critical civil society and a general "mindset of opposition" of the public as a challenge for the acceptance of bioenergy. Public opposition in Chile is not limited to bioenergy but equally applies to other (renewable) energy technologies, in particular hydropower and wind energy.

Direct local impact: This category addresses direct local impacts on nearby communities induced by bioenergy plants.

- *Traffic:* Experts mentioned increased traffic volumes through biomass transport as a direct impact on local communities situated nearby wood plantations and wood combustion plants. One interviewee reported that his company had to install a telephone hotline, which receives complaints of the residents with regard to trucks transporting the biomass, which regularly exceed the speed limit. Besides, increased traffic on unpaved roads creates dust and deteriorates the roads.

Local value creation: This category refers to all issues associated with the (lack of) local value creation for neighboring communities through wood combustion plants.

- *Employment in rural areas:* The creation of employment in rural areas was mentioned by several experts as an important local contribution of wood energy. Bioenergy creates employment in several areas, in particular in the production, the harvesting, and the transport of biomass. An expert further mentioned that mostly low-skilled jobs are required by the wood industry.

- *Negative impacts on tourism*: Experts stated that wood combustion plants have negative impacts on tourism. The south-central regions of Chile are very popular holiday destinations for both Chilean and foreign tourists. Therefore, the visual impact of larger plants and the associated transport movements of biomass might provoke public resistance in touristy areas.

- *Lacking local benefits:* Interviewees stated that little economic benefits for the south-central regions are created by the wood industry. Even though, the large forest companies occupy huge areas for wood plantations and freely use the local infrastructure, very little money stays in the region because the companies pay taxes in Santiago.

Effect on the environment: This category contains statements regarding environmental impacts of biomass combustion plants.

- *Emissions into the air:* The experts see the emissions induced by the bioenergy supply chain as an environmental challenge. In particular, the biomass transport with diesel trucks was mentioned critically.

- *Climate protection:* The experts addressed the advantages with regard to GHG emissions of biomass combustion plants over coal-fired power plants, which represent an important energy source in Chile.

- *Soil degradation:* The experts expressed concern that the removal of nearly all biomass residues from the forest plantations may affect nutrition cycles and lead to soil degradation in the long-term.

- *Impact on groundwater*: Several experts talked about potential impacts of the forest plantations on the ground water system. The cultivated species, especially eucalyptus, consume large amounts of water which might lead to sinking groundwater levels. The experts, however, added that water cycles are complex and depend on a lot of factors, of which the water demand by plantations is only one out of several.

Information and participation: This category comprises comments regarding the role of information and participation for public acceptance of bioenergy projects.

- *Information:* Experts named transparency as an important factor for public acceptance. The major instrument used so far to communicate with the public are environmental impact studies. These studies have been lately introduced by the Chilean Ministry of Energy to promote transparent communication with the public about new energy projects. These studies obligate the company to assess and disclose the expected impacts of the planned installation for the environment and the local community and develop respective action plans to mitigate those impacts.

- *Participation:* Public participation was named as relevant factor for public acceptance. However, the offered participation activities realized so far are again limited to public consultations in the context of the environmental impact studies, which are required by the Chilean Ministry of Energy. Moreover, the experts mentioned site visits as efficient measure to demonstrate the technology and to start the discourse with the public.

Trust: This category contains statements regarding the role of trust in the actors involved in bioenergy project for public acceptance.

- *Trust in project developers:* Experts noted a general distrust of the population towards industrial actors. There is the perception that especially large companies have the power to set up projects without considering the impacts on the local population. Certainly, this is a result of the persisting inequalities in the society despite the continuous economic growth of the country. This atmosphere of suspicion is also expressed in the category "public opposition" mentioned in the sub-category "critical public", which is actually a results of a severe distrust in economic actors and the government. The quotes in Table 3-6 illustrate that especially the population from lower classes immediately takes an opposite position against bioenergy projects. It is believed, that bioenergy projects occupy "their" space and pollute the environment, but do not offer any benefits, such as jobs, in return.

- *Trust in the forest industry:* The distrust towards the forest industry, as one of the largest industries in Chile, has been described as a precarious issue for public acceptance of bioenergy. The forest industry occupies large areas of land in the south-central regions for wood plantation. In consequence, many land use conflicts have occurred with the local population, particularly with the indigenous ethnic group Mapuche, who proclaim the land for themselves. One biomass supplier described the situation as follows: "Most of the people have sold [their land], but those who still live in the countryside are now encircled by a sea of plantations."

Table 3-6: Category framework based on inductive content analysis of the interviews from Chile

Main category	Sub-category	Quote
Societal aspects	Firewood as energy source for households	A lot of people depend on it [combustion of firewood in individual furnaces] to eat." (University)
	Knowledge	But the society does not have an idea of these new technologies and how they would benefit from them. (University)
	Critical public	There is a lot of opposition with regard to environmental issues in general. There is opposition with regard to dams, hydro-electricity, wind for everything there is opposition. (Consulting)
Direct local impacts	Traffic	The main conflict is associated with the use of gravel or earth roads. The traffic creates dust and deteriorates the roads. (Energy industry/ plant operator)
Local value creation	Employment in rural areas	Biomass generates a lot of labor. It creates jobs for the producer, the distributor, and jobs which require very little training. There are rather unskilled jobs, but with salaries exceeding the minimum wage in Chile because there is high demand for this type of labor. (Residents and local communities)
	Negative impacts on tourism	I think, if the projects are big, there's a problem for tourism. People do not differentiate between water vapor and pollutant emissions. Also, people do not like to see trucks in touristy places. In these zones we have a lot of tourism. (Consulting)
	Lacking local benefits	We all expect from a company as big as Arauco, with a tremendous consumption of wood, that they develop the value chains here. But no, they use our roads for which we pay the taxes. But they don't pay the taxes here in the city, they pay them in Santiago. (Biomass supplier/ farmer)
Effect on the environment	Emissions into the air	There is an issue with transportation […] because all the trucks are running with diesel. (Energy industry/ plant operator)

Main category	Sub-category	Quote
	Soil degradation	There are concerns that we take the nutrients out of the soil because before [the use of residues for bioenergy generation] all harvesting residues were left in the plantation. Now we take everything out. (Energy industry/ plant operator)
	Impact on groundwater	The plantations, in particular those of eucalyptus, have a high water demand. Therefore, some people are worrying about the effects on the groundwater. (University)
	Climate protection	Compared to carbon plants, which we have a lot in Chile, they [the bioenergy plants] are better because it is a renewable resource and in general emits less. (Energy industry/ plant operator)
Information and participation	Information	We make an environmental impact statement. […] The nearby community is usually interested in knowing what the impact of the project is. And if there are problems, mitigation measures can be applied so that the project can be unlocked and executed. (Energy industry/ plant operator)
	Participation	The local government […] decides together with the company if the project is beneficial for the location or not, without the community. They say that there has to be citizen participation but there is not. (Energy industry/ plant operator)
Trust	Trust in project developers	You have no idea. If it is an industrial project, the population immediately assumes a opposite position because the local community feels that they are going to occupy their space, that they are going to pollute and that they are not going to provide employment. This is the public perception in general. (University)
	Trust in the forest industry	I think that the resistance against the forest companies is a cultural issue. […] The forest companies are responsible for forest fires, are responsible for erosion, are responsible for water shortage, and for contamination. (Biomass supplier/ farmer)

3.1.1.3 Summary and Conclusions of the Interviews

To briefly summarize the findings of the interviews, the major influencing factors for public acceptance are: direct local impacts, local value creation, environmental impacts, information and participation, trust, siting and plant design, as well as specific societal aspects in Chile. These factors are in line with those factors identified in the review of the literature on explanatory variables (cf. section 2.4). Hence, the broader categories of influencing factors of public acceptance seem to be rather similar in all countries.

Comparing the interviews from the URR with those from Chile, it is however remarkable that in the URR environmental issues seem to occupy a much larger space in the interviews than in Chile. In contrast, the Chilean interviewees stressed the relevance of social issues for public acceptance, including the distribution of benefits and the lacking trust of the population in industrial and governmental actors. Environmental issues only played a subordinate role in the Chilean interviews. This is rather surprising considering the various environmental impacts of wood plantations which nowadays cover large areas of south-central Chile, for example described in Echeverria et al. (2006), Torres-Salinas et al. (2016), and van Holt et al. (2016). Especially, the topic of deforestation and the associated loss of biodiversity was not mentioned by the Chilean interviewees. This might be due to a biased sample as most of the interviewees themselves worked for or were somehow associated to the forest industry. Another reason could be that social aspects are simply in the foreground of the discussion in Chile due to high social inequalities and the persisting poverty (for more information see section 4.5.1.1).

3.1.2 Questionnaire Development

This section presents the process of the questionnaire development, which included the following four steps:

- Firstly, a literature research on social acceptance of renewable energies is conducted to define the scope of this work and to look for suitable theories (c.f. section 2). Measurement instruments, in particular questionnaire scales and items from other studies on public acceptance of renewable energies are reviewed. In this regard, it needs to be mentioned that despite the growing number of studies, most of the authors do not publish detailed information about the items and constructs they use in their questionnaires (cf. also section 6.3.2.2). This study combines measurement instruments from existing studies as far as available and indicates the sources of all items (cf. Appendix A).
- Secondly, semi-structured expert interviews are conducted in the URR and in Chile with participants of the biomass value chains. The interviews provide detailed information regarding relevant factors influencing public acceptance of biomass plants and help to familiarize with the energy political background in the four countries. The process of collecting empirical qualitative data through expert interviews is described in more detail in section 3.1.1.
- Thirdly, the information from the literature research and the expert interviews are combined to develop measurement scales for the questionnaire. The idea is to use items and constructs from the literature as far as available to increase comparability with other studies. If items are not available, new items are developed based on the insights from the expert interviews and the relevant theories. Moreover, the insights from the expert interviews are used to complement the scales from the literature and adapt the scales to the study context if required.
- Fourthly, the questionnaires are translated into the languages spoken in the survey regions. Special attention was required with respect to cultural considerations. To ensure reliability and comparability of the items in the different cultural contexts, all questionnaires were developed in an iterative team approach, with several translators and the author of this thesis

thoroughly discussing item equivalence (Harkness et al., 2004). Moreover, all language versions were pretested individually with native speakers from the respective study regions. The translation and pretesting process of the questionnaires is described in more detail in section 4.

Table 3-7 provides an overview of all constructs used in the questionnaires and their meaning. It is important to note that not all constructs were applied in all three case studies and that slight differences between the items contained in each of the constructs exist between the case studies. All items and construct are listed in Appendix A, the final questionnaires are displayed in Appendix B, and screenshots of the questionnaire are displayed in Appendix C.

Table 3-7: Constructs of the questionnaires

Construct	Concept
Advocacy of renewable energies	Support of renewable energy technologies in general and in the neighborhood
Perceived benefits of biogas plants	Perceived benefits of biogas plants for society and the individual
Perceived costs of biogas plants	Perceived costs of biogas plants for society and the individual
Odor	Frequency, intensity, and quality of the perceived odor emissions from the local plant
Trust in the plant operator	Trust in the plant operator with regard to perceived competencies, reliability, and intuitive appraisal
Perceived costs of energy crops	Perceived costs of monocultures and the use of agricultural crops for energy generation
Actual information and participation	Perceived information and participation possibilities during the planning and construction phase of the local biogas plant
Desired information and participation	Desired information and participation possibilities during the planning and construction phase of a local biogas plant
Engagement for renewable energies	Engagement with regard to convincing others, financial participation, and active support
Advocacy of energy autonomy	Support of approaches which lead to higher energy autonomy in general and at the local level

3.1.3 Statistical Methods

This section introduces the statistical methods applied for the analysis of the quantitative survey data in section 4. Firstly, information about the measurement scales, the distribution of the data, and the significance levels is provided. Secondly, the statistical methods applied in this thesis are briefly described. The methods comprise descriptive statistics, correlation analysis, linear multiple-regression analysis, and one-way analysis of variance (one-way ANOVA).

Measurement scales, data distribution and significance levels

The choice of an appropriate method to be applied in statistical analysis depends on the measurement scale on which the variable is assessed. In this thesis, the majority of variables are measured on a five-point Likert scale, which is assumed to have equidistant "spacing" in line with general social science practice and is hence treated as interval-scaled[4] (Greving, 2009, p. 72). The questionnaire contains constructs measured by several items on a five-point Likert scale. To test internal consistency of the constructs, an item analysis is conducted with the requirement that Cronbach's α exceeds the recommended threshold values of 0.70 (Bühner, 2011). If a construct consists of only two items, the Pearson-correlation coefficient is reported in addition. If the deviations from the desired value (Cronbach's $\alpha > 0.70$) are small, conceptual comprehensiveness is prioritized over internal consistency in the selection of items (Homburg, C., Müller, M., Klarmann, M., 2011; Little, T. D., Lindenberger, U., Nesselroade, J. R., 1999).

In addition to the measurement scale, the choice of the statistical method depends on the distribution of the data. In this work, parametric tests are applied. For parametric testing, an approximate normal distribution of the

4 There are discussions regarding the scale level of Likert scales. Some scholars claim that Likert-scales cannot be interpreted as interval-scaled and therefore parametric testing is not allowed (cf. Greving, 2009). However, Likert-scales are assumed to be interval-scaled in common social science practice. This hypothesis can be upheld as long as the statistical data analysis comes to meaningful interpretations of results (Westermann, 1985), which is the case for this thesis.

investigated variables is required, whereas nonparametric tests do not assume any specific distribution (cf. e.g., Sarstedt and Mooi, 2014, p. 142). In this work, the distribution of the variables of interest is checked visually with normal distribution plots. A deeper examination of the normal distribution assumption, e.g., by using the Shapiro-Wilk or Kolmogorov-Smirnoff test, is not performed. The reason is that these tests are rather conservative and tend to reject the hypothesis of normal distribution especially for large samples (Sarstedt and Mooi, 2014). Moreover, the parametric tests applied are relatively robust against violations of the assumption of normal distribution for sample sizes larger than 30 observations (Sarstedt and Mooi, 2014, pp. 148–149), which is the case in this work.

Moreover, the probability of error or significance level α is of high interest for statistical analyses. The significance level indicates the probability with which a true null hypothesis is incorrectly rejected (type 1 error). The smaller this value, the more reliable is the result of the statistical test. In this work, all tests are carried out to a significance level of 5% ($p\text{-value} < 0.05$).

Statistical methods

Univariate, descriptive methods are applied for a visual inspection and an analysis of the distribution of the data (e.g., normal distribution plots). Moreover, descriptive statistics, such as frequency distributions, calculation of arithmetic means (M), and standard deviations (SD) are used to describe the data and detect peculiarities with regard to cross-national differences.

The Pearson correlation coefficient (r_p) is used to measure the correlation between two variables. The Pearson correlation is the usual measure to describe the linear relationship between two at least interval-scaled variables. The value range of the coefficient is between -1 and 1. The direction of the influence is determined by the sign, the strength by the absolute value. At 0 there is no or a nonlinear relationship, at +1 and -1 there is a perfect relationship. As a rule of thumb a correlation below 0.30 is considered weak, between 0.30 and 0.49 moderate, and above 0.49 strong (Cohen, 2013). Before performing the analysis, the prerequisites for applying the Pearson correlation coefficient are tested. These are at least interval-scaled variables, a linear relationship between the variables, and an approximately normal distribution of the variables. (Sarstedt and Mooi, 2014, pp. 106–107)

The t-test for independent samples as well as the t-test for paired samples are used to compare means between two samples. The independent sample t-test is performed in case of two distinct groups, whereas the paired sample t-test is applied in case of comparing the means of two different variables for the same group of respondents. The prerequisites for conducting a t-test are that the variables are at least interval-scaled and approximately normally distributed (c.f. e.g., Sarstedt and Mooi, 2014, pp. 160–163). To indicate the size of the effect, Cohen's d is reported in addition to the significance level. Cohen's d ranges between 0 and 1. If Cohen's d is greater or equal 0.2, the effect is considered small; if Cohen's d is greater or equal 0.5, the effect is considered medium; and if Cohen's d is greater or equal 0.8 the effect is considered large (Cohen, 2013).

One-way ANOVA is performed to compare means of more than two samples. Before conducting the analysis, the prerequisites of at least interval-scaled variables, approximately normal distribution of the variables, and identical variances in each group are checked. Homogeneity of variances is tested using the Leven's test. If the assumption is violated, the Welch test is performed. Post-hoc analyses are used to obtain specific information with regard to differences between the groups. In case of homogeneity of variances, Tuckey's honestly significant difference test (short Tuckey's HSD) is used, and in case of heterogeneity of variances the Games-Howell test is applied to detect differences in means between the individual groups. Eta-squared (η^2) is reported as a measure of effect size. Eta-squared ranges between 0 and 1. Values below 0.30 are considered weak, values from 0.31 to 0.40 moderate, and values higher than 0.50 strong. (Sarstedt and Mooi, 2014, pp. 167-176)

Multiple regression analysis is carried out to test the influence of several dependent variables (presumed explanatory variables, cf. section 2.4) on an independent variable (public acceptance). Regarding multicollinearity, VIF values must be smaller than ten (or a corresponding tolerance value larger than 0.10) (Hair et al., 2014, p. 200). To check the independence of residues, Durbin-Watson statistics is required to be between one and three (Field, 2013,

p. 311). Linearity, homoscedasticity, and normality of the residues are assessed through an analysis of standardized residuals, standardized partial regression plots, and normal probability plots of the residuals. Finally, residuals are analyzed with regard to outliers and extreme outliers are excluded if reasonable (cf. Hair et al., 2014, pp. 216-219). As estimator of the effect size adjusted R^2 is reported. Coefficients between regression models with different dependent variables are compared according to the method suggested by Cohen et al. (2003).

3.1.4 Validation of Results

For cross-cultural research, it is vitally important that the interpretation of the collected data is validated in the respective cultural context. It needs to be acknowledged that every researcher brings in its own cultural background and thus feedback of persons from the study regions is required to draw appropriate conclusions. Therefore, the final step of the research process of this thesis consists in the conduction of stakeholder workshops with experts in the respective countries in which the research was conducted.

In total 6 stakeholder workshops, thereof two in Germany, one in France, one in Switzerland, and three in Chile were conducted. During the workshops the results from the expert interviews and the quantitative surveys were presented and put up for discussion. The discussions contributed significantly to the interpretation of results and were incorporated in the conclusions of the individual case studies presented in section 4.

Workshops in the URR

The results of the empirical investigations from the URR were presented during 4 workshops as part of the project OUI Biomasse. In April 2015, the results of the expert interviews (section 3.1.1) were discussed during three stakeholder workshops, one in each national sub-region of the URR. In total around 60 experts in the area of bioenergy from politics, industry, and science participated and provided valuable feedback. In addition, the results of case study 2 (section 4.3) were presented at a trinational workshop in June 2015 with around 50 participants from Germany, France, and Switzerland. The participants again were experts in the area of bioenergy and had various professional backgrounds. It needs to be acknowledged that the results from case study 1 (section 4.3) were not put up for discussion in the same setting. However, the lessons learned from the previous workshops were helpful for the interpretation of results of case study 1, too. Moreover, the aspect of cultural bias might not be too critical for the work conducted in the URR because during the whole process researchers from the three countries were involved throughout the project OUI Biomasse. Therefore, a constant exchange with researchers from the three countries was ensured, which minimizes the risk of interpretation bias.

Workshops in Chile

The empirical results of the expert interviews conducted in Chile (section 3.1.1) as well as the questionnaire-based survey (section 4.5) were validated during three workshops in Chile. The first presentation of results took place during a stakeholder workshop as part of the project SeMoBioEnergy in December 2017 with roughly 20 participants from science, industry, and politics. A few days later the results were put up for discussion during a stakeholder workshop of a related project[5] in which around 15 Chilean biomass suppliers and several Chilean researchers participated. The last presentation of final results of the expert interviews and the survey took place at a stakeholder workshop in January 2019. Around 20 Chilean bioenergy experts, most of them from science, attended this workshop.

[5] Project title "Modernizando el negocio de la leña: asociatividad, valor agregado y eficiencia energética" (English translation: "Modernizing the wood business: association, added value and energy efficiency")

3.2 Considerations Regarding the Study Scope

3.2.1 Selection of Countries

In this work three case studies are conducted in four countries. The study area includes the trinational URR, consisting of the territory of Alsace (France), the northwest region of Switzerland, a large part of Baden, and the south part of Rhineland-Palatinate (Germany), and the country of Chile.

The conduction of research in multiple countries is motivated by the fact that few studies have analyzed public acceptance of renewable energies in different national contexts in a systematic way so far (cf. also section 2.2). Thus, it is still not clear whether public acceptance is shared across countries and institutional settings or a country or project specific phenomena. From a methodological point of view, the investigation of several cases instead of one single case study significantly increases the quality of knowledge gained. Eisenhardt and Graebner (2007, p. 27) state that "adding three cases to a single-case study is modest in terms of numbers, but offers four times the analytic power. Thus, theory building from multiple cases typically yields more robust, generalizable, and testable theory than single-case research."

The choice of the investigated countries is justified by the similarities and differences that characterize them. On the one hand, the three national sub-regions of the URR share many characteristics. The sub-regions are characterized by similar geographic and socio-economic conditions and the rise of renewable energies during the last years in all three countries. Hence, the initial conditions for the development of renewable energies are rather comparable in the three sub-regions, whereas the policy frameworks (cf. section 4.2.3) and the cultural background of the inhabitants differ. On the other hand, the investigation of public acceptance in Chile adds another divergent case to the analysis. Chile differs substantially from the URR with regard to its geography, socio-economic issues, and the complete absence of public support schemes for renewable energies. Due to these commonalities and differences, the four countries provide an interesting combination of cases to explore public acceptance of renewable energies in different national contexts.

3.2.2 Selection of Renewable Energy Technologies

The main pillar of the future energy supply is renewable energy. These energy sources use the energy provided by the sun, gravity, and geothermal power. Renewable energies, in contrast to fossil fuels such as oil, coal, and gas, are energy forms that do not rely on finite resources and therefore are inexhaustible under human time horizons. (Gabler Wirtschaftslexikon, 2018; Quaschning, 2015)

This thesis examines public acceptance of renewable energies at the example of those sources that, apart from hydropower, account for around 66% of renewable electricity in Europe (Agora Energiewende, 2016; REN 21, 2017): wind (37%), solar (11%), and bioenergy (18%). With regard to technologies, it is differentiated between PV, including large-scale PV ground-installed systems (hereafter referred to as large-scale PV) and small-scale PV rooftop systems (hereafter referred to as small-scale PV), onshore wind energy plants (hereafter referred to as wind energy), and bioenergy, including biogas and wood combustion plants. The technologies are chosen as they potentially evoke direct interactions with the general public due to their high degree of decentralization and the potentially associated local impacts. Consequently, public acceptance is an important prerequisite for their implementation.

This work excludes hydropower, geothermal energy, marine energy, and offshore wind turbines from the study scope. The main reason is that due to their size, these renewable energy technologies lack the decentralized character of the other technologies examined in this study. In addition, hydropower plants have evoked strong social conflict during the last years in Chile (cf. section 4.5.1.1) and are therefore excluded for research ethical reasons. Geothermal energy was further excluded as the technology is not yet widely used in the URR and has not been implemented in Chile at all.

This thesis does not provide detailed technical descriptions of the investigated renewable energy technologies as this is not the research focus. However, to ensure that survey participants had an appropriate level of knowledge to answer the questions about the chosen renewable energy technologies, each of them is described in a short paragraph of the questionnaire (including a picture of a typical plant). The descriptions are available in the questionnaires in Appendix B. For additional information on the individual technologies see Quaschning (2015).

3.2.3 Selection of Hypotheses

As illustrated in section 1.2, public acceptance of renewable energies is approached in this thesis by comparatively testing several hypotheses across countries and technologies. To enable comparisons with the existing literature, the author decided to focus on often discussed topics of social acceptance, which are acceptance levels (H1) and dispositions to act (H2), public acceptance with regard to various acceptance dimensions, namely socio-political and community acceptance (H3), the relevance of spatial proximity of renewable energy plants to residential areas (H4), and the role of previous experiences with renewable energy projects for public acceptance (H5). From these issues the following five hypotheses are derived:

- H1: Renewable energies generally enjoy high public acceptance for future energy generation.
- H2: There is public disposition to act towards renewable energy plants in the neighborhood.
- H3: General public acceptance (socio-political dimension) exceeds public acceptance of plants in the neighborhood (community dimension).
- H4: Public acceptance of renewable energy plants is influenced by the distance of the plant to the respondent's home.
- H5: Public acceptance of renewable energy plants is higher among respondents with previous experience with renewable energy projects.

Based on the literature analysis conducted in section 2.3, the reviewed studies are assessed with respect to their coverage of the afore mentioned hypotheses. Table 3-8 presents the results.

Table 3-8: Coverage of hypotheses on public acceptance of REs by related empirical studies

Author	H1	H2	H3	H4	H5
Betakova et al. (2015)	–	–	–	✓	–
Bertsch et al. (2016)	✓	–	✓	✓	–
Kortsch et al. (2015)	✓	✓	–	–	–
Musall and Kuik (2011)	✓	–	–	–	–
Sonnberger and Ruddat (2017)	–	–	✓	✓	–
Zoellner et al. (2008)	✓	–	✓	✓	–
Kontogianni et al. (2014)	✓	✓	✓	✓	✓
Wolsink (2000)	✓	–	✓	–	–
Soland et. al. (2013)	–	–	–	–	✓
Sütterlin and Siegrist (2017)	✓	–	✓	–	–
Upreti (2004)	✓	✓	✓	–	–
Upreti and van der Horst (2004)	✓	–	✓	–	–
Upham and Shackley (2006)	✓	–	✓	–	–
Upham and Shackley (2007)	✓	–	✓	–	–
Upham (2009)	✓	–	✓	–	–
Petrova (2016)	✓	–	✓	✓	–
Jobert et al. (2007)	–	–	–	✓	–
Warren et al. (2005)	✓	–	✓	✓	✓
Aas et al. (2014)	✓	–	✓	–	–
Total frequency	15	3	14	8	3

Notes: ✓: the hypothesis is covered, – : the hypothesis is not covered.

The most often addressed issues in the reviewed studies are the assessment of acceptance levels and differences between socio-political and community acceptance. The relevance of distance is discussed by almost half of the studies. Several, but fewer studies are dedicated to investigate the disposition to act of the local population in addition to mere acceptance levels. This lacking interest in the disposition to act might also be due to the fact that there is no commonly agreed definition of acceptance and often no differentiation between various ways in which public acceptance can be expressed (cf. Busse and Siebert, 2018). Three out of the nineteen studies examine the relevance of experience for public acceptance.

Regarding the focus topic *"Bioenergy"*, the hypotheses are derived from the review of the literature on explanatory variables (cf. section 2.4) and the insights from the qualitative expert interviews (cf. section 3.1.1). The following hypotheses are made with regard to potential factors influencing public acceptance of locally installed bioenergy plants:

- H6: Advocacy of renewable energies
- H7: Perceived benefits of bioenergy plants
- H8: Perceived costs of bioenergy plants
- H9: Information and participation
- H10: Trust

In addition, case study 1 (section 4.3) and case study 3 (section 4.5) test the influence of perceived costs associated with the cultivation of dedicated energy crops for energetic use, and case study 2 (section 4.4) tests the influence of the additional factor perceived odor emissions on public acceptance of bioenergy plants.

- H11: Perceived costs of energy crops
- H12: Perceived odor emissions

The relevance of those hypotheses in the literature is assessed by analyzing related empirical studies on public acceptance of bioenergy plants in terms of their coverage of the afore mentioned hypotheses. Table 3-9 presents the results.

Table 3-9: Coverage of hypotheses on explanatory variables for public acceptance of bioenergy plants by related empirical studies

Author	H6	H7	H8	H9	H10	H11	H12
Kortsch et al. (2015)	✓	✓	–	✓	✓	–	✓
Zoellner et al. (2008)	✓	✓	✓	✓	✓	✓	–
Bertsch et al. (2016)	–	✓	–	–	–	–	✓
Wüste and Schmuck (2013), Wüste (2013)	–	✓	✓	–	–	✓	✓
Griesen (2010)	–	✓	–	–	✓	✓	✓
Soland et al. (2013)	–	✓	✓	✓	✓	–	✓
Upreti (2004),Upreti and van der Horst (2004)	–	✓	✓	✓	✓	–	✓
Upham (2009), Upham and Shackley (2006), Upham and Shackley (2007)	–	✓	✓	✓	✓	–	✓
Total frequency	2	8	5	5	6	3	7

Notes: ✓: the hypothesis is covered, – : the hypothesis is not covered.

The most often tested factors influencing public acceptance of bioenergy plants within the reviewed studies are perceived benefits of bioenergy plants and perceived odor emissions, followed by perceived costs of bioenergy plants, information and participation, and trust. In contrast, advocacy of renewable energies is only tested by two out of the twelve analyzed studies. The reason is assumed to be connected to the controversy around the NIMBY-theory. The theory is criticized for its oversimplification of use general attitudes towards renewable energies to explain attitudes towards local renewable energy projects (for more information see section 2.4.1). Only 3 out of the twelve reviewed studies test the influence of perceived costs of energy crops on public acceptance of bioenergy plants.

Regarding the focus topic *"Community Energy and Energy Autonomy"*, there are very few empirical investigations in the literature so far. Scholars have mostly focused on explaining phenomena of non-acceptance or rejection, without a deeper analysis of the different facets of positive acceptance and support (Batel et al., 2016; for a review, see Fast, 2013). The hypothesis of this thesis is therefore explorative and not based on any previous studies. The focus section's aim is to explore links, if any, between public acceptance of renewable energies and active support of renewable energies, and energy autonomy. Based on this idea the following hypothesis is formulated.

- H13: Public acceptance of renewable energies is linked to community energy and advocacy of energy autonomy.

4 Empirical Investigations Across Countries and Technologies

This section presents the three empirical, survey-based case studies, which assess public acceptance across several countries and technologies. To introduce the case studies, section 4.1 provides a brief overview of the three cases studies with regard to their geographical scope, the technologies, the dimensions of public acceptance covered, as well as the characteristics of the samples. Section 4.2 offers detailed information about the study regions regarding their geography, the current state of development of renewable energies, and relevant energy political frameworks conditions. Subsequently, each of the three studies is presented in detail including the materials and methods used and the obtained results. The results of the surveys are presented along the raised hypotheses (cf. section 3.2.3) and tested across national sub-regions and renewable energy technologies. Section 4.6.1 closes with a summary and conclusions of the afore presented case studies, including a comparison of findings between the case studies. Finally, the findings of the case studies are compared to those of the related literature.

4.1 Overview of the Case Studies

The three case studies conducted in this thesis differ in terms of their geographical scope, the technologies, the dimensions of public acceptance covered, as well as the characteristics of the samples. Table 4-1 provides an overview of the characteristics of the three case studies, which are presented in detail in the followings sections. For more information regarding the selection of cases see section 3.2.

Table 4-1: Characteristics of the case studies

	Case study 1	Case study 2	Case study 3
Study region	URR	URR	Chile
Technology	Small PV Large PV Wind energy Biogas plants	Biogas plants	Small PV Large PV Wind energy Wood combustion plants
Acceptance dimension	Socio-political & community	Community	Socio-political & community
Sample (size)	Population (n = 1.489)	Residents of 11 biogas plants (n = 667)	Population (n = 1.205)
Representativeness	Yes, with regard to age and sex on administrative district level	Yes, on case study level	Yes, with regard to age, sex, and social status on level of regions
Survey period	October 2015 to January 2016	November 2014 to March 2015	November 2017 to December 2017

4.2 Description of the Study Regions[6]

The national energy sectors of Chile, France, Germany, and Switzerland differ substantially with respect to their geography, state of development of renewable energies, and energy political frameworks. To assess the results of the three case studies regarding public acceptance, it is important to interpret them against the background of these national particularities. Therefore, the following section describes each of the study regions in detail and highlights communalities and differences between them.

4.2.1 Geography

Upper Rhine region

The tri-national URR is composed of the territory of Alsace (France), the northwest region of Switzerland, a large part of Baden, and the south part of Rhineland-Palatinate (Germany)[7] (cf. Figure 4-1). The region is populated by six million people and stretches across 21.517 square kilometers (km^2). Approximately 45% of the population lives in the German, 24% in the Swiss, and 31% in the French part of the URR (Deutsch-Französische-Schweizerische Oberrheinkonferenz, 2015). The three sub-regions are characterized by similar geographic and socio-economic conditions, and the rise of renewable energies during the last years in all three countries.

[6] Parts of this section have previously been published in Schumacher et al. (2019b) and Schumacher and Schultmann (2017).

[7] For simplicity reasons, it is either referred to the French, German, and Swiss sub-region, or to France, Germany, and Switzerland throughout this thesis.

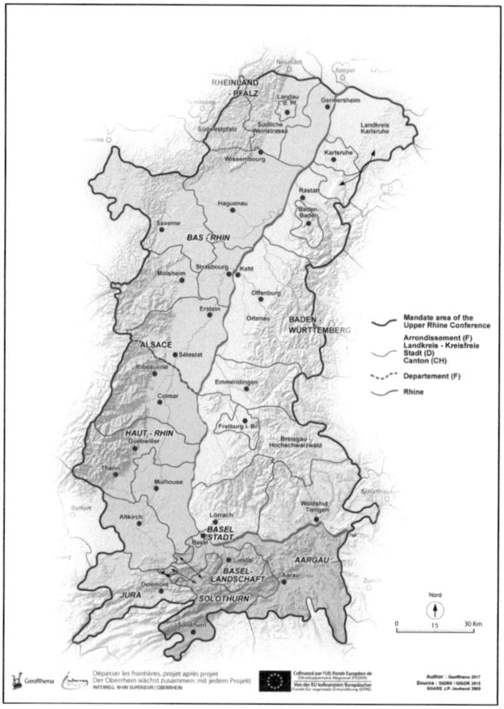

Figure 4-1: Map of the URR with three sub-regions (GeoRhena, 2017)

Chile

Chile is composed of 15 administrative regions, which are summarized to six larger geographical regions (see Figure 4-2). The country is populated by 17.6 million people (InE, 2017d) and stretches across 757,000 km². Approximately 87% of the population lives in urban areas, thereof 40% in the Metropolitan Region of Santiago (IEA, 2018b). Chile's geography is unique as it occupies a long and narrow coastal strip limited by the Pacific Ocean in the west and the Andean Mountains in the east. The country measures a north-south extension of approximately 4,300 km and an east-west extension of 175 km on average. In the north-south axis, Chile's climates range from the driest desert (the Atacama Desert), rainforests, lakes, and fjords to the glaciers of the Antarctica (IEA, 2018b). This variety of climates and geophysical conditions offers excellent conditions for virtually all forms of renewable energies, in particular solar, wind, hydropower, geothermal, and bioenergy (U.S. Department of Commerce, 2016).

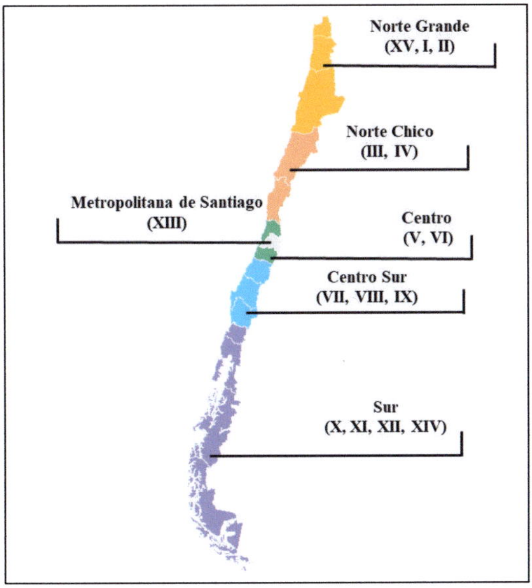

Figure 4-2: Map of Chile with six regions

4.2.2 Development of Renewable Energies

4.2.2.1 Growth of Renewable Energies

All four countries have defined ambitious targets for the development of renewable energies (cf. section 4.2.2.3), but the pace of growth differs substantially between the countries. Figure 4-3 illustrates the increase in installed electric capacities of renewable energies in the four countries from the year 2000 to 2017. Even though the installed capacity of renewable energies has been constantly increasing in all four countries, Germany experienced by far the strongest growth with a compound annual growth rate of 13% over the last decade. In Chile the installed renewable energy capacities grew by roughly 8% and in France by roughly 6% on average per year in the same time period. In Switzerland, annual growth rates are comparatively moderate with roughly 3% annual growth of renewable energies per year over the last 10 years (IRENA, 2018). This rather slow growth in Switzerland however needs to be seen at the background of the existing hydropower capacities, which already contribute a substantial share of roughly 60% of total electricity generation. (BFE, 2016a). The same is true for Chile, which already generates 30% of electricity from hydropower (cf. Figure 4-4).

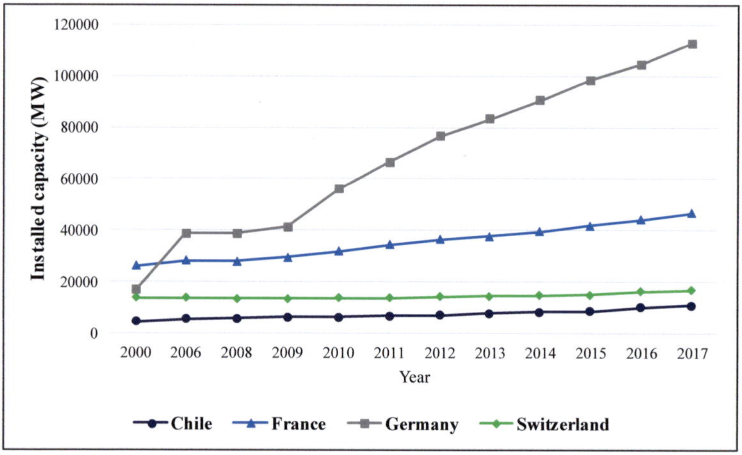

Figure 4-3: Growth of installed electric capacity of REs in Chile, France, Germany, and Switzerland (based on IRENA, 2018)

4.2.2.2 Current Electricity Generation Mix

Figure 4-4 shows the current electricity generation mix in the four countries. Due to favorable geographic conditions for hydropower, Switzerland currently has the largest share of renewable energies with 63% (thereof 60% from hydropower run-of-river and storage plants) in 2017 (BFE, 2016a). Chile is second with regard to the share of renewable energies. 56% of the country's electricity supply is based on fossil fuels and 43% on renewable energies, of which 30% is hydropower. The other renewable energies (PV, wind, and biomass) accounted together for 13% in 2017 (Watts Casimis and Pérez Odeh, 2018). Germany generated 29% of electricity with renewable energies in 2017 but still has substantial shares of coal, oil, and nuclear energy (Destatis, 2017). France produces the largest share from nuclear energy (76%) and has currently the smallest share (16%) of renewable energies, of which 10% came from hydropower in 2017 (RTE, 2016).

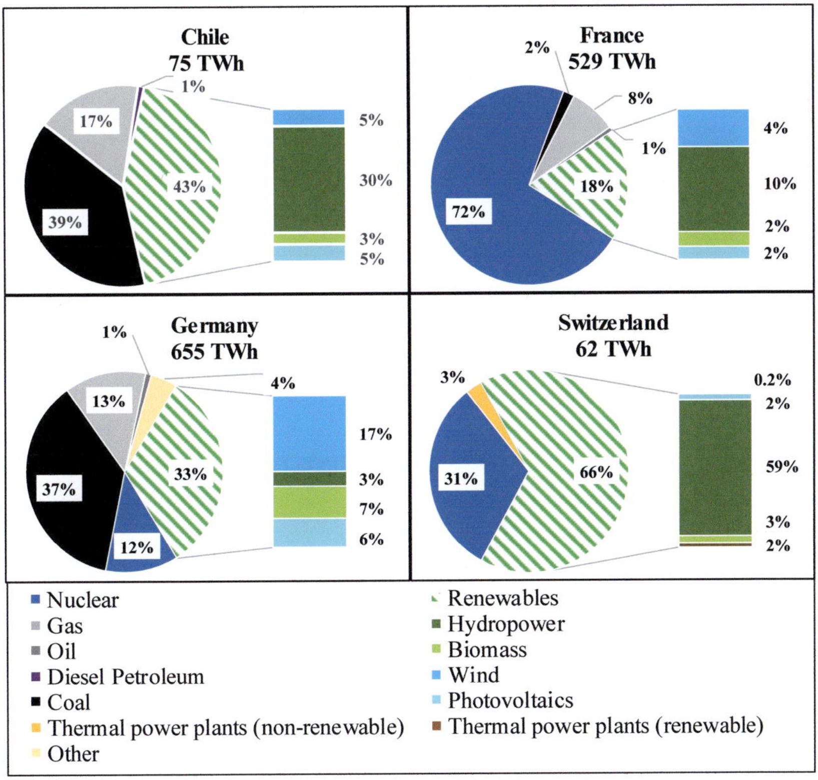

Figure 4-4: Electric energy generation in Chile (Watts Casimis and Pérez Odeh, 2018), France (RTE, 2017), Germany (Destatis, 2017), and Switzerland (VSE, 2019) in 2017

4.2.2.3 Targets for the Development of Renewable Energies

All four countries have defined ambitious targets for their future development of renewable energies. Table 4-2 provides an overview of the targets adopted by the individual countries.

Table 4-2: Targets for the development of REs adopted by Chile, France, Germany, and Switzerland

Country	Target	Target year
Chile	20% of electricity generation from non-hydro RES [a]	2025
	60% of electricity generation from RES [b]	2035
	70% of electricity generation from RES [b]	2050
France	40% of electricity demand met by RES [a]	2030
Germany	35% of gross electricity consumption from RES [c]	2020
	50% of gross electricity consumption from RES [c]	2030
Switzerland	24% of primary energy supply from "new" RES [a]	2020

Notes

[a] IEA (2019).

[b] Ministerio de Energía (2018).

[c] BMWi (2015).

Similar to Switzerland, Chile differentiates between large-scale hydropower and other "non-conventional" renewable energy sources (RES) which include geothermal, wind, solar, tidal, biomass and small hydroelectric power plants (IEA, 2016b). Based on this definition, Chile has formulated the goal to generate 20% of electricity from non-hydro RES by 2025. To further decrease import dependency and react to a quickly growing energy demand, Chile further sets the long-term target to increase the share of renewable energies to 60% by 2035 and at least 70% by 2050, including electricity from large-scale hydropower plants (IEA, 2018b). Germany aims at increasing the share of electricity demand met by renewable energies to 35% in 2020 and to 50% in 2030 (BMWi, 2015). Even though France is still holding on to nuclear energy, the country aims at increasing the share of renewables to 40% by 2030 (IEA, 2019). As afore mentioned, Switzerland enjoys favorable geographic conditions for hydropower and already generates a large share of energy from this source. But also the “new” RES, which are solar, wood, biomass, wind, and geothermal energy, are supposed to make and important contribution to the future Swiss energy supply (BFE, 2016b). To further develop those “new” RES, Switzerland is committed to increase the share of total primary energy supply to 24% by 2020.

4.2.3 Policy Frameworks

4.2.3.1 Policy Frameworks for Renewable Energies

To reach the afore described ambitious targets, the four countries rely on different policy instruments and market mechanisms, which are briefly presented in the following sections.

Germany

The fast development of renewable energies in Germany is mostly due to the decision to completely phase out nuclear energy by 2022 and the associated goals to increase the share of RES. Germany’s retail electricity market is liberalized and the whole sector is vertically unbundled. Whilst large fractions of non-renewable generation capacities are still owned and operated by the former “big four” utilities (EnBW, Vattenfall, E.ON (now uniper), and RWE), the majority of renewable generation capacity is accounted for by other actors than these four utilities, including private individuals, municipal utilities, farmers, and energy cooperatives (McKenna, 2018). The development of renewable energies in Germany has been heavily supported by the RES Act (Erneuerbare-Energien-Gesetz, EEG) in various versions since 1991 (previously the Electricity Feed-in Act, after 2000 EEG). The core of the Act is based on feed-in tariffs (FIT) for renewable electricity, combined with shared network connection and development costs between plant and network operators and priority dispatch for renewables. The FITs were initially fixed (EEG, 2000, 2004, 2009), before being supplemented by market and flexibility premiums (firstly with optional direct marketing in EEG, 2012), which later became compulsory (full direct marketing, EEG, 2014) to encourage more demand-oriented generation. In the most recent versions of the EEG (2014) and EEG (2017), tendering procedures for renewable electricity generation have been introduced (RES-LEGAL, 2017b). The most recent tendering procedures include special provisions for community energy: they do not require planning permission and in contrast to other (commercial) bidders receive the highest awarded price (rather than the bid). To finance the market and flexibility premiums, the electricity consumers have to pay a premium to the electricity price, the so-called "EEG-Umlage". This premium is defined by the transmission system operators and amounts to 6.405 €ct/kWh in 2019. Exceptions for companies for which electricity prices account for a high share of value added, train operators, and self-providers are possible. Household electricity prices in Germany are around 31 €ct/kWh (Eurostat, 2018).

Switzerland

Switzerland has a similar electricity market and energy-political framework to Germany, with liberalized retail markets and a vertically unbundled sector. It has fixed FITs, but no marketing/flexibility premiums, and direct marketing is being introduced in the context of the 2017 Energy Strategy (RES-LEGAL, 2017c). As in Germany, the costs of the renewable energy development in Switzerland are redistributed to all electricity consumers, with some exceptions. Household electricity prices are around 16 €ct/kWh (EICom, 2018). With regard to nuclear energy, Switzerland also decided a phase out but less radically than Germany – essentially no new nuclear plants will be built (UVEK, 2017). Existing nuclear plants may be operated as long as they meet the legal safety requirements. The Swiss Federal Nuclear Safety Inspectorate (ENSI) monitors the plants permanently and can request a shutdown if safety is no longer guaranteed (Swissnuclear, 2019).

France

Despite also being a liberalized retail electricity market, the French system is dominated on the supply side by EDF, the state-owned incumbent utility, as well as nuclear power (IEA, 2016a). In France the future of nuclear power continues to be discussed and no phase-out is currently planned. The energy-political framework for renewable energies in France is somewhat similar to that in Germany, though the level of the tariffs has not been as high, priority grid access is not guaranteed, and the costs are shared by all taxpayers as opposed to just electricity consumers (RES-LEGAL, 2017a). Household electricity prices amount to around 17 €ct/kWh (Eurostat, 2018).

Chile

In Chile the wish to decrease import dependency and the need to react to a quickly growing energy demand has led to a new institutional set-up with the creation of the Ministry of Energy in 2010. The ministry is responsible for the development and planning of the National Energy Policy 2050, which was launched by the government in 2015. Even though the development of renewable energies is strongly politically desired, there are no subsidies for renewable energies (IEA, 2018b). Instead, there is a "quota obligation" for electricity companies, which are imposed to generate a certain percentage (quota) of their total energy from "non-conventional" RES. Infringements against the quota are penalized with financial fines (IEA, 2016b). So far, the greatest share of renewable energy is generated by large-scale hydropower plants. Solar and wind energy are still in an early phase of development but have proven to be market-competitive without public financial support (IEA, 2018b). Especially for the development of PV, conditions are highly favorable due to strong solar radiation in the Atacama desert and the northern part of the country (Ministerio de Energía, 2018). Moreover, Chile has abundant woody biomass resources in the south-central regions in the form of wood plantations and natural forests. Whereas residues from wood plantations and sawmills are predominantly used for electricity generation in wood combustion plants (Rodríguez-Monroy et al., 2018), wood from natural forests is used as firewood by households (Ministerio de Energía, 2018). Household electricity prices are among the highest in Latin America and amounted to approximately 17 €ct/kWh in 2017 (IEA, 2018a), which is comparable to Switzerland and France.

4.2.3.2 Policy Frameworks for Bioenergy

As public acceptance of bioenergy plants is a focus topic of this thesis, it is worthwhile to briefly describe the differences in national support schemes in the four countries regarding bioenergy. Whereas the analysis in the URR refers to public acceptance of biogas plants, the analysis in Chile deals with the public acceptance of wood-combustion plants. Therefore, the following section firstly provides a brief description of the policy frameworks for biogas in Germany, France, and Switzerland, and secondly a description of the policy framework for wood combustion plants in Chile.

Biogas in Germany, France, and Switzerland

In the URR, biogas plants have experienced a substantial growth over the last decade. In all three countries, the biogas sector has received strong political support during the last years. The incentives provided through the introduction of cost-reflective feed-in tariffs for electricity produced from biogas by combined heat and power (CHP) plants pushed the growth of the national biogas sectors (Konsortium OUI Biomasse, 2015). The national incentive schemes, however, differ in extent and provisions, which led to specific developments in the three countries regarding the speed of growth and the implemented use concepts.

One major difference is the financial support of specific feedstock types for biogas production. In this regard, Germany has chosen a special path (Konsortium OUI Biomasse, 2015) by promoting the use of energy crops through the RES Act in 2000 (EEG, 2000). The incentives led to a strong growth of small and medium-sized agricultural biogas plants operated by local farmers dedicating parts of their arable land to produce energy crops for digestion, particularly corn (Markard et al., 2009). With the amendments of the German RES Act in 2014 (EEG, 2014), however, subsidies of energy crops were withdrawn for newly installed biogas plants, leading to a severe breakdown in the German biogas market (Markard et al., 2009). Without the subsidies, growth of the biogas sector in Germany now concentrates on biogas plants using residues and waste as well as on small plants with a maximum installed electric capacity of up to 75 kilowatts (kW_{el}) and running on manure from livestock farming. Moreover, the majority of existing biogas plants, which profited from the subsidies for energy crops, will not be profitable anymore after the expiration of the subsidy, which was limited to a term of 20 years (Hoffstede et al., 2018).

In contrast to this, France and Switzerland have focused on the use of residues and waste for the production of biogas. While the hierarchy of "food, feed, tank" is strictly applied in Switzerland, the legislative framework in France is more flexible, but does not explicitly support the use of energy crops for biogas production either. As a consequence, existing biogas plants in Switzerland exclusively process diverse organic residues from households, agriculture, and industry (Konsortium OUI Biomasse, 2015), whereas in France, biogas plants are allowed to use a small fraction of intermediate energy crops of up to 10% in combination with other residual feedstock or biogenic waste (Daniel and Bailly, 2015; Konsortium OUI Biomasse, 2015).

Sizes and growth rates also differ among the national sectors. Due to the provisions of the RES adopted in 2000, Germany experienced by far the fastest growth. From 2000 to 2013, the number of biogas plants grew from 1,050 to approximately 7,850 plants (German Biogas Association, 2014). In France and Switzerland, growth of the biogas sectors was much slower, which is also reflected by the number of plants in the three sub-regions of the URR (Table 4-3). In the French sub-region only five biogas plants had been installed in 2013. In the Swiss sub-region 14 plants were operated, whereas 74 biogas plants were run in the German state of Baden-Württemberg alone. Table 4-3 also reveals that the installed capacity and bioenergy provision per capita is significantly higher in Germany than in the other two sub-regions (2015).

Table 4-3: Energy provision of biogas plants in the French (Wolff and Muller, 2013), German (Konsortium OUI Biomasse, 2015), and Swiss (BFE, 2014) URR in 2013

	Germany (BW)	France	Switzerland
Number of plants	74	5	14
Total installed capacity (kW_{el})	100,837	2,625	3,600
Average installed capacity per plant (kW_{el}/plant)	1 363	525	257
Installed capacity per inhabitant (kW_{el}/capita)	37	1	2.58
Estimated bioenergy provision per year (6 000 h/y, electricity production of 1/3 of total) ($kWh_{(el+th)}$/year)	1,815,066,000	47,250,000	64,800,000
Estimated bioenergy provision per inhabitant per year ($kWh_{(el+th)}$/capita/year)	660	25	46

Wood combustion in Chile

Chile has abundant woody biomass resources in the central-southern regions (especially regions Maule VII, Bio-Bio VIII, and Araucania IX), which are predominantly used in two pathways:

(i) forest companies burn residues from their own plantations to generate electricity and heat for their own operations and feed excess electricity to the grid (Rodríguez-Monroy et al., 2018) and
(ii) households use firewood as major energy source for heating and cooking.

The burning of low-quality, humid wood by households has led to serious air pollution and health problems in many southern cities (IEA, 2018b). Therefore, the government encourages a shift to cleaner biomass conversion technologies for heat generation on the household level (Ministerio de Energía, 2018). The latter pathway needs to be mentioned because of its societal importance and potential side effects of industrial wood combustion plants, which might increase the competition for the resource of firewood.

Considering the large biomass potentials in Chile, the share of electricity generated from wood combustion is rather small. As afore mentioned, the existing wood combustion plants are usually owned and operated by companies from the forest and timber sector, which use residues from their own plantations of Radiata pine and eucalyptus to generate energy for their own operations and only feed excess electricity to the grid. Hence, the operation of wood combustion plants does not directly belong to their core business but is related to the resources they possess and their own high demand for electricity and heat (Rodríguez-Monroy et al., 2018). In February 2019, the installed electric capacity of woody biomass combustion plants amounted to roughly 359 Megawatt (MW). There are currently 22 plants in operation, which are diverse in size, ranging from 1.84 MW for the smallest and 60.70 MW electric installed capacity for the largest plant (CNE, 2019). With regard to those numbers it needs to be mentioned that the reported installed capacity does not include the additional capacities, which are used for auto-consumption by the forest industry but only accounts for the electricity fed into the grid.

4.3 Case Study 1: Public Acceptance of Renewable Energies in the Upper Rhine Region[8]

4.3.1 Materials and Methods

4.3.1.1 Survey and Questionnaire Design

The online survey was carried out in cooperation with a service provider for polls (Bilendi) from October 2015 to January 2016. The target population included all inhabitants of the URR of 16 years or older. The multi-cultural and multi-lingual conditions in the URR required the development of three linguistic versions of the questionnaire, one for each sub-region. Using a parallel approach to translation, the German source questionnaire was translated independently by two translators to French. Both translations were then thoroughly discussed within the team of translators and the first author. The Swiss language version was also slightly adapted to account for linguistic differences. Finally, all three language versions were pretested in the target regions and necessary adjustments were made to increase validity.

The questionnaire composes 77 questions covering socio-demographic information as well as motives and actions, personal attitudes and beliefs, perceptions and evaluations regarding renewable energies and energy autonomy (cf. Table A-1, Appendix A). The majority of questions deals with the respondent's attitude towards the most widely used renewable energy technologies in the URR, differentiating between large-scale and small-scale PV installations, wind power, and biogas plants. The focus was on those with which the wider population has the most direct interaction in the URR (cf. also section 3.2.2). Every technology was described in a short paragraph at the beginning of each section of the questionnaire and a picture of a typical plant was shown in order to ensure that all participants had a sufficient level of information to answer the questionnaire (cf. Appendix B and C). A separate

[8] Parts of this section have previously been published in Schumacher et al. (2019b).

section was dedicated to the focus topic "community energy and energy autonomy"[9], including aspects with regard to current or intended (financial) involvement in renewable energy projects. Several single items dealt with the respondent's self-perceived knowledge about renewable energies and the degree to which respondents are experienced with renewable energies in their neighborhood.

To increase comparability with other studies, all items and constructs are based as far as available on existing publications on the acceptance of various renewable energy technologies (cf. e.g., Bertsch et al., 2016; Griesen, 2010; Rau and Zoellner, 2008; Schweizer-Ries et al., 2010; Wüste, 2013). Some scales needed slight adaptation to the study context; some were newly developed by the author based on theoretical concepts from the literature and the expert interviews in the URR (cf. section 3.1.2). A list with all items is displayed in Table A-1, Appendix A. Most questions were answered on a five-point Likert scale to determine the degree to which the respondents agreed or disagreed with a proposed statement; a few questions also allowed for free-text answers. The option "don't know" was introduced wherever appropriate in order to avoid respondents choosing the "comfortable center" ("I am undecided" or "neutral") of the unevenly-numbered Likert scale. Because of the "don't know" option, the sample size differs for certain questions and analyses. At the end of the questionnaire, the respondents were asked to leave additional free text comments.

4.3.1.2 Sample Characteristics

The final sample contains 1,489 units of analysis and is representative relating to age and sex for all three sub-regions on the level of administrative districts (i.e. Landkreis in Germany, arrondissement in France, and Kanton in Switzerland). Of these, 33.2% live in Germany (n = 495), 33.6% in France (n = 501), and 33.1% in Switzerland (n = 493). Table 4-4 compares the socio-

[9] For energy autonomy the first question related to familiarity with the term. Subsequent questions related to the desirability and scales at which energy autonomy might be strived for. Before these subsequent questions, a short explanation of the term energy autonomy was given, in order to ensure that the participants were informed about the concept.

demographic characteristics of the sample to population statistics of the three sub-regions.

Table 4-4: Socio-demographic characteristics of the survey samples compared to population statistics (case study 1)

		France		Germany		Switzerland	
		sample	pop.	sample	pop.	sample	pop.
Male	(%)	47.7	48.9 [a]	46.7	49.0 [a]	47.9	49.4 [a]
Age	16-35 years (%)	33.3	30.6 [c]	32.3	29.9 [b]	33.9	29.5 [d]
	36-55 years (%)	30.5	34.8 [c]	30.9	35.0 [b]	33.5	35.3 [d]
	>56 years (%)	36.1	34.6 [c]	36.8	35.1 [b]	32.7	35.1 [d]
Home owners	(%)	61.5	65.1 [e]	49.9	52.5 [e]	41.4	44.0 [e]
Employment rate	(%)	64.7	50.1 [f]	64.4	61.6 [f]	63.3	68.0 [f]

Notes:

[a] Based on Deutsch-Französische-Schweizerische Oberrheinkonferenz (2015), includes male population aged 15 or younger, data on URR level.

[b] Own calculation based on Statistisches Landesamt Baden-Württemberg (2011), data on regional level without the German region "Südpfalz".

[c] Own calculation based on Institut national de la statistique et des études économiques (2015), data on regional level, deviating classes: 15-34, 35-54, >55 years.

[d] Own calculation based on Bundesamt für Statistik (2014), data on canton level.

[e] Based on Eurostat (2014), data on country level.

[f] Based on Deutsch-Französische-Schweizerische Oberrheinkonferenz (2015), includes working population from the age of 15, data on URR level.

Comparison with the statistical data reveals that the sample distribution represents the population quite precisely. However, some deviations with regard to employment and age classes are apparent. The strongest deviation was detected for the employment rate with an overrepresentation of the working population in France and Germany by 14.6 percentage points (pp) and 2.8 pp respectively and an underrepresentation in Switzerland by 5.1 pp However, tests showed that there are no statistically significant differences between employed and unemployed respondents with regard to acceptance levels of different renewable energy technologies. Another mentionable deviation was found in the age class "36-55 years" in the German and French sub-sample, which is slightly underrepresented by 4.1 and 4.3 pp respectively.

Also, a slight overrepresentation of the population class "16-35 years" by 4.4 pp was found in the Swiss sub-sample. Moreover, homeowner rates diverge slightly from the population statistics in all three sub-regions. This might also result from regional particularities of the URR, however, as the data for homeowner rates refers to the national level. The latter deviations are however considered as rather negligible (below 3 pp). To sum up, the sample represents the population living in the three sub-regions of the URR quite well. It however needs to be stressed that the obtained data does not claim representativeness for the three countries but only for the three sub-regions belonging to the URR.

4.3.1.3 Data Preparation and Analysis

The analysis of the survey data was carried out with the statistics Software SPSS (Version 21). To avoid measurement errors, the data was critically reviewed and units of analysis with a processing time less than four minutes (speeders) were removed (8% of the dataset).

The questionnaire contained several constructs which were measured by scales of several items. Table 4-5 lists all constructs and a short description of their meaning; the respective items are reported in Table A-1, Appendix A. All constructs were tested by an item analysis to assess internal consistencies for the overall sample and by sub-region (Table 4-6). In the overall sample, all values of Cronbach's α exceeded the recommended threshold of 0.70 (Bühner, 2011). In the French sub-sample, however, there were some slight deviations regarding the constructs "advocacy of renewable energies" ($\alpha = 0.626$), "perceived costs of energy crops" ($\alpha = 0.675$) and "advocacy of energy autonomy" ($\alpha = 0.664$). For conceptual reasons, the three constructs are still used, prioritizing conceptual comprehensiveness over internal consistency in the selection of scales.

Table 4-5: Constructs of the questionnaire (case study 1)

Construct	Concept
Advocacy of renewable energies	Support of renewable energy technologies in general and in the neighborhood
Perceived benefits of biogas plants	Perceived benefits of biogas plants for the society and the individual
Perceived costs of biogas plants	Perceived costs of biogas plants for the society and the individual
Perceived costs of energy crops	Perceived costs of monocultures and the use of agricultural crops for energy generation
Information and participation	Desired information and participation possibilities during the planning and construction phase of local biogas plants
Engagement for renewable energies	Engagement with regard to convincing others, financial participation, and active support
Advocacy of energy autonomy	Support of approaches which lead to higher energy autonomy in general and at the local level

Table 4-6: Internal consistency of constructs for the overall sample (URR) and by sub-region (case study 1)

Construct	Cronbach's α				Number of items
	France	Germany	Switzerland	URR	
Advocacy of renewable energies	.626	.758	.722	.71	2
Perceived benefits of biogas plants	.852	.903	.841	.87	5
Perceived costs of biogas plants	.746	.826	.721	.77	5
Perceived costs of energy crops	.675	.748	.701	.73	2
Information and participation	.882	.765	.753	.78	4
Engagement for renewable energies	.767	.723	.707	.73	3
Advocacy of energy autonomy	.664	.847	.81	.78	3

4.3.2 Results

In this section, the major findings of case study 1 are presented and discussed along the hypotheses (cf. section 3.2.3). Firstly, H1 to H5 are tested across the three sub-regions of the URR and the covered technologies. Subsequently, a closer look is taken at potential factors influencing the public acceptance of biogas plants (H6, H7, H8, H9, H11), which is particularly interesting due to differences in political frameworks in the three sub-regions (cf. section 4.2.3.2). To test H13, the link between public acceptance, engagement for renewable energies, and energy autonomy is empirically explored.

H1: Renewable Energies Generally Enjoy High Public Acceptance for Future Energy Generation.

In line with other studies (e.g., Bertsch et al., 2016; Gamma et al., 2017; Zoellner et al., 2008), the results show that on the socio-political dimension renewable energies are widely supported by the population in all three sub-regions for future energy provision (Figure 4-5). Solar energy enjoys highest approval with more than 85% of respondents being in favor. Bioenergy and geothermal energy rank lowest amongst the renewable energies, with the exception of the French sub-sample, where hydropower ranks significantly lower. This comparatively negative evaluation of bioenergy fits the findings of Butler et al. (2013) and Devine-Wright, 2003 (2003), who revealed that bioenergy was associated with fossil fuels and often not recognized as renewable energy source. Non-renewable energies lag far behind with less than 13% approval. In particular, coal suffers from a low popularity. This confirms the results of other studies, which show a decline in public acceptance of this energy carrier in Germany and increasing proportions of the population in favor of a complete phase out (Schumann et al., 2016).

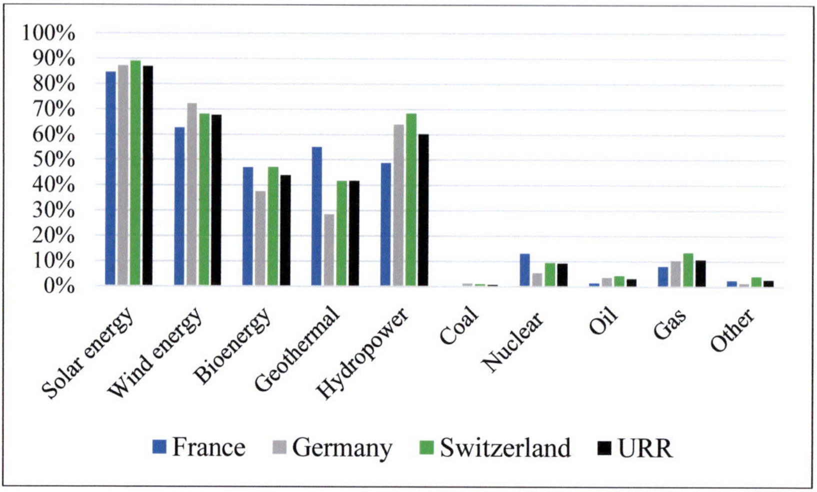

Note: Sample sizes: $n_{Germany} = 495$, $n_{Switzerland} = 493$, $n_{France} = 501$.

Figure 4-5: Frequency distribution of the answers to the question "In your opinion, which energy technologies should be preferably used in the future?" (case study 1)

H2: There is Public Disposition to Act Towards Renewable Energy Plants in the Neighborhood.

To assess H2, acceptance levels and dispositions to act are analyzed based on the definition of acceptance proposed by Schweizer-Ries et al. (2008) (cf. Figure 2-2). The four levels of acceptance are measured by the following three items: Firstly, the appraisal of a local plant is assessed by the item "How do you rate small-scale PV/ large-scale PV/ wind turbines/ biogas plants in your neighborhood?" on a five-point Likert scale with 1 = "very negative" and 5 = "very positive" as anchors (cf. Table A-1, Appendix A, item "appraisal of local plant"). Secondly, a filter on the first question to assess the action-oriented level of acceptance is applied in the following logic: in case of a *positive* appraisal, the successive item asks for the respondent's disposition to *actively support* a plant in the neighborhood. In case of a *negative* appraisal, the respondent's disposition to *actively oppose* a plant in the neighborhood is subsequently assessed (cf. Table A-1, Appendix A, item "active support" and "active resistance").[10]

Figure 4-6 presents the results by sub-region and technology. A visual inspection reveals a similar rank order of acceptance levels for the different technologies in all three sub-regions. Small- and large-scale PV plants are widely accepted, with 78% and 60% approval respectively on average in the URR. The highest rejection and resistance is demonstrated for wind and biogas plants, with 17% and 20% rejection respectively on average in the URR.

One-way ANOVA was performed to test for differences between the sub-regions with regard to acceptance levels and dispositions to act. The results are displayed by Table 4-7 and confirmed significant differences in mean acceptance values for all technologies, except for large PV plants. Eta-squared however revealed that all effects are very weak. Post hoc tests further showed significantly lower appraisal of small-scale PV and wind energy plants in the French compared to the German and Swiss sub-region. Especially for wind energy there was low acceptance and a high threat of active resistance against local projects in France. Based on the literature, this is assumed to be due to the historic "anti-wind-energy movement" in France, which saw the development of wind energy as a major threat to the "patrimoine" (national heritage) of the French landscape (Jobert et al., 2007). Generally, the data reveals that French respondents are more critical towards renewable energies than German and Swiss respondents.

[10] "(Active) support" is a sub-quantity of "(passive) approval", and "(active) resistance" a sub-quantity of "(passive) rejection" (cf. also Figure 2-2).

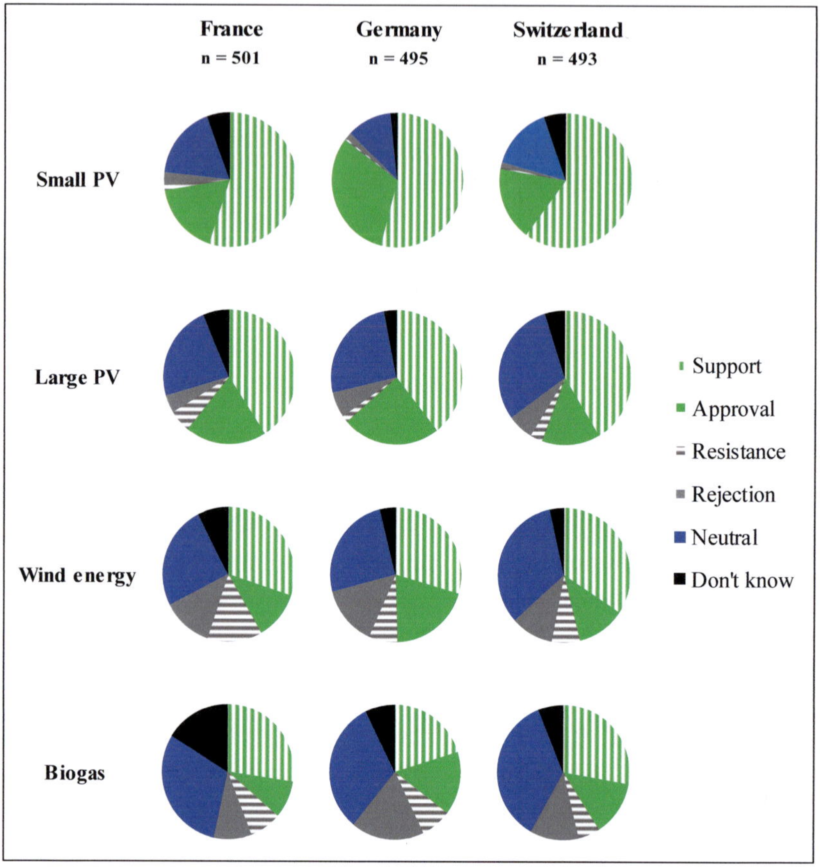

Note: Categories "approval" and "rejection" include the categories "support" and "resistance" respectively (cf. Figure 2-1).

Figure 4-6: Levels of acceptance and dispositions to act towards a RE plant in the neighborhood by sub-region and technology (case study 1)

Table 4-7: One-way ANOVA and post hoc analysis (Tukey) of differences in public acceptance of a RE plant in the neighborhood between sub-regions by technology

		France (n = 501)			Germany (n = 495)			Switzerland (n = 493)		
		n	M	SD	n	M	SD	n	M	SD
PV small	Approval/Resistance	473	3.98	.835	487	4.40	.784	467	4.30	.816
	of which support	363	1.24	.427	422	1.37	.483	383	1.23	.420
	of which rejection	21	1.71	.463	10	1.80	.422	8	1.75	.463
PV large	Approval/Resistance	469	3.72	.929	480	3.84	.946	469	3.72	.971
	of which support	305	1.33	.470	315	1.38	.486	274	1.26	.437
	of which rejection	48	1.44	.501	38	1.79	.413	46	1.67	.474
Wind	Approval/Resistance	463	3.2	1.16	476	3.46	1.17	476	3.45	1.12
	of which support	209	1.28	.449	245	1.40	.492	227	1.26	.437
	of which rejection	129	1.48	.502	106	1.67	.473	85	1.6	.493
Biogas	Approval/Resistance	420	3.29	1.02	459	3.17	1.14	463	3.39	1.04
	of which support	182	1.25	.433	175	1.43	.496	202	1.32	.468
	of which rejection	85	1.54	.501	126	1.71	.457	84	1.69	.465

		One-way ANOVA			Germany versus France			Germany versus Switzerland			France versus Switzerland		
		df[a]	p	η^2	ΔM	SE	p	ΔM	SE	p	ΔM	SE	p
PV small	Approval/Resistance	1,424	.000	.047	.422	.052	.000	.099	.053	.146	-.323	.053	.000
	of which support	1,165	.000	.021	.128	.032	.000	.140	.031	.000	.013	.033	.922
	of which rejection	36	.885	.007	.086	.174	.875	.050	.215	.971	-.036	.188	.980
PV large	Approval/Resistance	1,415	.086	.003	.115	.062	.150	.121	.062	.121	.006	.062	.994
	of which support	891	.005	.012	.052	.037	.332	.125	.039	.003	.072	.039	.149
	of which rejection	129	.002	.091	.352	.102	.002	.116	.103	.499	-.236	.097	.041
Wind	Approval/Resistance	1,412	.001	.011	.259	.075	.002	.008	.075	.993	-.251	.075	.003
	of which support	678	.001	.021	.127	.043	.010	.149	.042	.001	.022	.044	.872
	of which rejection	317	.012	.028	.189	.064	.010	.070	.071	.591	-.119	.068	.190
Biogas	Approval/Resistance	1,339	.008	.007	-.121	.072	.217	-.219	.070	.005	-.098	.072	.359
	of which support	556	.001	.024	.181	.049	.001	.107	.048	.069	-.75	.048	.262
	of which rejection	292	.033	.023	.165	.066	.035	.016	.067	.969	-.149	.073	.101

Note: [a]degrees of freedom between groups.

H3: General Public Acceptance (Socio-Political Dimension) Exceeds Public Acceptance of Plants in the Neighborhood (Community Dimension).

H3 was tested by assessing differences in public acceptance with regard to renewable energies in general (socio-political dimension) and acceptance of plants in the neighborhood (community dimension) across sub-regions and technologies. The questionnaire discriminated between general attitudes (cf. Table A-1, Appendix A, item "socio-political acceptance") and attitudes relating to locally installed renewable energy plants in the vicinity (cf. Table A-1, Appendix A, item "appraisal of local plant"). In analogy with other studies, vicinity was defined as a one kilometer radius from the respondent's home (cf. Hübner and Hahn, 2013; Musall and Kuik, 2011; Schumacher and Schultmann, 2017).

Table 4-8 shows the results for the t-test to compare public acceptance on the socio-political and the community dimension by sub-region and technology. Significant differences were confirmed for all technologies and sub-regions. Cohen's d revealed small to medium effects (Cohen's d between 0.44 and 0.78) for large-scale technologies (large PV, wind, and biogas plants) in all three sub-regions, and a medium effect (Cohen's $d = 0.52$) for small-scale PV in France. A notable result was that for small PV community acceptance was higher than socio-political acceptance, whereas for all other technologies it was the other way round. A possible explanation is, that small PV plants are likely to be (fully) owned by the respondents, whereas the respondents could at most have a share in large PV, wind, and biogas plants, but are unlikely to own them outright. Hence, this finding might be explained by the fact that people are more likely to accept a technology if they personally benefit from it. To further assess the role of (co-)ownership for public acceptance, it was analyzed if respondents that either own a renewable energy plant, are otherwise financially involved, or are part of an energy cooperative, reported higher public acceptance of local renewable energy plants than respondents that are not. A significant difference was detected on the community dimension for all technologies and hence confirmed a positive effect of (co-)ownership on public acceptance for local renewable energy plants.

Table 4-8: Paired sample t-test to compare public acceptance on the socio-political and the community dimension by sub-region and technology (case study 1)

Object of acceptance	Sub-region	n	Socio-political		Community		p-value	Cohen's d
			M	SD	M	SD		
	France	473	3.72	.949	4.19	.854	.000	.52
PV small	Germany	483	4.53	.735	4.63	.750	.000	.14
	Switzerland	471	4.45	.744	4.55	.767	.002	.13
	France	470	4.11	.847	3.70	1.004	.000	.44
PV large	Germany	478	4.47	.779	3.97	1.020	.000	.55
	Switzerland	469	4.37	.805	3.90	1.070	.000	.50
	France	475	3.79	1.049	3.19	1.265	.000	.52
Wind	Germany	484	4.34	.917	3.56	1.277	.000	.78
	Switzerland	474	4.23	.920	3.63	1.229	.000	.55
	France	428	3.76	.936	3.34	1.053	.000	.42
Biogas	Germany	462	3.78	1.112	3.20	1.271	.000	.49
	Switzerland	458	4.00	.917	3.52	1.103	.000	.47

H4: Public Acceptance of Renewable Energy Plants is Influenced by the Distance of the Plant to the Respondent's Home.

To approach H4, it was firstly assessed if distance to renewable energy plants was important for the different technologies at all. Table 4-9 displays the results to the question "To what extent is the distance between your house/ apartment and a small-scale PV/ large-scale PV/ wind energy/ biogas plant important to you?" by answer category, sub-region, and technology. The data revealed strong differences between technologies: Proximity was especially important with regard to wind and biogas plants with more than half of the respondents desiring a minimum distance to their homes, whereas the distance to small-scale PV was not relevant for the majority of respondents. In addition, sight-contact was named more often as a relevant issue for large-scale installations than for residential small-scale PV. It is therefore concluded that the relevance of proximity depends on the technology in question as larger plant sizes are associated with higher local impacts.

Table 4-9: Role of proximity for public acceptance of different RE plants in percent (%) of respondents by sub-region and technology

Response category	Sub-regions	Technology			
		Small PV	Large PV	Wind	Biogas
I do *not* accept the plant, independent of the distance.	France	2.8	4.4	14.4	12.6
	Germany	1	2.8	8.9	14.7
	Switzerland	1.6	5.1	8.1	9.3
The distance of the plant to my home is not relevant for me.	France	42.7	25	15.2	15.4
	Germany	74.9	38.8	21	13.9
	Switzerland	70.2	41.4	24.7	18.7
The distance is not relevant but the plant should not be visible from my home.	France	16.4	22.8	17.2	17.6
	Germany	7.9	23.6	16.6	21
	Switzerland	10.1	21.7	18.9	24.9
The plants should keep a minimal distance to my home.	France	38.1	47.9	53.3	54.5
	Germany	16.2	34.7	53.5	50.3
	Switzerland	18.1	31.8	48.3	47.1

Those respondents who indicated that renewable energy plants should keep a minimal distance to their homes (cf. Table 4-9) were subsequently asked to specify this distance in kilometers. Figure 4-7 displays the cumulated relative frequencies of the desired distance by technology. Results reveal that public acceptance increases with distance for all four renewable energy technologies, however, at different rates for the individual technologies. In a one kilometer distance, only 17% and 22% of respondents indicated to accept a biogas or a wind energy plant respectively. For large-scale PV plants, 38% of respondents stated to be willing to accept a plant in their vicinity (< 1 km distance). With regard to small-scale PV, however, 68% of respondents indicated to accept a plant in direct proximity to their homes. Even though the differences between technologies decrease with increasing distance, the rank order of technologies remains stable in all three sub-regions, with the smallest desired distance for small-scale PV and the largest for biogas plants. These results are in line with those reported by Bertsch et al. (2016), who found the same rank order of technologies for a representative sample in Germany. However, in their study Bertsch et al. (2016) reported considerably smaller desired mean minimal distances for solar PV modules, wind power stations, and biomass power plants.[11]

[11] Because of different research designs of the studies (e.g. sampling, items, and scales), a deeper interpretation of the differences between the reported numbers is not reasonable.

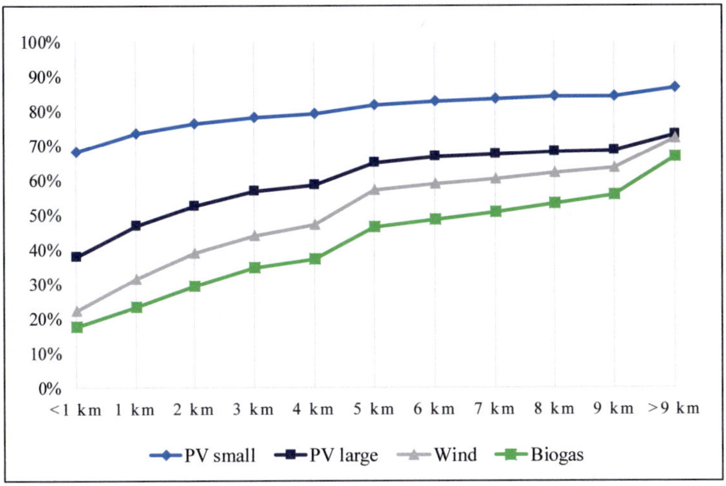

Notes:

Sample sizes: $n_{PV\ small} = 1{,}291$, $n_{PV\ large} = 1{,}090$, $n_{Wind} = 1{,}072$, $n_{Biogas} = 992$.

Includes responses "The distance of the plant to my home is not relevant for me." as 0 km.

Expressed as percentage of all responses (cf. Table 4-9).

Figure 4-7: Cumulated relative frequencies of the desired minimum distance of RE plants in the URR

H5: Public Acceptance of Renewable Energy Plants is Higher Among Respondents with Previous Experience with Renewable Energy Projects.

It was hypothesized that the acceptance of respondents already living with a renewable energy plant in their vicinity exceeds the acceptance of those without. Therefore, respondents were asked to indicate whether they were aware of renewable energy plants installed in their neighborhood (Table 4-10). Based on the responses, a t-test to compare public acceptance between respondents with and without renewable energy plant in their direct vicinity (Table 4-11) was performed.

Large differences between the sub-samples were found with regard to the number of respondents already living next to renewable energy plants: in Germany 62% indicated to live with some type of renewable energy plant in their vicinity, whereas in Switzerland 46% and in France only 19% did so.

Table 4-10: Share of respondents with RE plant in direct vicinity by sub-region and technology

		France	Germany	Switzer-land	URR
		(n = 501)	(n = 495)	(n = 493)	(n = 1489)
Plant in direct vicinity	total	94	310	228	632
	%	18.8	62.6	46.2	42.4
Thereof PV small	total	78	279	189	546
	%	83	90	82.9	86.4
Thereof PV large	total	23	52	42	117
	%	24.5	16.8	18.4	18.5
Thereof wind	total	14	102	23	139
	%	14.9	32.9	10.1	22
Thereof biogas	total	7	30	38	75
	%	7.4	9.7	16.7	11.9

Table 4-11 displays the results of the t-test to compare public acceptance between respondents with and without renewable energy plant in their direct vicinity. The results revealed statistically significant differences on the level of the URR for all technologies, except for biogas plants. On the level of the three sub-regions, however, significant differences could not be statistically proven for all cases, which could be due to small sample sizes in some of the sub-groups.

Table 4-11: T-test to compare public acceptance between respondents with and without RE plant in direct vicinity (case study 1)

Object of acceptance	Sub-region	*With* plant in vicinity			*Without* plant in vicinity			p-value	Cohen's d
		n	M	SD	n	M	SD		
REs	France	93	4.03	.902	376	3.87	.939	.133	.13
	Germany	307	4.58	.683	178	4.18	1.02	.000*	.25
	Switzerland	227	4.48	.772	252	4.37	.844	.149	.03
	URR	627	4.46	.773	806	4.10	.953	.000*	.14
Small PV plants	France	76	4.42	.753	410	4.14	.877	.008	.27
	Germany	278	4.80	.524	210	4.41	.940	.000*	.20
	Switzerland	187	4.63	.732	289	4.47	.799	.028*	.10
	URR	541	4.69	.650	909	4.31	.881	.000*	.24
Large PV plants	France	23	4.00	.853	464	3.66	1.02	.117	.32
	Germany	51	4.35	.890	434	3.91	1.05	.004	.38
	Switzerland	42	4.38	.936	432	3.84	1.08	.002	.46
	URR	116	4.29	.904	1330	3.80	1.05	.000	.43
Wind energy plants	France	14	3.71	1.27	474	3.15	1.27	.099	.43
	Germany	101	4.00	1.13	385	3.44	1.29	.000*	.34
	Switzerland	23	3.96	1.22	455	3.62	1.23	.213*	.26
	URR	138	3.96	1.16	1314	3.40	1.27	.000*	.40
Biogas plants	France	7	3.86	.690	450	3.30	1.06	.168	.52
	Germany	30	3.50	1.33	437	3.19	1.26	.189	.23
	Switzerland	38	3.61	1.15	433	3.49	1.11	.546	.10
	URR	75	3.59	1.19	1320	3.33	1.15	.056	.21

Note: *Welch-Test because of variance heterogeneity.

To further explore the role of experiences with renewable energy plants, the relationship between experience and desired distance was analyzed. It was found that the average reported desired distance to a local renewable energy plant was lower for respondents with a plant in a one kilometer radius than for respondents without. However, due to the small numbers of participants with plants in a one kilometer radius, the effect was only statistically significant for small PV plants, being the largest sub-sample. Furthermore, respondents with an equivalent plant in a one kilometer radius were less likely to reject such a plant in their vicinity than respondents without. On the level of sub-regions, a similar observation was made: the average desired distance to a renewable energy plant was significantly larger in the French (4.8 km) compared to the Swiss (3.9 km) and the German (3.6 km) sub-region (cf. Figure 4-7). Hence, there was empirical evidence that public acceptance was higher among respondents with previous experience than among those without.

H6 to H12: Factors Driving the Acceptance of Bioenergy Plants

The comparison of public acceptance of biogas is particularly interesting as the policy frameworks in Germany, France, and Switzerland vary substantially (cf. section 4.2.3.2). Consequently, differences in public acceptance can be assumed if, inter alia, political frameworks were to play a role for social acceptance. Therefore, the questionnaire contained a dedicated section to assess public acceptance of biogas with several items and constructs (cf. Table 4-5 and Table 4-6).

Multiple linear regression was used to examine which factors significantly influence social acceptance of biogas plants. Table 4-12 shows the results of two regression models, one with self-reported acceptance on the socio-political level (item "Biogas plants are a suitable form of energy generation") as dependent variables, and another with community level (item "I support biogas plants in my neighborhood") as dependent variables. To test the influence of the hypothesized factors (cf. section 3.2.3), the acceptance factors "advocacy of renewable energies" (H6), "perceived benefits of biogas plants" (H7), "perceived costs of biogas plants" (H8), "information and participation" (H9), and "perceived costs of energy crops" (H11) were included in the model. The factors "trust" (H10) and "perceived odor emissions" (H12) were not included in the model as they refer to specific, already existing bioenergy plants, which are not covered in case study 1.

Moreover, the respondents' sex (female/male), the home owner status (yes/no) and the existence of a biogas plant in the neighborhood (yes/no) were included as control variables in the model. By introducing two dummy variables ("Dummy France" and "Dummy Switzerland") for the respondents' country of residence it was tested for differences between the sub-regions. The dummies assumed the value one, if the respondent was living in the respective country, and zero if not.

Both models fulfil the assumptions of multiple linear regressions (cf. section 3.1.3). A visual inspection of residuals showed no critical violations of the assumption of normal distribution of residuals and no indication of violations of the linearity assumption (Hair et al., 2014, pp. 216–219). The VIF statistics showed no noteworthy indication of multicollinearity and are far below the upper acceptable bound (VIF model "socio-political acceptance" ≤ 1.461, VIF model "community acceptance" ≤ 1.471) (Hair et al., 2014, p. 200). A visual inspection of the residual scatter diagrams indicated homoscedasticity (Hair et al., 2014, p. 217). As the data is no time series data, auto correlation was not expected to be a critical issue, which was confirmed by the Durbin-Watson-test (Durbin-Watson model "socio-political acceptance" = 2.025, Durbin-Watson model "community acceptance" = 2.056) (Field, 2013, p. 311).

The results showed that the by far most important factor for the acceptance of biogas plants was "perceived benefits of biogas plants" (H7) with highly significant positive effects on the socio-political ($B = 0.805$, $p < 0.001$) as well as on the community dimension ($B = 0.819$, $p < 0.001$). Moreover, "advocacy of renewable energies" (H6) was revealed as significant factor with a positive effect on the socio-political ($B = 0.102$, $p < 0.01$) and the community dimension ($B = 0.078$, $p < 0.05$) and "perceived costs" (H8) was detected as significant factor on both the community ($B = -0.238$, $p < 0.001$) and the socio-political ($B = -0.073$, $p < 0.05$) dimension.

Using the method suggested by Cohen et al. (2003) to compare coefficients of regression models with different dependent variables, it was revealed that the influence of "perceived costs" was more important on the community than on the socio-political dimension whereas "perceived benefits" were more important on the socio-political dimension. A potential explanation is the so-called "low-cost hypothesis" (Diekmann and Preisendörfer, 2003), which states a decreasing importance of attitudinal factors with increasing behavioral costs. For example, while biogas plants in general might be positively evaluated due to their benefits for climate protection and the energy system, the community impacts of those plants are perceived to be relatively high and therefore superpose rather abstract general benefits.

Moreover, there was a weak positive effect of "perceived costs of energy crops" (H11) ($B = -0.076$, $p < 0.01$) on the socio-political level. This finding fits the explanation that the debate on "food versus fuel" is an ethical debate, which might therefore not be relevant for the impacts of biogas plants on the community level.

A weak negative effect was revealed for "information and participation" (H9) on public acceptance ($B = -0.080$, $p < 0.05$). It is assumed that this can be explained by the fact that the item asked for the *desired* information and participation. Hence, it is possible that the *real* level of information and participation was lower than the *desired* level and hence the coefficient turned negative.

Interestingly, the effects of the dummy variables for the countries France and Switzerland were not significant. Hence, no significant influence of the respondents' country of origin was confirmed on either dimension.

The regression model for socio-political acceptance explained 53% and the one for community acceptance 45% of the variance in the respective dependent variables. Hence, R^2 is in an acceptable range compared to other empirical studies of the field (cf. Kortsch et al., 2015; Sonnberger and Ruddat, 2017; Zoellner et al., 2008).

To sum up, all hypothesized factors were proven to significantly predict public acceptance either on both the community and the socio-political or on one of the two dimensions.

Table 4-12: Multiple linear regression of public acceptance of biogas plants in the URR (case study 1)

Dependent variable	Socio-political acceptance (n = 1,206)		Community acceptance (n = 1,225)	
	B	β	B	β
Sex (1=m)	.091*	.046*	-.005	-.002
Home-owner (1=yes)	.055	.028	.093	.041
Biogas plant in vicinity (1=yes)	.016	.004	-.013	-.003
Advocacy renewable energies	.102**	.076**	.078*	.050*
Perceived benefits of biogas plants	.805***	.655***	.819***	.576***
Perceived costs of biogas plants	-.073*	-.055*	-.238***	-.154***
Perceived costs of energy crops	-.076**	-.071**	-.023	-.019
Information and participation	.016	.012	-.080*	-.051*
Dummy France	-.060	-.028	.103	.042
Dummy Switzerland	.014	.007	.100	.041
F	138,057***		103,732***	
R^2	.534		.459	
Adjusted R^2	.530		.454	

Note: *** p < .001. ** p < .01; * p < .05.

H13: Public Acceptance of Renewable Energies is Linked to Community Energy and Advocacy of Energy Autonomy.

Another specific area of interest of this case study is in the connection, if any, between public acceptance and active support of renewable energies, community energy, and energy autonomy respectively. The term energy autonomy (Deuschle et al., 2015; McKenna et al., 2014; McKenna et al., 2015; McKenna et al., 2016; Rae and Bradley, 2012) is employed here to also include energy autarky (Müller et al., 2011), self-sufficiency (Balcombe et al., 2015; Deuschle et al., 2015), and integrated community energy systems (Koirala et al., 2016). Community energy is defined here as local participation in renewable energy initiatives and is measured using the construct "engagement for renewable energies" (cf. Table A-1, Appendix A). This section therefore explores the findings in relation to these three aspects, with a particular focus on the links between them.

In the German and Swiss sub-sample, around 10% of respondents reported to be already engaged in community energy of some kind, compared to just 4% in the French sub-sample, whereby the differences between the countries are highly significant. These findings are in stark contrast to the willingness to get involved (cf. Table A-1, Appendix A, item "general active support of renewable energies") in renewable energy projects, which 43% of respondents expressed. However, only 22% thereof are actually currently involved (cf. Table A-1, Appendix A, item "community energy") with significantly lower involvement in the French sub-sample than in the other two samples. Hence the expressed willingness strongly exceeds the actual involvement in renewable energy projects. At least for Switzerland, these results seem to confirm insights from other studies. For example, whilst over 60% of the population (in a survey of around 1,000 people) would have an interest in participating in such projects, only 2% have already done so (Gamma et al., 2017). In France, the Renewable Energy Cooperative (REScoop, 2017) project refers to about 60 community energy initiatives. In Germany, around 46% of renewable energy capacity can be classified as community energy and is owned by private individuals and farmers (Klaus Novy Institut e.V. & trend:research, 2011) and 718 energy cooperatives have been founded since 2006 (DGRV, 2014).

Regarding energy autonomy, 42% of the respondents stated that they are familiar with the term itself (cf. Table A-1, Appendix A, item "familiarity with energy autonomy"), whereby this fraction differed strongly between national sub-samples and levels of education. Surprisingly, with 63% a lot more respondents were familiar with the term in the French than in the German and Swiss sub-sample with 35% and 28% respectively. It is however assumed that the extremely high familiarity of French respondents might be due to a wrong understanding of the term "energy autonomy". Due to the structure of the energy sector in France (cf. section 4.2.3.1), energy autonomy might be associated with the exclusive use of domestic energy sources for the country as a whole, including non-renewable sources, such as nuclear energy. In addition, significant differences for the respondents' sex and year of education were found: 51% of male respondents claimed to be familiar with the term compared to just 34% of females, and respondents with more years of education were more likely to be familiar with the term than people with fewer years. Ultimately, familiarity seems to play an important role in the general evaluation of energy autonomy. People who already were familiar with the term evaluated approaches to more energy autonomy significantly more positively. Furthermore, people who were already involved with renewable energy for environmental reasons, showed an interest in getting financially involved or were willing to actively support renewable energy, were significantly more often familiar with the concept and rated concepts for more energy autonomy significantly more positively. Hence, there is empirical evidence that engagement for renewable energies and advocacy of autonomy are related concepts.

Generally, there was a strong spontaneous approval of approaches to local energy autonomy in all three sub-regions, with a significantly higher approval in the German than in the Swiss and French sub-samples. Respondents with a renewable energy plant in their neighborhood approved concepts for more local energy autonomy significantly more positively than those without. Even though familiarity with energy autonomy seems to play an important role, many respondents indicated a spontaneous positive appraisal without a deeper knowledge of the concept. Overall, it is difficult to compare these results with the literature, as to the author's knowledge very few if any studies have analyzed these relationships.

A further question asked which scales were considered sensible to achieve energy autonomy (Figure 4-8). With the exception of Switzerland, where at least every third respondent stated their preference for energy autonomy at the Canton or national level, the preferred scales were at or below the regional level. Especially the level of village/ municipality/ city was selected as being most favorable, in most cases over twice as favorable as the other levels. This roughly corresponds to findings in the literature where projects aim at a local energy autonomy at the municipality level (McKenna et al., 2014; McKenna et al., 2015; McKenna, 2018).

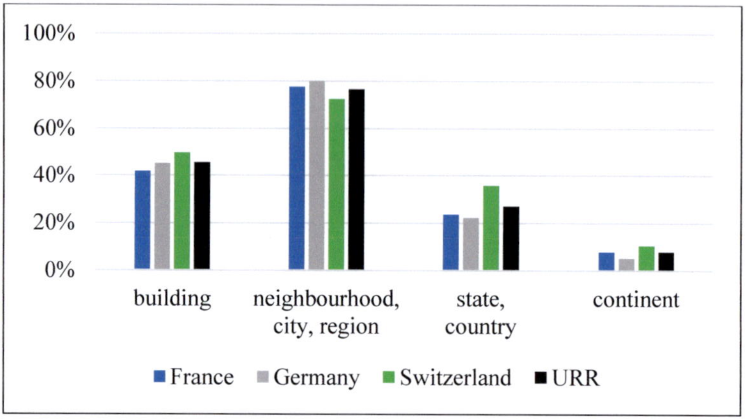

Note: Sample sizes: $n_{Germany} = 495$, $n_{Switzerland} = 493$, $n_{France} = 501$.

Figure 4-8: Frequency distribution of the answers to the question "On what level do you find energy autonomy most appropriate?"

Having examined community energy and energy autonomy individually, attention is now turned to the relationships between those concepts. Table 4-13 shows the correlations between the three constructs "advocacy of renewable energies", "engagement for renewable energies", and "advocacy of energy autonomy". The results show that:

- For "advocacy of energy autonomy" and "advocacy of renewable energies", there is a significant moderate to strong positive correlation on the level of all three sub-regions and the URR as a whole.
- For "advocacy of energy autonomy" and "engagement for renewable energies", there is a significant but very weak correlation, on the level of the German sub-region and the URR as a whole.
- For "advocacy of renewable energies" and "engagement for renewable energies", there is a significant but very weak correlation for the French and German sub-region and the URR as a whole.

The first finding is hardly surprising, given that higher levels of energy autonomy are typically achieved with more locally installed renewable energy technologies. It seems reasonable to suppose that if people accept one of these, they generally accept both. The second finding is more interesting, however, as it points to a very weak relationship between "approval of energy autonomy" and active "engagement for renewable energies". It also points to acceptance of renewable energies as a prerequisite for energy autonomy, but not necessarily an active engagement – even though it is difficult to derive causality from any correlation. The third finding seems to suggest that, with the exception of Switzerland, advocacy and engagement of renewable energy go hand in hand. In other words, the "approval" and "support" groups in Figure 4-6 are not nearly as distinct as the "rejection" and "resistance" ones. This would seem to confirm the results of Musall and Kuik (2011), who found that, compared to a case without community ownership (or co-ownership) the level of public acceptance in the local community is higher with it. There are also local benefits that can motivate German municipalities towards energy autonomy through community energy projects, such as tax revenues, environmental awareness and independence from private utilities (Engelken et al., 2016). Overall, the findings would seem to confirm what Fast (2013, pp. 860–863) highlights as the role of public acceptance in "the guiding narrative of energy independent regions in Austria and Switzerland", whereby these initiatives act to "bind residents more tightly to existing municipal or territories, in effect hardening these boundaries".

Table 4-13: Pearson's correlation coefficient (r_p) between the constructs "advocacy of energy autonomy", "advocacy of REs", and "engagement for REs"

	France		Germany		Switzerland		URR	
	r_p	n	r_p	n	r_p	n	r_p	n
"advocacy of REs" and "advocacy of energy autonomy"	.466**	467	.518**	467	.466**	471	.480**	1,405
"advocacy of energy autonomy' and "engagement for REs"	.089	469	.183**	468	.061	471	.106*	1,408
"advocacy of REs" and "engagement for REs"	.123**	494	.109*	493	.065	487	.080**	1,474

Note: ** $p < .01$, * $p < .05$.

4.4 Case Study 2: Community Public Acceptance of Biogas Plants in the Upper Rhine Region[12]

4.4.1 Materials and Methods

4.4.1.1 Survey Design

The survey was conducted from November 2014 to March 2015 and covered resident households living less than one kilometer away from eleven biogas plants installed in the URR. In order to obtain comparable samples for the three sub-regions, the sample points were identified by applying several selection criteria: The first criterion was the existence of a significant number of households within a distance of one kilometer around the plant, which was assessed though a GIS (Geographical Information System) analysis. Further selection criteria included the year of installation, the plant size, and the type of technology. Regarding the year of installation, the plants were required to have approximately the same age (the year of installation within the sample ranges from 2006 to 2014). As regards the plant sizes, each national sub-sample covers several installed capacities ranging from 100 kW_{el} to 530 kW_{el}. Concerning the technology, only biogas plants digesting organic waste, energy crops, agricultural residues, manure from livestock farming or other biogenic residues (e.g., from the food industry) were included in the sample. Biogas plants fed with sewage sludge were not considered for this survey because they are associated with other acceptance issues due to their integration into waste water treatment plants.

Applying the above selection criteria, eleven plants were chosen. Three of them are located in Northwestern Switzerland (Fischbach-Göslikon, Ormalingen/ Gelterkinden, Liesberg), four in Baden-Württemberg (Sinzheim, Forchheim, two plants in Schwanau), and four in the Alsace region (Obernai, Littenheim, Lohr, Friesenheim). Ten of the eleven plants are located in rural

[12] Parts of this section have previously been published in Schumacher and Schultmann (2017).

areas, one plant is a demonstration plant situated in a medium-sized city (Obernai). Ten of the selected plants produce electricity through CHP; one plant feeds gas into the natural gas grid (Forchheim). All selected plants only marginally use the waste heat from the CHP process, e.g., to provide process heat for the digester and to heat own or neighboring houses. More detailed information about the selected plants is displayed in Table 4-14.

In analogy with similar studies (cf. Hübner and Hahn, 2013; Soland et al., 2013), all households situated within a radius of one kilometer from the biogas plant were defined as local residents as they might potentially experience the strongest negative impacts from the production site, such as odor or noise nuisances from the biogas plant and the associated biomass transport. The standardized questionnaire was consequently distributed within a one kilometer radius around the plant in a mixed mode procedure, using a combination of personal interviews and paper-pencil questionnaires. In six communities a full census and in four communities a partial census was conducted. The individual households were preselected by means of a GIS analysis (Figure 4-9 and Figure 4-10) and precise walking routes were defined for the interviewers (Figure 4-11). In case of the partial census, a random selection of households was made by providing the interviewers with random numbers indicating the households to be skipped on their walking route. All 24 interviewers were trained in advance and fluently spoke the language in which they conducted the personal interviews.

Table 4-14: Characteristics of the sample sites

Country	Location	Technology	Substrate	Year of installation	Heat use
Germany	Forchheim	Biomethane fed into the gas grid	Energy crops	2006	No heat use
Germany	Schwanau (plant 1)	Biogas with CHP	Manure	2006	Own use
Germany	Schwanau (plant 2)	Biogas with CHP	Energy crops, manure	2010	Local heating network
Germany	Sinzheim	Biogas with CHP	Manure, residues	2007	No information
Switzerland	Fischbach-Göslikon	Biogas with CHP	Manure and organic waste	2007	Own use
Switzerland	Liesberg	Biogas with CHP + Organic Rankine Cycle (ORC)	Manure, organic waste, residues	2011	No heat use
Switzerland	Ormalingen/ Gelterkinden	Biogas with CHP	Manure, organic waste, residues	2008	Local heating network
France	Friesenheim	Biogas and CHP	Manure, energy crops, residues,	2013	Own use
France	Littenheim	Biogas and CHP	Manure, intermediate crops, residues	2012	Own use
France	Lohr	Biogas and CHP	Manure, intermediate crops	2014	Own use
France	Obernai	Biogas and CHP	Organic waste, manure, intermediate crops, residues	2013	Local heating network with nearby food business

Figure 4-9: Sample of Schwanau by interviewer area (DigitalGlobe, 2014; OSM, 2014)

Figure 4-10: Sample of Schwanau, interviewer area 1 (DigitalGlobe, 2014; OSM, 2014)

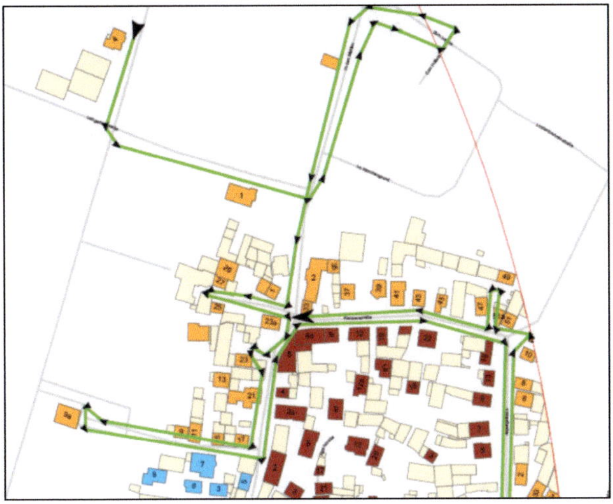

Figure 4-11: Forchheim, walking route of interviewer 1 (DigitalGlobe, 2014; OSM, 2014)

Each household was contacted as follows: Firstly, the target person was asked to participate in an oral interview on the spot. If the person agreed, the interview was carried out immediately; if the person refused, a printed questionnaire was handed out for later reply by mail. In the event of a complete refusal to respond, no questionnaire was given. If no personal contact was possible, the interviewer left an envelope with a cover letter, the questionnaire, and a prepaid, self-addressed envelope in the mailbox. All personal contacts were documented by the interviewers in contact protocols.

In total, 218 interviews were conducted orally (69 in Germany, 45 in Switzerland, and 104 in France) and 449 questionnaires were answered in writing (225 in Germany, 131 in Switzerland, and 93 in France). The return rate was 20.5%, also accounting for the oral contacts documented in the contact protocols. The obtained sample was further restricted by three exclusion criteria. Firstly, the respondents needed to be aware of the local plant prior to the survey; secondly, they needed to live at their current address before the plant was built; and thirdly, they were required to have no relation to the plant operator through an employment, customer, or other business relationship. The analysis showed that 24.4% of the respondents were not aware of the biogas plant (n = 163), 8.8% of the respondents were not living at the current address before the biogas plant was built (n = 59), and 4.8% of the respondents had a business relationship to the plant operator (n = 32). These three criteria reduced the sample from 667 to 433 respondents (64.9%).

For the data analysis, the individual sample communities are subsumed according to the three national sub-regions of the URR. To be able to draw conclusions based on comparisons between sub-regions, it is necessary to avoid bias from the characteristics of the individual sample points. Hence, the assumption must be proven that sample points within the same national sub-regions are more similar to one another than the samples points from different national sub-regions. A one-way ANOVA for testing homogeneity of sample points within the three national sub-regions with regard to "self-reported acceptance" was therefore conducted (Table 4-15). Results showed that in the French and Swiss sub-sample, no statistically significant differences exist between the individual sample points regarding the "self-reported acceptance". In the German sub-sample, a significant difference was detected between the samples of Schwanau and Sinzheim (Tuckey test, $p = 0.002$, $\eta^2 =.064$) but not between the other samples pairs. However, with and eta-squared of .064, the effect was small. Hence, it is concluded that the national sub-samples are rather homogenous and can be subsumed per sub-region in the following analysis of results.

Table 4-15: One-way ANOVA for regional sub-samples with regard to "self-reported acceptance"

Country	Sample point	n	M	SD	df1[a]	df2[b]	F	p
Germany	Schwanau	68	2.5	1.1	2	187	6.41**	.002**
	Forchheim	34	3.0	1.2				
	Sinzheim	88	3.1	1.1				
France	Friesenheim	16	3.1	1.0	3	2.58	2.58	.059
	Obernai	23	3.0	1.2				
	Littenheim	18	3.7	1.0				
	Lohr	34	3.7	1.0				
Switzerland	Fischbach-Göslikon	43	3.9	1.1	2	1.75	1.75	.179
	Liesberg	43	3.6	1.1				
	Ormalingen/Gelterkinden	36	4.0	.9				

Notes: *** $p < .001$, ** $p < .01$, * $p < .05$.

[a] degrees of freedom between groups.

[b] degrees of freedom within groups.

4.4.1.2 Questionnaire design

Three specific versions of the questionnaire were developed for the sub-regions in Germany, France, and Switzerland to meet the multi-cultural and multi-lingual conditions of the study region (cf. section 3.1.2). In a parallel approach, cross-cultural considerations from the three countries were included when drafting the German source questionnaire (Harkness et al., 2010). To ensure reliability and comparability of the questions in different cultural contexts, the French target version was developed in an iterative team approach, with two translators and one researcher thoroughly discussing item equivalence (Harkness et al., 2004). Moreover, all three language versions were pretested individually with native speakers in the respective sub-region.

In total, the questionnaire consisted of 38 items and seven main constructs. The questions covered personal attitudes, beliefs, perceptions, and evaluations regarding renewable energies in general and the local biogas plant in particular. To increase comparability of results, the items and constructs were taken to the largest possible extent from existing studies covering the acceptance of various renewable energy technologies in different countries (items were taken from Kontogianni et al., 2014; Musall and Kuik, 2011; Rau et al., 2012; Rau and

Zoellner, 2008; Schweizer-Ries et al., 2010; Soland et al., 2013; Wüste, 2013; Zoellner et al., 2008). Several of the scales already existing in academic literature were adapted to the biogas context. Other scales were newly developed on the basis of a thorough literature review (cf. section 2.4) and the expert interviews (cf. section 3.1.1). The questionnaire ended with personal questions on socio-demographic variables. To respect the participant's anonymity, for some of the socio-demographic variables rather broad classes were applied (e.g., age and occupational status).

Table 4-16 lists the main constructs and provides a short summary of their meaning. Despite the rejection of the NIMBY theory as unidimensional explanation for local resistance (cf. section 2.4.1), the construct "advocacy of renewable energies" (H6) was included. Distributive justice was measured by the constructs "perceived benefits of biogas plants" (H7), "perceived costs of biogas plant" (H8), and "perceived odor" (H11). Procedural justice was covered by the constructs "trust in the plant operator" (H10), "actual information and participation", as well as "desired information and participation" (both of the latter refer to H9). A list of the individual items belonging to the respective scales is available in Table A-2, Appendix A.

Additionally, several single items were used to analyze the individual affectedness by asking for the respondent's awareness of the local plant, the relationship to the plant operator, the visibility of the plant from the respondent's home, and the desired distance of the home to a biogas plant. Referring to the acceptance model presented in section 2.1 (Figure 2-2), the respondent's willingness to actively support or oppose a local biogas plant was asked for.

The majority of the questions used a five-point Likert scale to determine the degree to which the respondent agreed or disagreed with a proposed statement, with the answer categories "entirely incorrect" (1), "rather incorrect" (2), "I am undecided" (3), "partly correct" (4), "completely correct" (5). Other answer formats included scales ranging from "very negative" (1) to "very positive" (5) as well as more particular answering formats for specific questions, e.g., for perceived odor ranging from "very strong" (1) to "very weak" (5). It was assumed that some respondents might have a low level of information and knowledge about biogas plants. To avoid a disproportionately frequent use of the "comfortable center" of the five-point Likert scale ("I am undecided" or "neutral"), the answer category "don't know" was introduced wherever appropriate. During the personal interviews, the interviewers could also use the answer category "refused". At the end of the questionnaire, the respondents were asked to leave additional free-text comments.

Table 4-16: Constructs of the questionnaire (case study 2)

Construct	Concept
Advocacy of renewable energies	Support of renewable energy technologies in general and in the neighborhood
Perceived benefits of biogas plants	Perceived benefits of biogas plants for the society and the individual
Perceived costs of biogas plants	Perceived costs of biogas plants for the society and the individual
Perceived odor	Frequency, intensity, and quality of the perceived odor emissions from the local plant
Trust in plant the operator	Trust in the plant operator with regard to perceived competencies, reliability, and intuitive appraisal
Actual information and participation	Perceived information and participation possibilities during the planning and construction phase of the local biogas plant
Desired information and participation	Desired information and participation possibilities during the planning and construction phase of a local biogas plant

4.4.1.3 Sample Characteristics

The final sample comprises 433 local residents of biogas plants in Germany, France, and Switzerland. Of these, 46.9% lived in Germany (n = 203), 23.1% in France (n = 100), and 30% in Switzerland (n = 130). 416 of the respondents reported their gender, age, and place of residence. For an overview of the socio-demographic characteristics of the obtained samples compared to population statistics see Table 4-17. Comparison with statistical data revealed some deviations, which are briefly discussed below.

Table 4-17: Socio-demographic characteristics of the survey sample compared to population statistics (case study 2)

			Germany		France		Switzerland	
			sample	pop.	sample	pop.	sample	pop.
Male		(%)	67.2	49.0 [a]	57.1	48.9 [a]	57.9	49.4 [a]
Age	16-30 years	(%)	1.0	22.3 [b]	10.2	22.5 [c]	6.3	16.5 [d]
	31-50 years	(%)	27.6	33.5 [b]	36.7	33.1 [c]	24.6	48.7 [d]
	>51 years	(%)	71.4	44.2 [b]	53.1	44.3 [c]	69.0	34.8 [d]
Home owners		(%)	90.0	52.5 [e]	89.7	65.1 [e]	77.8	44.0 [e]
Employment rate		(%)	62.6	52.8 [f]	62.2	41.5 [f]	65.6	60.4 [f]

Notes:

[a] based on Deutsch-Französische-Schweizerische Oberrheinkonferenz (2015), includes male population aged 15 or younger, data on URR level.

[b] own calculation based on Statistisches Landesamt Baden-Württemberg (2011), data on regional level without Südpfalz.

[c] own calculation based on INSEE (2015), data on regional level, deviating classes: 15-29, 30-49, >50 years.

[d] own calculation based on Bundesamt für Statistik (2014), data on canton level.

[e] based on Eurostat (2014), data on country level.

[f] based on Deutsch-Französische-Schweizerische Oberrheinkonferenz (2015), includes working population of the age of 15, data on URR level.

Of the 416 respondents, 62% were male (n = 258) and 38% were female (n = 158). Compared to statistical data of the respective communities, men are overrepresented in particularly in the samples of Schwanau and Forchheim (Statistisches Landesamt Baden-Württemberg, 2011), Ormalingen (BFS, 2014), and Lohr (INSEE, 2015). Judging from experiences gained in similar studies, where men were also overrepresented (cf. e.g., Griesen, 2010; Hübner and Hahn, 2013; Upham, 2009; Wüste and Schmuck, 2013), it is assumed that women passed the questionnaire on to their husbands, who are more likely to represent the interests of the household to the outside community and may feel better informed about the biogas plant.

Moreover, the age of the sample population exceeds the statistical average age of the respective communities. In particular, the age class 16 to 20 years is strongly underrepresented, whereas the age class 61 to 70 years is strongly overrepresented. This overrepresentation of elderly respondents is assumed to result from a higher preparedness to respond to the questionnaire if the respondent feels strongly attached to the community and place of residence. This assumption is also supported by the fact that the home ownership rate of the sample of 86.2% exceeds national averages (Eurostat, 2014) and that the respondents lived in the community for 31.9 years on the average. Moreover, it needs to be considered that the oral interviews have been conducted during daytime, which may lead to a higher representation of retired persons. The employment rate of the sample, however, exceeds the statistical average of the population, which might result from the overrepresentation of men.

Despite the described deviations from statistical data, the obtained sample is considered as suitable to assess the defined hypotheses. Moreover, comparison of the obtained sample with statistical data on the regional or country level only is an approximation because the exact socio-demographic characteristics of the households situated in a one kilometer radius around the biogas plant are unknown. Hence, the statistical data do not precisely reflect the characteristics of the target population. As regards representativeness, however, some limitations might also result from the sampling procedure. Due to the use of mixed modes and the various exclusion criteria (cf. section 4.4.1.1), the probability of selection bias, such as (positive and negative) self-selection effects, is quite high. Even though rigorous randomization and sampling procedures were applied, the obtained data might not be fully representative of the considered communities.

4.4.1.4 Data Preparation and Analysis

All constructs were tested through an item analysis to assess internal consistencies for the overall sample and sub-regions (Table 4-18). For the overall sample, Cronbach's α exceeds the recommended threshold values of .70 for all constructs with the exception of "advocacy of renewable energies". However, the Pearson-correlation of the two items belonging to the construct "advocacy of renewable energies" is strong with $r = .527$ ($p < .001$, $n = 420$). For the sub-samples, two constructs are below the recommended threshold. The deviations from the desired values, however, are quite small. For conceptual reasons (cf. section 2.4), the three concerned constructs were still included in the regression analysis. This decision was based on suggestions in academic literature to prioritize conceptual comprehensiveness over internal consistency in the selection of items (Homburg, C., Müller, M., Klarmann, M., 2011; Little, T. D., Lindenberger, U., Nesselroade, J. R., 1999).

Table 4-18: Internal consistency of constructs for the overall sample (URR) and by sub-region (case study 2)

Construct	Cronbach's α				Number of items
	Germany	France	Switzer-land	URR	
Advocacy of renewable energies	.552	.710	.769	.660	2
Perceived benefits of biogas plants	.905	.841	.888	.893	4
Perceived costs of biogas plants	.716	.545	.724	.710	3
Perceived odor emissions	.831	.841	.846	.838	3
Trust in plant operator	.877	.911	.903	.890	3
Actual information and participation	.909	.783	.923	.902	5

To deal with non-response rates of some items, the hot deck method was applied to impute missing values. The percentage of missing data for the individual items ranged between 0.5% and 5.5% and amounted to roughly 2% on the average for the considered items (excluding the answer category "don't know"). Hot deck imputation involves replacing a missing value of one dataset ("donee") by the value of another dataset ("donor") that matches the "donee" in researcher-determined categories (Myers, 2011). For this study, socio-demographic characteristics were used as deck variables (sex, age, place of residence, home-owner status, family status, education, and employment status), assuming similarity of answers of respondents from similar social backgrounds. Through hot deck imputation, missing values were substantially reduced, but not all data gaps could be filled. For this reason, the number of observations of the regression analysis was further restricted through pairwise exclusion of incomplete datasets.

The survey data were analyzed using the statistics Software SPSS (Version 21). Descriptive methods were used for cross-national comparisons, such as frequency distributions, calculation of means (M) and standard deviations (SD). In addition, a qualitative inductive analysis of the participants' free text comments was conducted. To test the hypothesized relationship between "self-reported acceptance" and presumed influencing factors, multiple regression analysis was carried out for the overall sample.

4.4.2 Results

In this section, the major findings of case study 2 are presented along the selected hypotheses (cf. section 3.2.3). Case study 2 differs from case study 1 and 3 as it exclusively investigates public acceptance of biogas plants by local residents. Therefore, H1, H2, H3, and H4 are tested with regard to the public acceptance of biogas plants across the three sub-regions of the URR. H5 is not relevant as all respondents live in a one kilometer radius around the biogas plants (cf. section 4.4.1.1) and thus, already have experiences with the investigated technology. Subsequently, the hypotheses on potential factors influencing public acceptance of biogas plants (H6, H7, H8, H9, H10, H12) are investigated. Moreover, an inductive analysis of free text comments of supporters and resisters is conducted to qualitatively further interpret each of the factors. Finally, a closer look is taken at the role of information and participation (H9) by comparing the actual information and participation possibilities with regard to the existing biogas plants and the desire of local residents to participate in such projects.

H1: Renewable Energies Generally Enjoy High Public Acceptance for Future Energy Generation.

To draw a general picture of the level of advocacy of renewable energies in the three sub-regions, the respondents' preferences regarding multiple energy technologies was queried. The frequency distribution in Figure 4-12 clearly shows that renewable energies are overall supported by the sample population. In all three sub-regions, solar energy ranks the highest (Germany with 91%, n = 185; France with 72%, n = 72; Switzerland with 90%, n = 117), followed by hydropower in Germany (87%, n = 176) and Switzerland (82%, n = 106), and wind energy in France (70%, n = 70). Bioenergy ranks third in Switzerland (77%, n = 100) and fourth in France (63%, n = 63) and Germany (51%, n = 104). The lowest preference was expressed for geothermal energy. The proposed non-renewable energies (char and nuclear) are far lagging behind in all sub-regions.

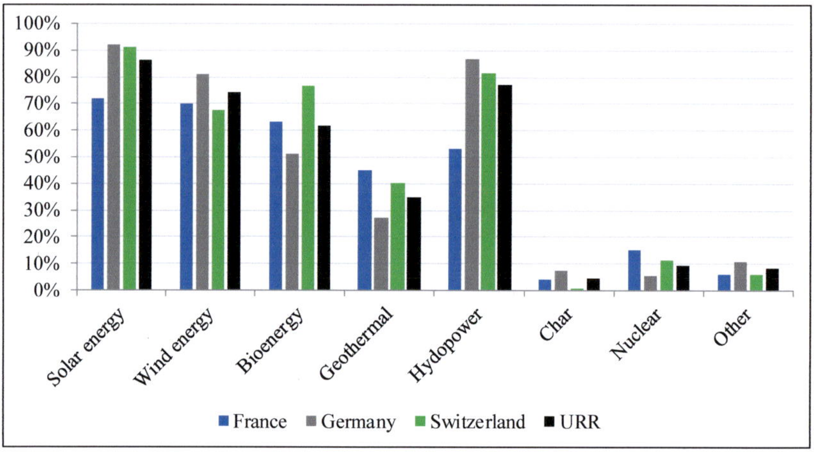

Note: Sample sizes: $n_{Germany} = 203$, $n_{Switzerland} = 130$, $n_{France} = 100$.

Figure 4-12: Frequency distribution of the answers to the question “In your opinion, which energy technologies should be preferably used in the future?” (case study 2)

H2: There is Public Disposition to Act Towards Renewable Energy Plants in the Neighborhood.

To assess H2, the same logic as afore presented in case study 1 (cf. section 4.3.2.2) was applied. Firstly, the appraisal of the local biogas plant was assessed by the item “How positive or negative do you rate the biogas plants in your neighborhood?” on a five-point Likert scale with 1 = “very negative” and 5 = “very positive”as anchors (cf. Table A-2, Appendix A, item “appraisal of local plant”). Secondly, a filter on the first question to assess the action-dimension of acceptance was applied in the following logic: in case of a *positive* appraisal, the next item asked for the respondent's willingness to *actively support* a biogas plant in the neighborhood. In case of a *negative* appraisal, the next item asked about the respondent's willingness to *actively oppose* a biogas plant in the neighborhood. (cf. Table A-2, Appendix A, items "active support" and "active resistance").[13]

The results are displayed in Figure 4-13 which revealed differences between the sub-regions with regard to acceptance levels,. In Switzerland 68% (n = 89) of respondents assessed the local biogas plant positively or very positively, 52% (n = 51) of the respondents in France, but only 30% (n = 61) in Germany did so. Accordingly, 32% (n = 65) of respondents in Germany had a negative assessment of the local plant, whereas 16% (n = 16) in France and 12% (n = 15) in Switzerland expressed a negative appraisal. The group of respondents that had a neutral attitude towards the local plant was largest in Germany with 30% (n = 61), followed by 25% (n = 25) in France, and 16% (n = 21) in Switzerland. Hence, the majority of respondents in the French and Swiss sub-regions demonstrated a positive appraisal of the local biogas plant. In the German sub-sample, this only applies to less than one third of the respondents. One-way ANOVA confirmed statistically significant differences between the three national sub-samples regarding "self-reported acceptance" ($F(2, 405) = 26.47$, $p = 0.00$, $\eta^2 = 0.12$).

With respect to dispositions to act, French and Swiss respondents were found to have the highest disposition to actively support the local biogas plant with 31% (n = 31) and 32% (n = 42), respectively, whereas only 16% (n = 32) of respondents in Germany claimed to be active supporters. Accordingly, a relatively high percentage of 20% (n = 40) of German respondents answered that they were prepared to actively oppose a biogas plant in the neighborhood, whereas only 10% (n = 10) and 3% (n = 4) agreed with this in France and Switzerland, respectively. The percentage of still undecided respondents regarding an active involvement is relatively high on the positive appraisal side. In Germany, 10% (n = 20), in France 8% (n = 8), and in Switzerland 20%

[13] "(Active) support" is a sub-quantity of "(passive) approval", and "(active) resistance" a sub-quantity of "(passive) rejection".

(n = 26) declared to have a positive appraisal, but were undecided as to whether they wanted to be actively involved or not. On the negative appraisal side, the percentage of undecided respondents was much smaller (in Germany 4%, n = 9; in France 2%, n = 2; in Switzerland 2%, n = 2).

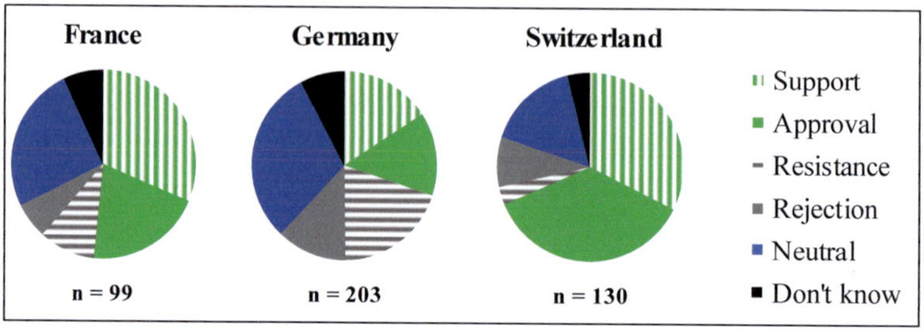

Note:

Categories "approval" and "rejection" include the categories "support" and "resistance" respectively (cf. Figure 2-1).

Figure 4-13: Levels of acceptance and dispositions to act towards a biogas plant in the neighborhood by sub-region (case study 2)

H3: General Public Acceptance (Socio-Political Dimension) Exceeds Public Acceptance of Plants in the Neighborhood (Community Dimension).

In analogy to case study 1 (cf. section 4.3), H3 was tested by comparing public acceptance of biogas plants in general (socio-political dimension) and acceptance of biogas plants in the neighborhood (community dimension) across the three sub-regions. The questionnaire differentiated between general attitudes towards biogas plants (cf. Table A-2, Appendix A, item "socio-political acceptance") and specific attitudes towards the locally installed biogas plants in the neighborhood (cf. Table A-2, Appendix A, item "appraisal of local plant").

Table 4-19 displays the results for the t-test which confirmed a significant difference between public acceptance on the socio-political and the community dimension for all three sub-regions. Cohen's d revealed a small effect in the

French and Swiss sub-region (Cohen's d = 0.34 and 0.49 respectively) and a large effect in Germany (Cohen's d = 0.82). Hence, H3 was confirmed in all cases.

Table 4-19: Paired sample t-test to compare public acceptance of biogas plants on the socio-political and community dimension by sub-region (case study 2)

Sub-region	Socio-political			Community			p-value	Cohen's d
	n	M	SD	n	M	SD		
France	68	4.0	.938	68	3.5	1.099	.001	.34
Germany	183	3.6	1.320	183	2.9	1.196	.000	.82
Switzerland	118	4.3	.934	118	3.8	1.070	.000	.49
URR	369	3.9	1.189	369	3.3	1.207	.000	.63

H4: Public Acceptance of Renewable Energy Plants is Influenced by the Distance of the Plant to the Respondent's Home.

Another goal of the study was to obtain a deeper understanding of the relevance of the distance between the respondents' homes and the biogas plant for public acceptance. Figure 4-14 displays the cumulated relative frequencies of the desired distance to a biogas plant in the neighborhood. Results indicate that the distance has a high relevance to the majority of respondents, if the plant is situated closer than one kilometer to the respondent's home. Still, 19% in Germany, 30% in Switzerland, and 33% in France of the respondents also accept a biogas plant in their direct vicinity (< 1 km distance). A distance of three kilometer or more is perceived to be large enough by the large majority of respondents (90% in Germany, 93% in Switzerland, and 96% in France). One-way ANOVA demonstrated statistically significant differences between the three national sub-samples with regard to desired distance ($F(2, 418) = 5.85$, $p = 0.003$, $\eta^2 = 0.03$). The Games-Howell test further indicated a statistically significant difference between the German and the French sub-sample ($p = 0.012$), as well as the German and the Swiss sub-sample ($p = 0.015$).

It is noted that German respondents desired the longest distance to the biogas plant, whereas French and Swiss respondents had similar preferences. From the free text comments, it might be assumed that this could be connected to the different feedstock used to run the biogas plants in the three sub-regions (cf. Table 4-14). Whereas all considered plants in France and Switzerland predominantly run on manure, organic waste, other residues, as well as intermediate crops, two of the investigated German plants exclusively use energy crops. In the case of already existing agricultural activities for producing the feedstock themselves (e.g., through livestock farming), transport distances are minimum and local impacts can thus be avoided. Biogas plants running on energy crops, by contrast, require continuous feeding from the area around the plant, which may potentially result in noise and traffic, changes of rural landscapes, and potential odor nuisances. Hence, German respondents are likely to experience stronger direct impacts from the biogas plant in the vicinity and might therefore prefer longer distances to residential areas.

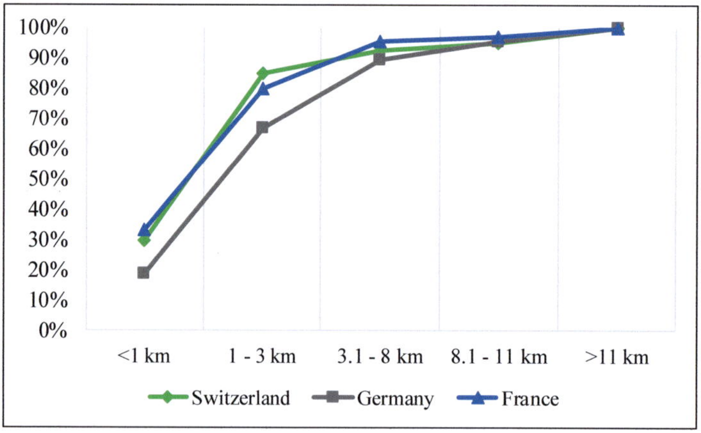

Note: Sample sizes: $n_{Germany} = 195$, $n_{France} = 96$, $n_{Switzerland} = 125$.

Figure 4-14: Cumulated relative frequencies of the desired minimum distance of biogas plants in the URR

H6 to H12: Factors Driving the Acceptance of Bioenergy Plants

The following section aims at identifying factors which influence public acceptance of locally installed biogas plants. Multiple regression analysis was used to quantitatively assess potential factors and a qualitative content analysis of free-text comments was conducted to add more depth to the interpretation of the quantitative regression model.

Multiple Regression Analysis

Multiple regression analysis was conducted to detect factors having a statistically significant influence on public acceptance. The "self-reported acceptance" was measured by the item "How do you rate the biogas plant in your neighborhood?" on a five- point Likert scale with 1 = "very negative" and 5 = "very positive" as anchors and included in the regression model as dependent variable. All other constructs (cf. Table 4-16), which correspond to H6, H7, H8, H9, H10, and H12, were included as independent variables with the exception of the "desired information and participation" for conceptual reasons[14]. It has to be noted that H11 was not included in the model as the hypothesis was developed on the basis of the gained insights during the research process of case study 2.

The multiple linear regression model contained two blocks of variables (Table 4-20). In a first step, four control variables were included in the model: The mode of data collection (oral/ written), the sex of the respondent (female/ male), the ownership status (owner/ tenant), and the view (direct/ indirect) with the biogas plant from the respondent's home. These variables were included to control possible effects of diverging levels of affectedness, interviewer effects, and the respondent's gender. In a second step, all constructs measuring advocacy of renewable energies (H6), distributive (H7, H8, and H12), and procedural justice (H9), as well as trust in the plant operator (H10) were added to the model. In addition, dummy variables for the countries were created to

[14] The scale "desired information and participation" refers to a theoretical disposition for participation instead of an actual evaluation of the participation process with regard to the local biogas plant. Therefore, the scale "actual information and participation" was used to account for procedural aspects during the planning and construction phase of the local plant.

test the hypothesized effect of the respondent's country of residence. To this end, the variable "country" was recoded into three dummies, "Dummy Germany", "Dummy France", and "Dummy Switzerland". The dummies assumed the value one, if the respondent was living in the respective country and zero, if the respondent was living in another country. The variables "Dummy France" and "Dummy Switzerland" were included in the second block of the regression model as the descriptive analysis provided empirical evidence that the German sub-sample might differ from the other two sub-samples regarding public acceptance.

The regression model fulfils the underlying assumptions of multiple linear regressions (cf. section 3.1.3). A visual inspection of residuals showed no critical violations of the assumption of normal distribution of residuals and no indication of violations of the linearity assumption (Hair et al., 2014, pp. 216–219). The VIF statistics gave no noteworthy indication of multicollinearity and are far below the upper acceptable bound ($VIF = 2.563$) (Hair et al., 2014, p. 200). A visual inspection of the residual scatter diagrams indicated homoscedasticity (Hair et al., 2014, p. 217). As the data is no time series data, auto correlation was not expected to be a critical issue, which was confirmed by the Durbin-Watson-test (Durbin-Watson = 1.837) (Field, 2013, p. 311).

The analysis revealed highly significant positive effects of the scales "advocacy of renewable energies" ($B = .203$, $p < .001$) (H6), "perceived benefits of biogas plants" ($B = .351$, $p < .001$) (H7), and "trust in the plant operator" ($B = .245$, $p < .001$) (H10). A highly significant negative effect on public acceptance was found for "perceived odor emissions" ($B = -.188$, $p < .001$) (H12). The effects of the dummy variables for the countries France ($B = .279$, $p < .05$) and Switzerland ($B = .345$, $p < .01$) also were significant, confirming the hypothesis of differences between the sub-regions with regard to the level of public acceptance. The regression model explained 64% of the variance in the variable "self-reported acceptance" of the local biogas plant.

Table 4-20: Multiple linear regression of public acceptance of biogas plants in the URR (case study 2)

Variable	B	β
Sex	.090	.037
Home owner	.151	.043
Survey mode	.175	.065
Visual contact	-.076	-.026
Advocacy of renewable energies	.203***	.139***
Perceived benefits of biogas plants	.351***	.348***
Perceived costs of biogas plants	-.052	-.050
Perceived odor emissions	-.188***	-.185***
Trust in the plant operator	.245***	.260***
Actual information and participation	-.022	-.023
Dummy France	.279*	.099*
Dummy Switzerland	.345**	.133**
F	48.947***	
R^2	.650	
Adjusted R^2	.637	

Notes: n = 329; *** p < .001, ** p < .01, * p < .05.

Qualitative Content Analysis of Free-Text Comments

A qualitative inductive analysis of the participants' free text comments at the end of the questionnaire was carried out. The focus was on those respondents, who had indicated their disposition to become actively involved, including both support and resistance. The aim was to understand their motives and identify issues relevant to public acceptance. An overview of the absolute frequencies of responses grouped in categories is provided in Table 4-21 and Table 4-22. The qualitative analysis serves to complement the quantitative multiple regression analysis above and is therefore discussed along the tested hypotheses with regard to the influencing factors of public acceptance of bioenergy plants.

Table 4-21: Positive free text comments of active supporters and active resisters by sub-region

Positive comments regarding the local biogas plant	Germany (n = 72)	France (n = 35)	Switzer-land (n = 52)	URR (n = 159)
Avoidance/ no additional odor emissions (from private household waste and livestock farming)	1	3	1	5
Effective use of waste resources	-	-	3	3
Visual impact is negligible	-	2	-	2

Note: Ordered by absolute frequencies.

Table 4-22: Negative free text comments of active supporters and active resisters by sub-region

Negative comments regarding the local biogas plant	Germany (n = 72)	France (n = 35)	Switzer-land (n = 52)	URR (n = 159)
Odor emissions	6	6	6	18
Lack of information and participation possibilities	-	3	8	11
Ethical concerns regarding the use of food for fuel	5	-	-	5
Lacking heat use concept	2	5	-	7
High density of plants/ site selection	6	1	-	7
Mistrust (in the plant operator, local and control authorities, and politics)	6	-	1	7
Environmental concerns (emissions into air and groundwater, monocultures etc.)	7	-	-	7
Traffic and noise emissions (destruction of roads)	3	1	-	4
Safety concerns	2	1	-	3
Loss in value of nearby houses and properties	1	-	1	2
Reduction of the quality of life	1	-	-	1

Note: Ordered by absolute frequencies.

- *Advocacy of renewable energies (H6)/ perceived costs of energy crops (H11)*
  Regarding general advocacy of renewable energies, the analysis revealed that several supporters stressed their support of renewable energies and biogas in general, but pointed out that food should not be used as feedstock for energy generation. Particularly in Germany, the ethical debate about "food versus fuel" production was frequently brought up in this context.

- *Perceived benefits (H7)*
  Perceived benefits from the efficient use of resources were particularly reported by Swiss respondents welcoming the use of private food waste and green waste for energy generation. Another potential benefit mentioned by several German and French respondents was the shared use of waste heat. It was highlighted that possibilities for private use of waste heat from the plant through a local heating network would be appreciated.

- *Perceived costs (H8)*
  Perceived costs were mentioned with regard to noise emissions and the destruction of roads by the traffic for feedstock delivery. In addition, German respondents, supporters and resisters alike, expressed concerns about the sustainability of monocultures and the environmental friendliness of biogas plants using energy crops. Furthermore, several respondents expressed fears about possible safety risks from the local plant.

- *Information and participation (H9)*
  Another issue addressed in France and Switzerland was the lack of information about participation possibilities in the planning and operation of the local plant. One respondent mentioned that no information had been provided in the early planning phase. Another respondent suggested offering site visits in order to increase transparency about the plant's operations. One respondent criticized that the site selection process had neglected wind directions, thus leading to high odor emissions in the nearby residential area, which could have been prevented through a careful and cooperative site selection process.

- *Trust (H10)*
  Regarding trust in the plant operator, several German respondents expressed concerns about lacking compliance of the local plant with environmental protection regulations as well as insufficient supervision by the responsible authorities. Moreover, German respondents criticized the heavy subsidization of biogas plants as unjust, in particular with respect to the use of energy crops.

- *Perceived odor (H12)*
  One controversially issue in all sub-regions was perceived odor emissions. Supporters living near biogas plants using manure as a feedstock pointed out that odor emissions from pig farming are comparable or even more disturbing than the smell from the biogas plant. They also stated that most people in rural areas are used to odor emissions and, hence, tolerate them as part of living in the countryside. Some respondents also mentioned that they were not able to clearly attribute the smell to the source, because manure was applied to the fields for fertilization. One Swiss respondent explained that the frequency of organic waste collection had doubled since the plant had been installed, which is why odor emissions from private collection systems had been reduced. However, one resister claimed that odor emissions were too strong and therefore reducing quality of live. Resisters also expressed fears of a loss in value of their houses and properties, indicating a link between perceived odor and perceived costs.

- *Distance of the plant to the respondent's home (H4)*
  With regard to proximity to the plant, French respondents mentioned that the visual contact of the plant was negligible. Some French supporters even explicitly stated that they did not perceive the plant as unaesthetic, but well integrated into the rural landscape. German respondents in contrast critically mentioned the high density of plants. This might however result from the fact that in one of the German sample communities (Schwanau), two plants were installed in close proximity.

H9: Role of Information and Participation

To gain a deeper understanding of the role of information and participation, actual participation was analyzed in comparison to the desired participation relating to the local biogas plants. Based on the participation pyramid by Rau et al. (2012) (Figure 2-3), respondents were asked for both their actual participation in the planning and construction phase of the local biogas plant and their desire of participation on all four levels of involvement (reception of information, consultation, cooperation, and assumption of responsibility).

Results show that all mean values of the desired participation surpass the actual possibilities offered in all three sub-samples (Figure 4-15 and Table 4-23). The gap was largest in the French sub-sample, closely followed by the German sub-sample, whereas respondents from Switzerland reported the smallest gap. One-way ANOVA confirmed statistically significant differences between the three national sub-samples on all levels of involvement with the exception of "desired information" (cf. Table 4-22).

Besides the existence of a participation gap, the results also reveal that mean values of desired participation decreased with increasing assumption of responsibility in all three sub-samples. Hence, participation possibilities with a low involvement level (desired information and consultation) were generally preferred to the participation options, which require higher activity and assumption of responsibility (cooperation and assuming responsibility). The strongest decline was observed on the level of desired assumption of responsibility.

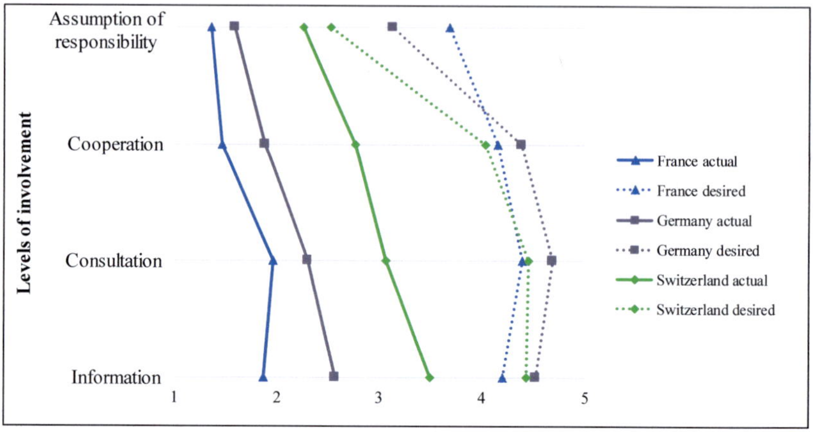

Figure 4-15: Mean values for actual and desired information and participation on the four levels of involvement by sub-region (five-point Likert scale with 1 = "entirely incorrect" and 5 = "completely correct" as anchors)

Table 4-23: One-way ANOVA for national sub-samples with regard to information and participation

		Germany			France			Switzerland					
		N	M	SD	N	M	SD	N	M	SD	df1[a]	df2[b]	F
Actual	Information	148	2.6	1.5	91	1.9	1.1	85	3.5	1.4	2	321	32.02***
	Consultation	148	2.3	1.4	84	2.0	1.3	75	3.1	1.5	2	304	26.68***
	Cooperation	163	1.9	1.2	77	1.5	1.0	72	2.8	1.4	2	309	24.85***
	Assumption of responsibility	161	1.6	.9	85	1.4	.7	78	2.3	1.2	2	321	20.49***
Desired	Information	193	4.5	.9	98	4.2	1.1	123	4.4	1.0	2	411	2.94
	Consultation	198	4.7	.7	96	4.4	.8	126	4.5	.9	2	417	5.26**
	Cooperation	195	4.4	.9	95	4.2	1.1	123	4.1	1.2	2	410	4.85**
	Assumption of responsibility	184	3.3	1.3	91	3.7	1.4	118	2.5	1.1	2	390	21.60***

Notes:

[a] degrees of freedom between groups.

[b] degrees of freedom within groups.

*** $p < .001$, ** $p < .01$, * $p < .05$.

4.5 Case Study 3: Public Acceptance of Renewable Energies in Chile[15]

4.5.1 Materials and Methods

4.5.1.1 Socio-Economic Context

As the socio-economic context in Chile strongly affects the interpretation of the survey data, this section provides an overview of relevant issues.

With regard to renewable energies, there have recently been some public conflicts in Chile. Lacking participation and sharing of benefits has led to public resistance, especially with regard to large renewable energy projects. Especially hydropower projects are seen highly critical and are often blamed for destroying unique landscapes and ecosystems and provoke land use conflicts with other economic activities, such as tourism, and the local population (Consejo de Defensa de la Patagonia Chilena, 2018), cf. e.g., hydropower projects Altomaipo (CIEL, 2017), Hydroaysén (Emol, 2014), and Rio Cuervo (Rodrigo Fuentes, 2017). However, other renewable energies are also seen with some skepticism because of their impacts on the environment and the quality of life of local residents, cf. e.g., biomass plant in Cabrero (Rocío Parraguez, 2014).

The International Energy Agency (2018b, p.12) recommends that the Chilean government should strive to 'allay nimbyism ("not in my backyard") and reduce the number of projects blocked in courts' by introducing regulations, which provide guidance for projects with regard to local economic development and land use planning. However, societal opposition to renewable energy projects cannot only be explained by selfish NIMBY-motives. Chile still faces a large social gap within its population and participation in decision making of the lower social classes has been largely neglected. Despite great progress in terms of economic development and welfare levels, inequality remains an important issue. Chile ranks first in Latin America in the Human

[15] Parts of this section have previously been published in Schumacher et al. (2019a).

Development Index (HDI) that is published annually by the UNDP, but falls back twelve positions in the HDI world ranking if the index is adjusted for inequality (PNUD, 2017; UNDP, 2018). This social gap and the perceived unfairness regarding siting decisions for renewable energy projects has led to a highly critical perception and a general distrust, especially towards large infrastructure projects (cf. also section 3.1.1.2). This shortcoming has been recognized by the Chilean government through the creation of the Division of Participation and Social Dialogue within the Ministry of Energy in 2014. The division has the task to "promote inclusive, timely and transparent participation in the development of energy policies, plans, programs and projects, and also incorporate the indigenous relevance into these developments" (IEA, 2018b, p. 25). Putting this into practice, a nation-wide public consultation process has been carried out as part of the development of the National Energy Policy 2050, which has emerged as an outstanding example for public consultation on energy policy issues (IEA, 2018b).

4.5.1.2 Survey and Questionnaire Design

The online survey was carried out in November 2017 in cooperation with the data collection company Netquest. The Netquest panel is one of the largest in Chile counting more than 200,000 participants of 18 years or older. The panel is recruited via invitation and uses incentivized participation only, which means that every respondent is compensated with redeemable points for its participation. To obtain a good representation of the Chilean population, quota sampling was used with regard to age, sex, social class, and region (on the level of the 15 administrative regions of Chile). Netquest invited 4,627 randomly chosen panel members via e-mail to participate in the survey. The response rate was 34.7%, which produced a final sample of 1,205 observations (excluding 154 overquotas and 284 respondents who failed quality checks).

The questionnaire consists of 77 questions covering personal attitudes and dispositions to act regarding a set of renewable energy technologies as well as socio-demographic information. Special focus sections are dedicated to: knowledge of respondents with respect to renewable energies, acceptance of biomass combustion plants, societal participation and justice in renewable energy projects; and the use of firewood by households for heating purposes.[16] Moreover, a quality check was introduced at a random point of the survey to test the attention of the participant with a simple math question.

The majority of questions refer to attitudes towards four renewable energy technologies: large- and small-scale PV, wind power, and biogas plants. The focus is on those technologies as they often evoke direct interactions with the general public due to their decentralized location and associated local impacts. (for more information on the selection of investigated technologies cf. section 3.2.2). To ensure that the participants had an appropriate level of knowledge to answer the questions about the four chosen renewable energy technologies, each of the technologies was described in a short paragraph and a picture of a typical plant was displayed.

The items and constructs were taken as far as possible from existing studies (cf. e.g., Kontogianni et al., 2014; Ministerio de Energía, 2016; Musall and Kuik, 2011; Rau et al., 2012; Schumacher et al., 2019b; Schumacher and Schultmann, 2017; Soland et al., 2013; Zoellner et al., 2008) to allow for comparability of results with other studies. Some scales required adaptation to the Chilean context, some were newly developed using theoretical concepts from the literature (for more information see section 3.1.2). The majority of items used a five-point Likert scale including the option "don't know", wherever appropriate, to avoid respondents choosing the "comfortable center" ("I am undecided" or "neutral") of the unevenly-numbered Likert scale. In consequence, sample sizes differ for certain calculations. At the end of the questionnaire, the respondents were asked to leave a free text comment. All constructs, items and literature sources are listed in Table A-3, Appendix A.

To ensure validity, the questionnaire required adaptation to the study context through pretesting. A source questionnaire was developed in English which was then translated to Spanish in a cooperative approach between the author and a professional translator. Finally, the questionnaire was pretested in the

[16] The results of the two focus sections societal participation and justice in renewable energy projects and use of firewood by households for heating purposes are not presented in the following as they go beyond the scope of this thesis.

Chilean population (with support of Chilean researchers as multipliers). Based on the pretest results, adjustments were made to ensure comprehensibility and suitability of the questionnaire for the Chilean context.

4.5.1.3 Sample Characteristics

Table 4-24 compares the socio-demographic characteristics of the sample to population statistics of the Chilean population. The comparison reveals that the sample distribution represents the population quite precisely. Notwithstanding, the existing deviations deserve critical analysis and are therefore briefly discussed hereinafter.

The largest deviations consist in the share of home owners and employment status: home owners are strongly underrepresented by 13 pp, whereas the working population is strongly overrepresented by 8 pp. At the same time there are some minor deviations regarding age groups: the younger population (18-24 years) is overrepresented by 2 pp, whereas the elderly population (> 55 years) is underrepresented by 3 pp. It is hence concluded that there might be a selection bias with a slight overrepresentation of young working people, which do not yet possess their own houses, and an underrepresentation of retired persons, which are more likely to be home owners already. It is assumed that this results from the data collection mode via the internet as younger persons are more likely to be reached than elderly. The collection mode might further be a reason for the slight underrepresentation of persons of the lowest social class (E) by 4 pp, and the slight overrepresentation of members of the higher social classes (D, C2/C3, ABC1), assuming that internet access might be more limited for persons from the lower social status classes. Moreover, the most important ethnic group in Chile, the Mapuche, is slightly overrepresented in the sample by 2 pp, all other ethnic groups are not represented in the sample at all, except for the Aimara. However, the overall deviations with regard to ethnicity are rather negligible. With these limitations in mind, it is still concluded that the sample is a fairly good representation of the Chilean population in terms of sex, age, social status, and administrative regions on the level of the individual administrative 16 regions of Chile.

Table 4-24: Socio-demographic characteristics of the survey sample compared to population statistics (in %) (case study 3)

		Sample	Population
Male		49.8	49.5[a]
Age	18-24 years	17.1	14.8[a]
	25-34 years	20.6	21.1[a]
	35-44 years	19.3	18.4[a]
	45-54 years	18.9	18.3[a]
	> 55 years	24.1	27.5[a]
Social status	E	15.9[b]	20.3[c]
	D	35.7[b]	34.8[c]
	C2/C3	39.9[b]	37.8[c]
	ABC1	8.5[b]	7.2[c]
Region	Norte Grande (régiones XV, I, II)	6.3	6.5[a]
	Norte Chico (régiones III, IV)	5.6	5.9[a]
	Metropolitana de Santiago (XIII)	40.2	40.9[a]
	Centro (régiones V, VI)	15.5	15.4[a]
	Centro Sur (régiones VII, VIII, IX)	23.5	23.1[a]
	Sur (X, XI, XII, XIV)	8.8	8.4[a]
Ethnicity	Alacalufe (Kawashkar)	0	.02[d]
	Atacameño	0	.14[d]
	Aimara	.41	.32[d]
	Colla	0	.02[d]
	Mapuche	6.22	4.00[d]
	Quechua	0	.04[d]
	Rapa Nui	0	.03[d]
	Yámana (Yagán)	0	.01[d]
	None of the above	93.36	95.42[d]
Home owner rate		49.5	62.3[e]
Employment rate		63.7	55.7[f]

Notes:

[a] Own calculation based on InE (2017b), data from 2015.

[b] Social status is measured by "household size" and "income" with E being the lowest and ABC1 being the highest social status classes.

[c] Based on Adimark (2017), Census 2002, social status is measured by "material possession" and "highest level of education of the head of the household" with E being the lowest and ABC1 being the highest social status class.

[d] Own calculation based on InE (2017a), Census 2002.

[e] Based on Ministerio de Desarrollo Social (2016), data from 2015.

[f] Own calculation based on InE (2017c), data from 2017.

4.5.1.4 Data Preparation and Analysis

The data analysis was carried out using the statistics Software SPSS (Version 21). To avoid measurement errors, the data was critically reviewed and speeders and respondents who failed the quality check were eliminated. The questionnaire contained constructs measured by several items. Table 4-25 provides an overview of all constructs and their meaning. The exact items are reported in Table A-3, Appendix A. An item analysis was conducted for the constructs to assess internal consistency (Table 4-26). All values of Cronbach's α exceeded the recommended threshold of 0.70 (Bühner, 2011) with exception of the construct "perceived costs of energy crops", which lacks internal consistency ($\alpha = 0.448$) and is therefore not used in the regression analysis. Instead the item "energy crops from forest plantations" is included in the model to assess the influence of using wood from dedicated plantations.

Table 4-25: Constructs of the questionnaire (case study 3)

Construct	Concept
Advocacy of renewable energies	Support of renewable energy technologies in general and in the neighborhood
Perceived benefits of bioenergy plants	Perceived benefits of wood combustion plants for the society and the individual
Perceived costs of bioenergy plants	Perceived costs of wood combustion plants for the society and the individual
Perceived costs of energy crops	Perceived costs of monocultures and the use of agricultural crops for energy generation
Information and participation	Desired information and participation possibilities during the planning and construction of local wood combustion plants

Table 4-26: Internal consistency of constructs (case study 3)

Construct	Cronbach's α	Number of items
Advocacy of renewable energies	.798	2
Perceived benefits of biogas plants	.775	5
Perceived costs of biogas plants	.797	5
Perceived costs of energy crops	.448	2
Information and participation	.879	4

4.5.2 Results

Knowledge of Renewable Energies

So far, little empirical research regarding the public acceptance of renewable energies in Chile has been done. Hence, for explorative research it is essential to ensure that the object of the investigation is actually known by the respondents. Therefore, the level of knowledge of respondents was assessed (Figure 4-16), before starting to inquire the acceptance of renewable energies. For the question "Based on what you know, what you have seen, read or heard, what is renewable energy?" several answers were suggested, of which only one was correct. Roughly 70% of respondents were able to identify the correct definition, 30% did not. Compared to the results of a survey conducted in 2016 by the Chilean Ministry of Energy in 2016, which asked exactly the same question, there was an improvement of right answers to the question within the population by 15 pp (Ministerio de Energía, 2016). Hence, even if it cannot be assumed that every person is familiar with renewable energies in detail, the level of knowledge has been substantially improved over the last years.

Subsequently, the respondents were asked to assess their own level of knowledge with regard to renewable energies on a Likert scale with 1 = "very bad" and 5 = "very good" as anchors (Figure 4-17). Surprisingly, 39% of respondents assessed their level of knowledge as good or very good, 49% as medium, and only 12% as bad or very bad. Hence, the large majority of respondents consider themselves to have at least some knowledge on the topic of renewable energies.

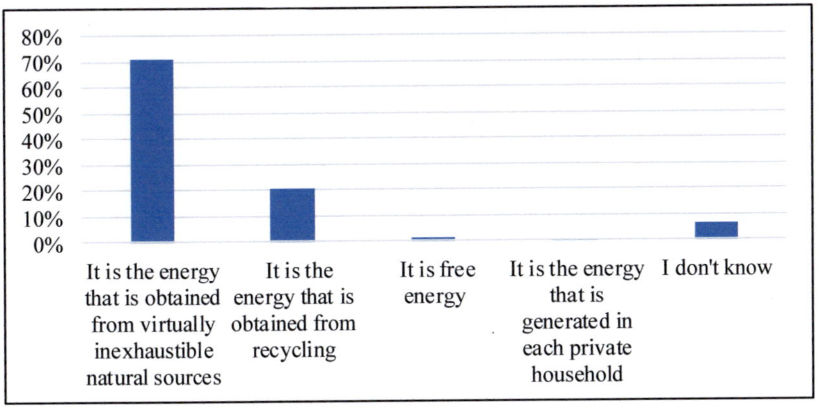

Figure 4-16: Frequency distribution of the answers to the question "Based on what you know, what you have seen, read, or heard, what is renewable energy?" (n=1,205)

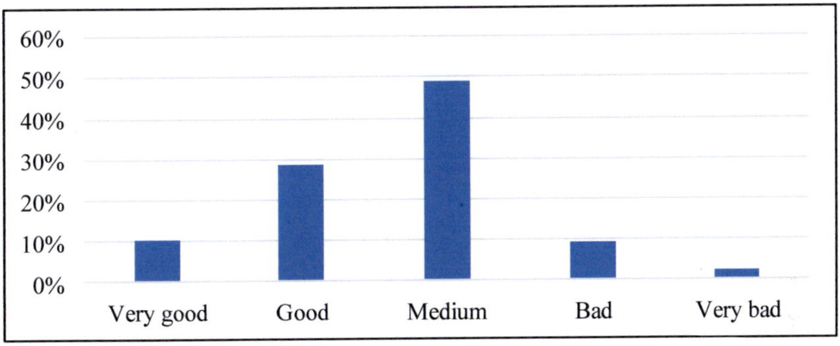

Figure 4-17: Frequency distribution of the answers to the question "How would you rate your general knowledge regarding renewable energy?" (n=1,205)

In addition, it was presumed that low or lacking knowledge could introduce biases to the respondents' assessment of renewable energies. Looking at the literature, the findings regarding the role of knowledge for public acceptance are divergent. A study conducted in southern Finland for example found that lacking knowledge was associated with a negative attitude towards electricity transmission lines (Soini et al., 2011). In contrast, other studies did not find any effect or even report contradictory results. For example, Ellis et al. (2007)

find that many opponents of an offshore wind farm proposal in Northern Ireland seemed to be very well informed and Aitken (2010) concludes from a review of the literature on public acceptance of wind energy that the relatively high level of knowledge has led to both opposition and support.

Thus, to understand the impact of knowledge in this study, it was necessary to statistically test whether the self-reported knowledge (item "knowledge of renewable energies", Table B-4) was correlated to public acceptance (item "local support", Table B-4). The test results, did not reveal any significant effect ($p = .959$). It is hence concluded, that the relatively low level of knowledge does not bias the answers of the survey and that respondents are sufficiently informed to legitimize the conduction of a meaningful opinion survey on renewable energies in Chile.

Furthermore, it is argued, that public acceptance is not necessarily explicable on a factual basis but is rather traced back to subjective valuations, which do not necessarily go hand in hand with technical knowledge (Bertsch et al., 2016). However, Bertsch et al. (2016) found that the respondent's level of education (which includes knowledge about renewable energies) influences the consistency of answers given with respect to the acceptance of renewable energies. Hence, a low level of knowledge might influence the reliability of answers. Keeping these limitations in mind, the analysis is able to provide an overall picture of current public attitudes towards renewable energies in Chile, for which it is less relevant whether the knowledge of participants is objectively high, but rather whether there is a certain level of awareness concerning renewable energies. The latter enables the formation of public opinion and has been confirmed by the above performed analysis.

H1: Renewable Energies Generally Enjoy High Public Acceptance for Future Energy Generation.

The data collected to assess H1 revealed that renewable energies generally received wide support by the Chilean population for future energy provision (Figure 4-18). Solar (91%) and wind energy (75%) enjoyed by far the highest support, whereas bioenergy (25%), geothermal (23%), hydropower (23%), and natural gas (21%) were less popular for the future energy mix. Coal (2%), nuclear (4 %), and oil (3%) had very little support in the Chilean population.

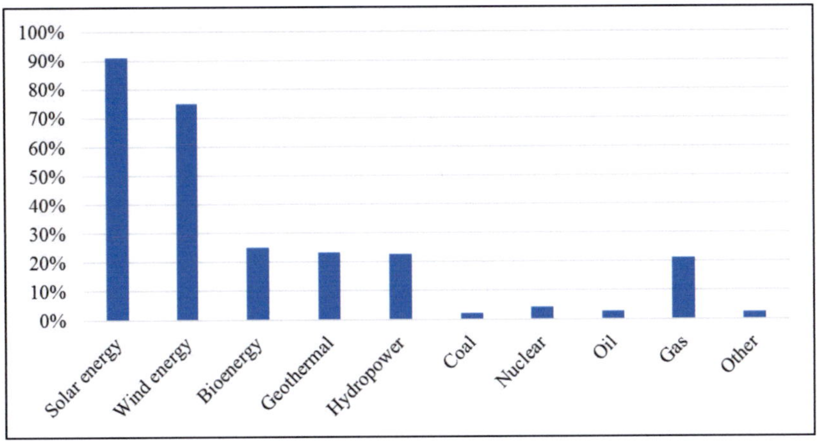

Figure 4-18: Frequency distribution of the answers to the question "In your opinion, which energy technologies should be preferably used in Chile in the future?" (n = 1,205)

H2: There is Public Disposition to Act Towards Renewable Energy Plants in the Neighborhood.

To assess H2, the concept by Schweizer-Ries et al. (2008) (c.f. Figure 2-1) was applied following the same logic as afore presented in case study 1 and 2. The concept defines acceptance by an appraisal and an action dimension, which were translated into three items. Firstly, the appraisal of the respective technology was assessed (ranging from negative to positive); secondly, a filter to assess the disposition to act was applied in the following logic: If a respondent's appraisal towards a local plant of a certain technology was *positive*, then the subsequently question asked if the respondent was prepared to *actively support* a local plant. If a respondent's appraisal towards a local plant of a certain technology was *negative*, then the subsequent question asked if the respondent was prepared to *actively oppose* a local plant.

Figure 4-19 shows the results by renewable energy technology which revealed a high approval of locally installed small PV (94%) and large PV (80%) plants as well as a high dispositions to act in favor of locally installed small PV (89%) and large PV (73%) plants. Wind energy plants also enjoyed high approval (71%) and high level of support (64%). However, the percentage of resisters (4%) was also slightly higher compared to small PV (0.3% resisters) and large PV (3% resisters). For local bioenergy plants the picture was quite different: here 46% of respondents rejected a local plant and 12% of respondents even indicated to be willing to actively resist a local bioenergy plant in their neighborhood compared to 16% active supporters.

These divided findings with respect to the individual technologies were discussed during two stakeholder workshops in Chile (cf. section 3.1.4). Participants were Chilean experts in the area of bioenergy from science, administration, and industry. They shared the opinion that there is strong distrust within the population towards large renewable energy projects as well as towards the forest industry (cf. section 3.1.1.2), which is often blamed for environmental damage and land use conflicts with the ethnic group of Mapuche, especially in the Regions Bío Bío and Araucanía in south-central Chile (Torres et al., 2015; Torres-Salinas et al., 2016). It is therefore assumed that both of the latter influenced the public image of wood combustion plants and led to a negative perception within the population.

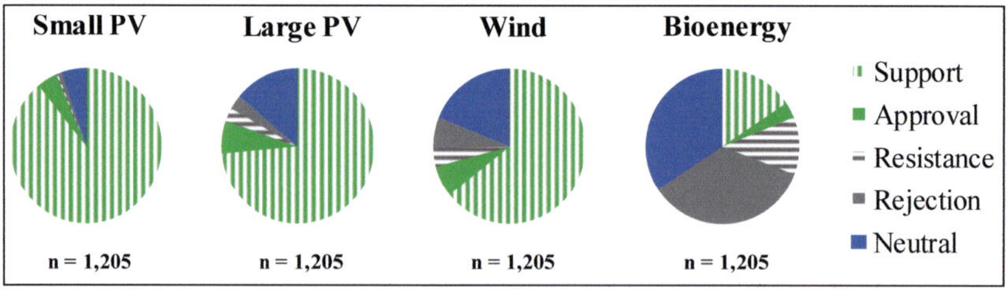

Note:

Categories “approval” and “rejection” include the categories “support” and “resistance” respectively (cf. Figure 2-1).

Figure 4-19: Levels of acceptance and dispositions to act towards a RE plant in the neighborhood by technology (case study 3)

H3: General Public Acceptance (Socio-Political Dimension) Exceeds Public Acceptance of Plants in the Neighborhood (Community Dimension).

H3 was assessed by testing differences in public acceptance of renewable energies in general (socio-political dimension) and public acceptance of plants in the neighborhood (community dimension) for all covered renewable energy technologies. The questionnaire distinguished between general attitudes (cf. Table A-3, Appendix A, item "socio-political acceptance") and attitudes relating to locally installed renewable energy plants in the vicinity (cf. Table A-3, Appendix A, item "appraisal of local plant"). In analogy with other studies, vicinity was defined as a one kilometer radius from the respondent's home (cf. Hübner and Hahn, 2013; Musall and Kuik, 2011; Schumacher and Schultmann, 2017).

Table 4-27 displays the results of the t-test, comparing public acceptance with regard to the socio-political and the community dimension by technology. Significant differences were detected for all technologies. For large PV, wind energy, and bioenergy plants public acceptance on the socio-political dimension significantly exceeded public acceptance on the community dimension. Cohen's d further revealed a small effect (Cohen's d between 0.24 and 0.48). Surprisingly, for small PV plants the effect was in the opposite direction with community public acceptance exceeding the socio-political dimension. The effect-size was however negligible (Cohen's $d = 0.12$). A possible explanation for this result is that small PV plants are likely to be owned by individuals of the local community, whereas large-scale technologies such as large PV, wind, and bioenergy plants are mostly owned by external companies. Hence, it seems reasonable to suppose that the willingness to accept a plant on the community level is higher if respondents expect a direct local or personal benefit. Another notable result was that the effect was largest for bioenergy plants (Cohen's $d = 0.48$), which again underlines the finding that biomass plants are perceived particularly negative on the community level (cf. findings for H2).

Table 4-27: Paired sample t-test to compare public acceptance on the socio-political and the community dimension by technology (case study 3)

Object of acceptance		Socio-political		Local		p-value	Cohen's d
	n	M	SD	M	SD		
Small PV	1,176	4.36	1.099	4.48	1.000	.000	.12
Large PV	1,167	4.36	1.131	4.09	1.082	.000	.24
Wind	1,154	4.36	1.025	3.97	1.142	.000	.36
Bioenergy	1,105	3.19	1.221	2.61	1.186	.000	.48

H4: Public Acceptance of Renewable Energy Plants is Influenced by the Distance of the Plant to the Respondent's Home.

To assess H4, a two-step approach was used: In a first step, it was assessed whether proximity to a renewable energy plant is an issue at all for the respondent. The answers to the question "To what extent is the distance between your house/ apartment and a small-scale PV/ large-scale PV/ wind energy/ bioenergy plant important to you?" are displayed by Table 4-28. It was again striking that bioenergy plants were seen a lot more critically than the other renewable energies with roughly 39% of respondents indicating to reject a local bioenergy plants independent from the distance to their home. In contrast, roughly 51% and 41% of the respondents stated that the distance to small and large PV plants respectively was not important for them at all. For wind turbines, visibility of the plants was important with 19% of respondents demanding that the plant should not be visible from their homes (compared to 11% for small PV, 16% for large PV, and 16% for biomass plants).

Table 4-28: Role of proximity for public acceptance of different RE plants in percent (%) of respondents by technology

Response category	Technology			
	Small PV	Large PV	Wind	Bioenergy
I do *not* accept the plant, independent of the distance.	1.7	2.2	4.9	38.6
The distance of the plant to my home is not relevant for me.	50.5	41.3	29.0	9.3
The distance is not relevant but the plant should not be visible from my home.	11.1	15.9	18.8	15.7
The plants should keep a minimal distance to my home.	36.7	40.5	47.2	36.4

In a second step, those respondents who answered "The plant should keep a minimal distance to my home." were asked to indicate the respective distance at which they would accept a certain type of renewable energy plant in their vicinity. The scale ranged from "less than 1 km" to "more than 9 km" as anchors. Figure 4-20 presents the cumulated relative frequencies of the desired distance for the investigated renewable energy technologies. It was confirmed that acceptance increased with distance for all four renewable energy technologies. Again, it was striking that for bioenergy plants the desired distance was substantially larger than for all other renewable energies, which is in line with the low public acceptance of biomass combustion plants (cf. H2). Even at a nine kilometer distance, only 46% of respondents indicated to accept a bioenergy plant in their vicinity.

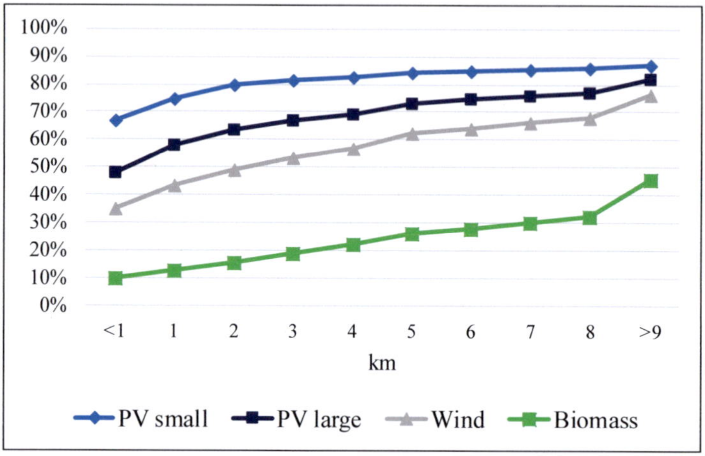

Notes:

Sample sizes: $n_{PV\ small} = 1{,}050$, $n_{PV\ large} = 986$, $n_{Wind} = 919$, $n_{Biomass} = 551$.

Includes responses "The distance of the plant to my home is not relevant for me." as 0 km.

Expressed as percentage of all responses (cf. Table 4-28).

Figure 4-20: Cumulated relative frequencies of the desired minimum distance of RE plants in Chile

H5: Public Acceptance of Renewable Energy Plants is Higher Among Respondents with Previous Experience with Renewable Energy Projects.

To test H5, respondents were firstly asked whether they already live with an renewable energy plants installed in their neighborhood (Table 4-29). Secondly, a t-test was conducted to compare public acceptance between respondents with and without renewable energy plants in their direct vicinity (Table 4-30).

Roughly 38% of respondents indicated to be living with some type of renewable energy plant in their vicinity, thereof the large majority (88%) with small PV plants, 12% with wind energy plants, and only a minority (less than 5%) indicated to be aware of any other type of renewable energy plant in their vicinity. This result is interesting given the critical evaluation and high disposition to resist towards bioenergy plants on the community level (cf. H2), which hence, cannot be traced back to former personal negative experiences but rather to expected impacts and the negative perception of bioenergy plants (cf. H1).

Table 4-29: Share of respondents with RE plant in direct vicinity by technology in Chile

One or more RE plant(s) in direct vicinity	total	454
	%	37.7
Thereof small PV	total	400
	%	88.1
Thereof large PV	total	23
	%	5.1
Thereof wind power	total	55
	%	12.1
Thereof biomass combustion plant	total	8
	%	1.8
Thereof geothermal plant	total	16
	%	3.5
Thereof hydroelectric power plant	total	13
	%	2.9
Thereof other RE plants	total	10
	%	2.2

Note: n = 1,205.

The t-test to compare public acceptance between respondents with and without renewable energy plant in the neighborhood (cf. Table 4-30) revealed statistically significant differences for renewable energies in general, small PV, and wind energy, whereas for large PV and bioenergy plants no significant effect was found. Cohen's d only revealed a noteworthy small-sized effect for wind energy plants (Cohen's $d = 0.31$). It however needs to be kept in mind that some sub-samples, especially those of residents of large PV and bioenergy plants, were very small, which might have influenced the test results.

Table 4-30: T-test to compare public acceptance between respondents with and without RE plant in direct vicinity (case study 3)

Object of acceptance	*With* plant in vicinity			*Without* plant in vicinity			p-value	Cohen's d
	n	M	SD	n	M	SD		
REs	453	4.49	1.142	731	4.33	1.176	.025	.14
Small PV	400	4.58	.978	787	4.43	1.007	.012*	.15
Large PV	23	4.22	1.166	1,150	4.08	1.078	.556	.13
Wind energy	54	4.26	.828	1,107	3.95	1.152	.011*	.31
Bioenergy	8	3.25	1.488	1,126	2.60	1.178	.120	.48

Note: *Welch-Test because of variance heterogeneity.

To further investigate the role of experiences for public acceptance, the relationship between experience and desired distance (cf. Figure 4-20) was analyzed with an interesting result: If respondents lived with a small PV plant in their direct vicinity, desired average distance decreased from 2.7 km to 1.7 km ($p = 0.049$, Cohens'd = 0.48). For the other technologies, no such effect was found, which might however be due to the small sample sizes for residents of the other technologies (cf. Table 4-29). Furthermore, it was assessed whether respondents with an equivalent plant in a one kilometer radius were less likely to reject such a plant in their vicinity than respondents without. A significant effect was found for wind energy ($p = 0.000$, Cohen's d = 0.17). None of the respondents living with a wind energy plant in the neighborhood indicated to reject a wind energy plant as such (cf. item "I do not accept the plant, independent of the distance", Table 4-28). To sum up, the empirical evidence points to higher levels of public acceptance if respondents were already living in direct vicinity to the respective plant and thus, H5 is confirmed.

H6 to H12: Factors Driving the Acceptance of Wood Combustion Plants

Multiple linear regression was performed to identify factors which significantly influence social acceptance of biomass combustion plants. Table 4-31 shows the results of the regression analysis with self-reported acceptance on the socio-political level (item "Biomass plants are a suitable form of energy generation") and the community level (item "I support biomass plants in my neighborhood") as dependent variables. Based on the existing literature (cf. section 2.4), the factors "advocacy of renewable energies" (H6), "perceived benefits of biomass combustion plants" (H7), "perceived costs of biomass combustion plants" (H8), and "information and participation" (H9) were included in the model (Kortsch et al., 2015, Schumacher and Schultmann, 2017, Soland et al., 2013). One additional item was included to account for "perceived costs of monocultures" (H11) as it was assumed from the results of the expert interview analysis (cf. section 3.1.1.2) that perceived impacts from the mono-cropping practices of the wood companies might play a role for public acceptance.[17] The factors "trust" (H10) and "perceived odor emissions" (H12) were not tested in this model as they refer to specific bioenergy projects, which are not covered in case study 3. Moreover, the respondents' sex (female/ male), the home owner status (yes/ no) and the existence of a biomass combustion plant in the neighborhood (yes/ no) were added as control variables to the model.

Both models fulfil the underlying assumptions of multiple linear regressions (cf. section 3.1.3). A visual inspection of residuals showed no critical violations of the assumption of normal distribution of residuals and no indication of violations of the linearity assumption (Hair et al., 2014, pp. 216-219). The VIF statistics gave no noteworthy indication of multicollinearity and are far below the upper acceptable bound (VIF model "socio-political acceptance" $\leq$ 1.485, VIF model "community acceptance" $\leq$ 1.515) (Hair et al., 2014, p. 200). A visual inspection of the residual scatter diagrams indicated homoscedasticity (Hair et al., 2014, p. 217). As the data is no time series data, auto correlation was not expected to be a critical issue, which was confirmed by the Durbin-Watson-test (Durbin-Watson model "socio-political acceptance" = 1.953, Durbin-Watson model "community acceptance" = 1.918) (Field, 2013, p. 311). To handle outliers, a first run of the regression model identified observations with residuals less than or equal to 3 and greater than or equal to 3 which were removed from the

[17] The construct "perceived costs of energy crops", lacked internal consistency with $\alpha = 0.448$ and is therefore not used for the regression analysis (cf. Table 4-26).

dataset before the final calculation was performed (cf. Hair et al., 2014, pp. 216-219). For the socio-political acceptance model five outliers were eliminated, for the community acceptance model two outliers were removed.

The results of the regression analysis revealed "perceived benefits of biomass combustion plants" as the by far most important factor with a highly significant positive effect on both the socio-political ($B = 0.845$, $p < 0.001$) and the community level ($B = 0.656$, $p < 0.001$). The second most important factor differed between the two models. In the socio-political model, "advocacy of renewable energies" ($B = 0.148$, $p < 0.001$) and in the community model "perceived costs of biomass plants" ranked second ($B = -0.237$, $p < 0.001$). The factor "perceived costs of biomass plants", however, was also identified as significant in the socio-political model ($B = -0.119$, $p < 0.05$). Using the method suggested by Cohen et al. (2003) to compare coefficients of regression models with different dependent variables, it was found that the influence of "perceived costs of biomass plants" was more important on the community than on the socio-political level ($p = 0.002$), whereas the factor "advocacy of renewable energies" was more important on the socio-political than on the community level ($p = 0.012$). Interestingly, the factors "perceived costs of monocultures" and "information and participation" did not have a significant influence in neither model. The differences between the two models support the findings of Sonnberger and Ruddat (2017) for the acceptance of wind farms in Germany. To explain differences between public acceptance on the socio-political and the community level, they refer to the so-called "low-cost hypothesis" (Diekmann and Preisendörfer, 2003), stating that attitudinal factors decrease with increasing behavioral costs. Applied to the presented results of the two regression models, this means that advocacy of renewable energies as an attitudinal factor is more relevant for socio-political acceptance, whereas perceived costs of biomass plants are more relevant on the community level because behavioral costs increase with the necessary toleration of direct impacts from local plants.

The regression model for socio-political acceptance explained 39% and the one for community acceptance 29% of the variance in the respective dependent variable. Hence, R^2 is in an acceptable, however rather low range compared to other empirical studies of the research field (cf. Kortsch et al., 2015; Sonnberger and Ruddat, 2017; Zoellner et al., 2008).

Table 4-31: Multiple linear regression of public acceptance of biomass combustion plants (case study 3)

	Socio-political acceptance (n = 790)		Community acceptance (n = 784)	
Dependent variable	B	β	B	β
Sex (1=m)	-.047	-.018	.068	.028
Home-owner (1=yes)	-.133	-.054	-.013	-.005
Biomass plant in vicinity (1=yes)	-.087	-.035	.018	.008
Advocacy renewable energies	.148***	.138***	.041	.040
Perceived benefits of biomass plants	.845***	.562***	.656***	.445***
Perceived costs of biomass plants	-.119*	-.081*	-.237***	-.163***
Perceived costs of monocultures	.055	.046	-.066	-.041
Information and participation	-.002	-.001	.035	.031
F	62.999***		40.229***	
R^2	.392		.293	
Adjusted R^2	.389		.289	

Note: *** $p < .001$. ** $p < .01$; * $p < .05$.

4.6 Discussion of Case Study Results

This section sums up and discusses the principal findings of the three previously presented case studies (sections 4.3, 4.4, and 4.5). Section 4.6.1 starts with a comparison of results between the case studies themselves and interprets them in terms of differences and communalities. Section 4.6.2 broadens the discussion of findings by comparing the empirical findings of this thesis with those from related literature (cf. section 2.3).

4.6.1 Comparison Between the Case Studies

This section compares the findings of the three case studies conducted in this thesis and discusses their communalities and differences along the thirteen raised hypotheses (cf. section 3.2.3). The results from the three case studies are presented jointly and in a condensed form and no details of the methods used are provided. For information on the methodology, the reader is referred to the explanations presented in the respective sections of the case studies (cf. sections 4.3, 4.4, and 4.5).

The comparison of results of the three case studies is particularly interesting, because a similar research design was applied, which allows for meaningful comparisons across countries, technologies, and dimensions of acceptance. Thus, the usual uncertainty regarding the comparability of study designs and measurement instruments is eliminated (cf. section 2.2). However, it needs to be acknowledged that measurement instruments differ slightly between the case studies because of adaptations to the study context. Hence, if measurement scales are adapted, the local context was prioritized over exact comparability of measurement instruments (cf. also section 6.1.2). Still, all deviations are transparently indicated (cf. Appendix A) and discussed with respect to their influence on the comparison.

The subsequent discussion is divided into two parts: Firstly, a comparison of findings for H1 to H5, and secondly, a comparison of findings for H6 to H12 is provided. The separation is made as H1 to H5 refer to public acceptance of a set of renewable energy technologies, whereas H6 to H12 exclusively focus on factors influencing public acceptance of bioenergy plants.

H1 to H5: Comparison Between the Case Studies

This section analyzes the three case studies of this thesis with regard to their findings for H1 to H5 (cf. section 3.2.3). Table 4-32 provides an overview of findings. As some findings vary with respect to the acceptance dimension, it is distinguished between socio-political and the community acceptance. Table 4-32 is followed by a detailed discussion of results for each of the hypotheses.

Table 4-32: Comparison of findings for H1 to H5 by case study

Study	Dimension	H1	H2	H3	H4	H5
1	Socio-political	Yes	N/A	Yes, except small PV	N/A	Yes
1	Community	N/A	Yes	Yes, except small PV	Yes	Yes
2	Socio-political	Yes	N/A	N/A	N/A	N/A
2	Community	N/A	Yes	N/A	Yes	N/A
3	Socio-political	Yes	N/A	Yes, except small PV	N/A	Yes
3	Community	N/A	Yes	Yes, except small PV	Yes	Yes

Notes:

Yes: The hypothesis has been confirmed.

No: The hypothesis has been rejected.

N/A: The hypothesis has not been addressed or is not applicable for the study.

H1: Renewable Energies Generally Enjoy High Public Acceptance for Future Energy Generation.

Figure 4-21 shows the results for H1 of the three case studies in comparison. A visual inspection of the frequency distribution of the answers to the question "In your opinion, which energy technologies should be preferably used in the future?" shows that some of the technology preferences of Chilean respondents diverged rather strongly to those of respondents from the URR. Whereas solar energy and wind energy were similarly often cited in all countries, there was substantially lower support for bioenergy, geothermal, and hydropower in Chile compared to the URR. In contrast, gas was rated more positively in Chile than in the URR.

Moreover, the comparison of results of the population sample (case study 1) with the sample of residents of biogas plants (case study 2) revealed some interesting differences with regard to bioenergy and hydropower. For both of the latter public acceptance was noticeably higher among residents than among the general public. As case study 2 refers to specific sample-points and not to the whole URR (cf. section 4.4.1.3), this could be due to sampling error. However, the largest gap, which was observed for bioenergy, still deserves some attention. Indeed, it is an interesting result that bioenergy was named more often as future energy source by residents of biogas plants than by respondents of a representative population sample. This points to a potential relation between experiences with bioenergy plants and their public acceptance (cf. the subsequent discussion regarding H5).

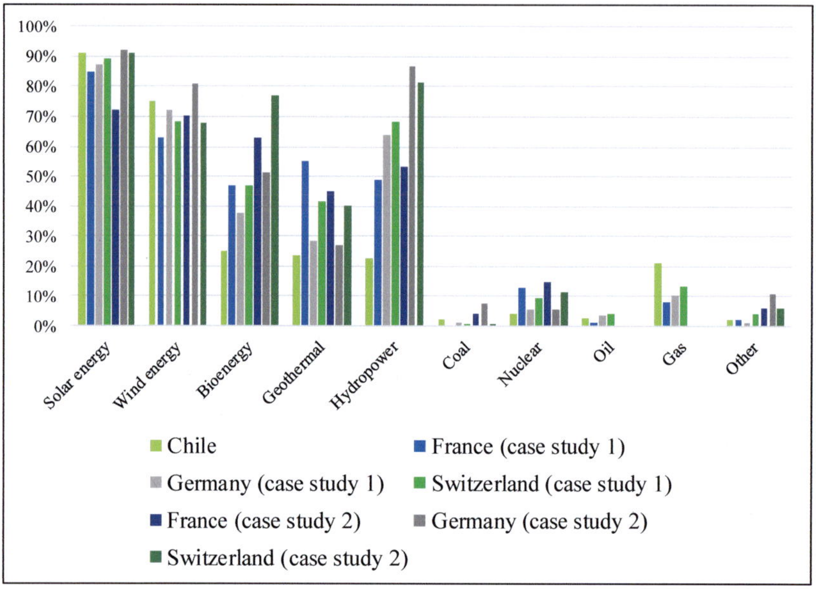

Notes:

Case study 1: $n_{Germany} = 495$, $n_{Switzerland} = 493$, $n_{France} = 501$.

Case study 2: $n_{Germany} = 203$, $n_{Switzerland} = 130$, $n_{France} = 100$.

Case study 3: $n_{Chile} = 1{,}205$.

Figure 4-21: Frequency distribution of the answers to the question "In your opinion, which energy technologies should be preferably used in the future?" (all case studies)

H2: There is Public Disposition to Act Towards Renewable Energy Plants in the Neighborhood.

The results of the three case studies for H2 are jointly displayed by Figure 4-22. Comparing the results for the general public in Chile (case study 3) with those for the URR (case study 1), it is obvious that Chilean respondents expressed more extreme positions regarding the individual technologies: on the one hand, Chile's share of approval is substantially higher for small PV (94%), large PV (80%), and wind energy (71%) compared to the URR (78% for small PV, 60% for large PV, and 46% for wind); on the other hand, rejection towards biomass plants is substantially higher in Chile (47%) than in the URR (20%), whereas resistance is on a comparable level in Chile (12%) and the URR (7%). The comparison between the three case studies further supports the conclusion that bioenergy is perceived particularly negative by the Chilean public (cf. sections 3.1.1.2 and 4.5.2).

Another interesting result is revealed by the comparison of results of case studies 1 and 2 with respect to bioenergy plants. In both France and Switzerland approval levels are higher among residents of biogas plants (case study 2) than the general public (case study 1). The largest deviation is observed for the Swiss sample with 68% of residents compared to 41% of the general public indicating to approve a biogas plant in their neighborhood. At the same time, the share of respondents with a "neutral" evaluation of biogas is substantially lower among local residents (16%) than the general public (36%) in the Swiss sample. The same is true in the French sample, but with smaller deviations between the approval by residents (52%) and the general public (36%). Another notable difference was found with respect to resistance in the Swiss sample which was substantially lower among local residents (3%) than the general public (5%). To sum up, residents of biogas plants in France and Switzerland show a more positive appraisal and less resistance towards local biogas plants than the general public.

Interestingly, for the German sub-region, the same comparison revealed the reversed effect: Whereas 35% of the general public approved a hypothetical biogas plant in their neighborhood, only 30% of local residents do so. Likewise, the share of rejection was slightly higher among local residents

(32%) than among the general public (26%). The strongest deviation however is revealed for the disposition to actively resist a local biogas plant: 20% of residents in contrast to 8% of the general public indicate to be active opponents of biogas plants.

To conclude, the combined results of the case studies show substantial differences in terms of acceptance levels and disposition to act between technologies, countries, and sub-groups of the public. An interesting finding is revealed by the comparison between case study 1 and 2 for biogas. It seems that experience with a local biogas plant can potentially lead to both more positive appraisal and higher support or more negative appraisal and higher rejection. This suggest that the quality of the actual experience with a local plant is decisive for its evaluation.

Moreover, some general conclusions can be drawn from the joint investigation of results of acceptance levels and dispositions to act. Firstly, it is remarkable that the rank order of technologies with respect to their approval is similar in all countries with only slight deviations. Secondly, in all three case studies the reported disposition to support exceeds the disposition to resists for all technologies, with the exception of biogas in Germany rated by local residents. The strength of the latter effect is dependent on the technology in question: Whereas the reported disposition to support is particularly pronounced for small and large-scale PV, the disposition to resist increases for wind and bioenergy. Thirdly, a notable share of respondents is undecided ("neutral") regarding the appraisal of local renewable energy plants, especially with regard to medium- and large-scale technologies (large PV, wind, and bioenergy).

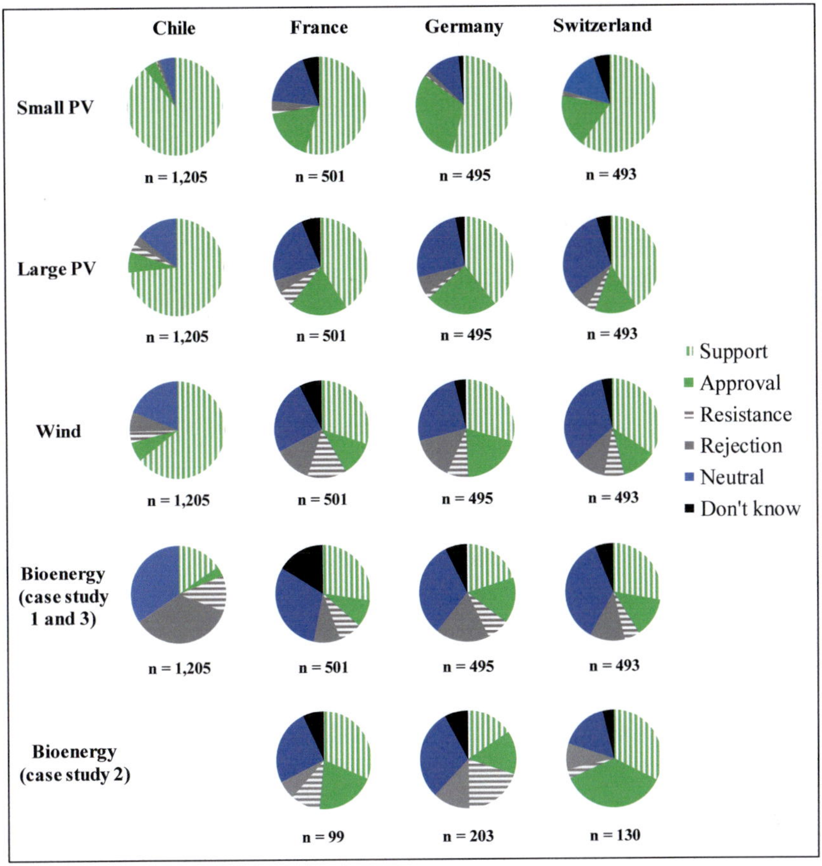

Notes: Categories "approval" and "rejection" include the categories "support" and "resistance" respectively (cf. Figure 2-1).

For bioenergy, the data for Chile refers to wood combustion plants, whereas the data for the URR refers to biogas plants.

Figure 4-22: Levels of acceptance and dispositions to act towards a RE plant in the neighborhood by study region and technology (all case studies)

H3: General Public Acceptance (Socio-Political Dimension) Exceeds Public Acceptance of Plants in the Neighborhood (Community Dimension).

All three case studies found significant differences between socio-political and community public acceptance for all technologies and countries. For the covered medium to large-scale technologies (large PV, wind, and bioenergy) H3 was unanimously confirmed. However, effect-sizes varied between case studies and technologies. Whereas all effects found for large PV, wind and bioenergy in the URR (case study 1) and Chile (case study 3) were small to medium (Cohen'd ≤ 0.8), a large-sized effect (Cohen'd $= 0.82$) was revealed in the German sub-sample of residents of biogas plants (case study 3). This result again underlines the finding that German residents of biogas plants were most critical towards those plants.

Another notable result was that in contradiction to H3, community acceptance of small PV plants exceeded socio-political acceptance in all four countries. A plausible interpretation of this finding was already presented for H3 in sections 4.3.2 and 4.5.2: whereas small PV plants are likely to be (fully) owned by the respondents or community members, large PV, wind, and biogas plants are in most cases owned by commercial actors. Hence, respondents could at most have a share in those plants, but are very unlikely to own them outright. This suggests that persons might be more willing to accept a renewable energy plant in their vicinity if they personally benefit from it (cf. also results for H13 in section 4.3.2).

To sum up, H3 was unanimously confirmed for the medium and large-scale technologies (large PV, wind energy, and bioenergy), and unanimously rejected for small-scale PV by all three case studies.

H4: Public Acceptance of Renewable Energy Plants is Influenced by the Distance of the Plant to the Respondent's Home.

To interpret the findings of the three case studies for H4, the results are visualized in several combined figures. Figure 4-23 displays the results of the representative population surveys in the URR (case study 1) and in Chile (case study 3). A visual inspection reveals that the average desired distance was notably smaller in the Chilean sample for all technologies, except for wood combustion plants. Especially for wind energy and large PV plants, smaller distances were desired by the Chilean population than by the inhabitations of the URR. Desired distances for small PV are only slightly smaler in the Chilean than in the URR sample. This result is in line with the findings for H2, which showed that small and large PV as well as wind energy plants were assessed more positively by the Chilean population, whereas bioenergy was confronted with substantially higher levels of rejection in Chile than in the URR.

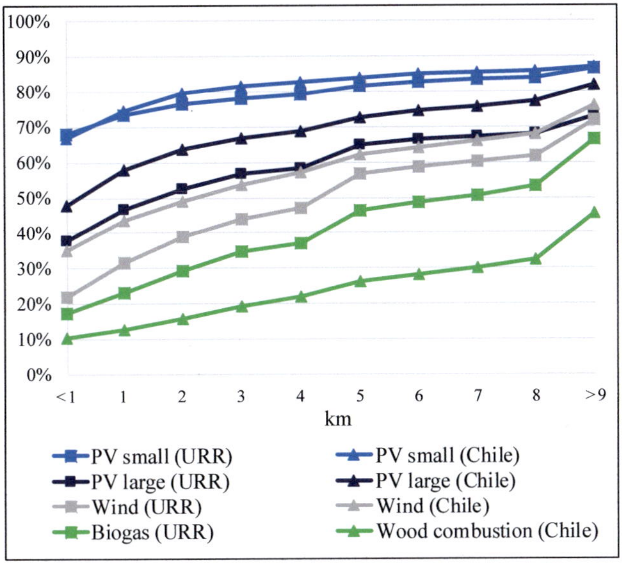

Notes:

Sample sizes Chile: $n_{\text{PV small}} = 1{,}050$, $n_{\text{PV large}} = 986$, $n_{\text{Wind}} = 919$, $n_{\text{Biomass}} = 551$.

Sample sizes URR: $n_{\text{PV small}} = 1{,}291$, $n_{\text{PV large}} = 1{,}090$, $n_{\text{Wind}} = 1{,}072$, $n_{\text{Biogas}} = 992$.

Includes responses “The distance of the plant to my home is not relevant for me.” as 0 km.

Figure 4-23: Cumulated relative frequencies of the desired minimum distance of RE plants in the URR (case study 1) and Chile (case study 3)

Figure 4-24, Figure 4-25, and Figure 4-26 display the minimum distance to renewable energy plants desired by the general public (case study 1) and residents of local biogas plants (case study 2) by sub-region of the URR. It is striking that residents of biogas plants in all three sub-regions demanded by far smaller distances for biogas plants than the general public. Hence, respondents who were actually living with a biogas plant in their vicinity appeared to be less critical regarding proximity than respondents answering a hypothetical question. Interestingly this finding holds also true for the German sub-region. This is rather surprising given that German residents assessed a local biogas plant more critically than the general public (cf. results for H2). This could mean that even though German residents probably had negative experiences with the biogas plant in their vicinity, they still did not reject the technology as such. On the contrary, they even desired smaller distances between the plant and their home than the general public. Therefore, it is assumed that other characteristics related to the specific biogas plant in their vicinity, such as perceived costs and benefits, aspects of procedural justice as well as trust, might be the reason for the negative appraisal of local residents.

Moreover, some general conclusions can be drawn from the joint observations of the three case studies. Firstly, it is noticeable that the rank order of desired distances for the four renewable energy technologies is the same in all three case studies with the largest desired distance for bioenergy plants and the smallest for small-scale PV plants. Secondly, all of the three case studies share the observation that public acceptance increases with larger distances of the plants to the respondent's home. This leads to the conclusion that proximity is a relevant factor for local public acceptance and thus H4 is confirmed.

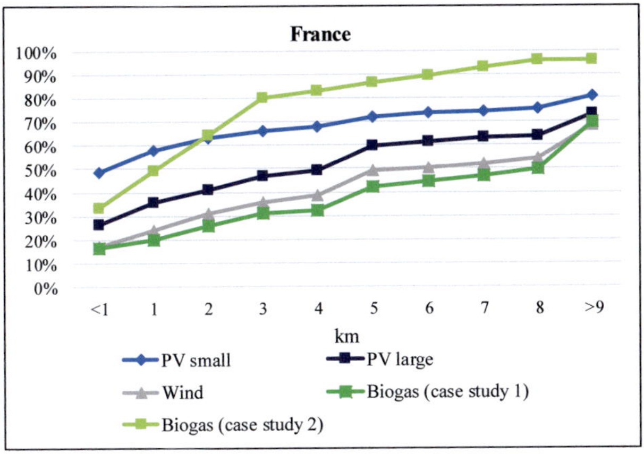

Notes: Sample sizes: n $_{\text{PV small}}$ = 501, n $_{\text{PV large}}$ = 501, n $_{\text{Wind}}$ = 501, n $_{\text{Biogas (case study 1)}}$ = 501, n $_{\text{Biogas (case study 2)}}$ = 96.

Includes responses "The distance of the plant to my home is not relevant for me." as 0 km.

Figure 4-24: Cumulated relative frequencies of the desired minimum distance of RE plants in France

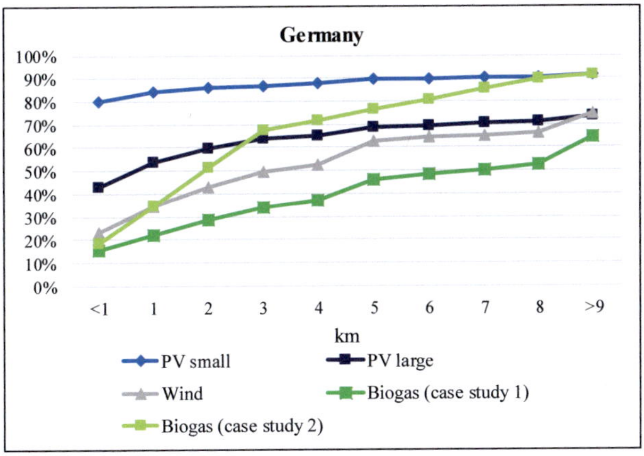

Notes: Sample sizes: n $_{\text{PV small}}$ = 495, n $_{\text{PV large}}$ = 459, n $_{\text{Wind}}$ = 495, n $_{\text{Biogas (case study 1)}}$ = 495, n $_{\text{Biogas (case study 2)}}$ = 195.

Includes responses "The distance of the plant to my home is not relevant for me." as 0 km.

Figure 4-25: Cumulated relative frequencies of the desired minimum distance of RE plants in Germany

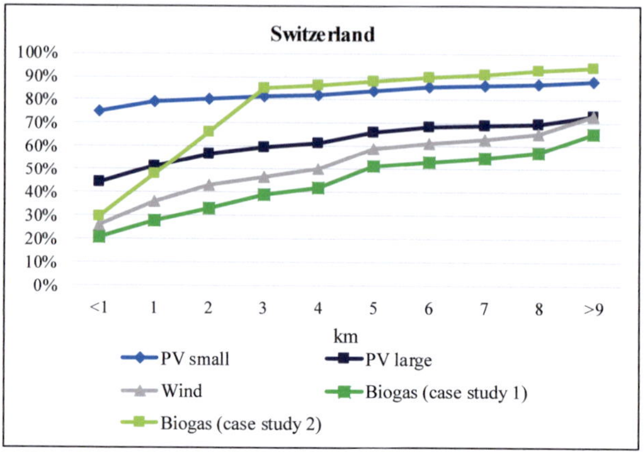

Notes: Sample sizes: $n_{\text{PV small}} = 493$, $n_{\text{PV large}} = 493$, $n_{\text{Wind}} = 493$, $n_{\text{Biogas (case study 1)}} = 493$, $n_{\text{Biogas (case study 2)}} = 125$.

Includes responses "The distance of the plant to my home is not relevant for me." as 0 km.

Figure 4-26: Cumulated relative frequencies of the desired minimum distance of RE plants in Switzerland

H5: Public Acceptance of Renewable Energy Plants is Higher Among Respondents with Previous Experience with Renewable Energy Projects.

The results of both case study 1 and 3 point to a link between public acceptance and experience of the respondents. Both studies only confirmed statistical differences for some technologies leaving doubt about the generalizability of results. The test results are also questionable due to small sample sizes in some sub-groups of respondents living next to certain renewable energy plant (cf. results for H5, sections 4.3.2 and 4.5.2). To obtain a larger and more meaningful sample, all answers of respondents of the three case studies are combined in the following analysis. This substantially increases the number of observations in the critical groups of residents and thus adds explanatory power to the data.

Table 4-33 displays the results of the t-test to compare public acceptance between respondents of all three case studies with and without a renewable energy plant in direct vicinity. For all technologies the test results confirm significantly higher acceptance for respondents living with a plant in vicinity than for those without, although the effects are all rather small (Cohen's d between .13 and .39). Hence, H5 is confirmed based on the extended dataset for all covered renewable energy technologies.

Table 4-33: T-test to compare public acceptance between respondents with and without RE plant in direct vicinity (combined data from case study 1, 2, and 3)

Object of acceptance	Sub-region	*With* plant in vicinity			*Without* plant in vicinity			p-value	Cohen's d
		n	M	SD	n	M	SD		
Small PV	France	76	4.42	.753	410	4.14	.877	.008	.27
	Germany	278	4.80	.524	210	4.41	.940	.000*	.20
	Switzerland	187	4.63	.732	289	4.47	.799	.028*	.10
	URR	541	4.69	.650	909	4.31	.881	.000*	.24
	Chile	400	4.58	.978	787	4.43	1.007	.012*	.09
	All	941	4.64	.807	1,696	4.36	.943	.000*	.17
Large PV	France	23	4.00	.853	464	3.66	1.016	.117	.32
	Germany	51	4.35	.890	434	3.91	1.045	.004	.38
	Switzerland	42	4.38	.936	432	3.84	1.076	.002	.46
	URR	116	4.29	.904	1,330	3.80	1.050	.000	.43
	Chile	23	4.22	1.166	1,150	4.08	1.078	.556	.13
	All	139	4.28	.948	2,480	3.93	1.072	.000	.31
Wind energy	France	14	3.71	1.267	474	3.15	1.266	.099	.43
	Germany	101	4.00	1.131	385	3.44	1.288	.000*	.34
	Switzerland	23	3.96	1.224	455	3.62	1.225	.202	.26
	URR	138	3.96	1.155	1,314	3.40	1.273	.000*	.40
	Chile	54	4.26	.828	1,107	3.95	1.152	.011*	.26
	All	192	4.05	1.080	2,421	3.65	1.250	.000*	.30
Bioenergy	France	103	3.52	1.275	450	3.30	1.064	.100*	.16
	Germany	230	3.26	1.516	437	3.19	1.263	.518*	.03
	Switzerland	163	4.12	1.221	433	3.49	1.106	.000	.37
	URR	496	3.60	1.425	1,320	3.33	1.153	.000*	.15
	Chile	8	3.25	1.488	1,126	2.6	1.178	.12	.55
	All	504	3.59	1.425	2,446	2.99	1.219	.000*	.39

Notes:

*Welch-Test because of variance heterogeneity.

For small PV, large PV, and wind energy the data from case studies 1 and 3 was merged; for bioenergy the data from case study 1, 2, and 3 was merged.

Bioenergy refers to biogas plants in the URR and to wood combustion plants in Chile.

H6 to H12: Comparison Between the Case Studies

The subsequent section analyzes the findings of the three case studies with regard to factors influencing public acceptance of bioenergy plants. Table 4-34 provides an overview of findings for H6 to H12 of the three case studies by acceptance dimension. The table is followed by a comparison of findings of the three case studies for H6 (advocacy of renewable energies), H7 (perceived benefits), H8 (perceived costs), H9 (information and participation), and H11 (perceived costs of energy crops). As H10 (trust) and H12 (perceived odor) are exclusively considered in case study 2, a comparison of results is not possible.

Table 4-34: Comparison of findings for H6 to H12 by case study

Case study	Dimension	H6	H7	H8	H9	H10	H11	H12
1	Socio-political	Yes	Yes	Yes	No	N/A	Yes	N/A
	Community	Yes	Yes	Yes	Yes	N/A	No	N/A
2	Community	Yes	Yes	No	No	Yes	N/A	Yes
3	Socio-political	Yes	Yes	Yes	No	N/A	No	N/A
	Community	No	Yes	Yes	No	N/A	No	N/A

Notes:

Yes: The hypothesis has been confirmed.

No: The hypothesis has been rejected.

N/A: The hypothesis has not been addressed or is not applicable for the study.

H6: Advocacy of Renewable Energies

Regression analysis confirmed a significant positive effect of "general advocacy of renewable energies" for all three case studies. The factor "general advocacy of renewable energies" ranked second as predictor in case study 1 and 3 (for the latter only on the socio-political dimension) and fourth in case study 2. Surprisingly, H6 was not confirmed in the model "community acceptance" of case study 3. This deviating result suits the "low-cost hypothesis" (Diekmann and Preisendörfer, 2003), which states that attitudinal factors decrease with increasing behavioral costs (cf. results for H6 in sections 4.3.2 and 4.5.2). Hence, the abstract general attitude of general support of renewable energies is assumed to be superposed by other factors which exert a direct impact on the community level, such as perceived costs or odor emissions of bioenergy plants. To conclude, advocacy of renewable energies was confirmed as important factor for public acceptance, however, with a stronger influence on the socio-political than on the community dimension.

H7: Perceived Benefits

The construct "perceived benefits" of bioenergy plants was unanimously confirmed to be the by far strongest predictor for public acceptance in all three case studies with regard to both the socio-political and the community dimension. However, it needs to be acknowledged that there were slight differences between the constructs used in the case studies. Case study 2 measured "perceived benefits" by four items addressing the aspects of distributive justice, climate protection, regional economic development, and benefits for the community. In contrast, case study 1 and 3 additionally covered the aspects of import dependency and environmental protection but did not address benefits for the community (cf. Appendix A). Due to these differences in measurement scales, the effects are not directly comparable. Considering the importance of perceived benefits as predictor for public acceptance, future research should explore in more depth which benefits are most relevant for the public and on that basis further refine the measurement instruments (cf. also section 6.3.2.2).

H8: Perceived Costs

The three case studies revealed mixed findings for the influence of "perceived costs" on public acceptance of bioenergy plants. Case study 1 and 3 found a significant negative effect for both the socio-political and the community dimension, whereas case study 2 did not confirm the effect. Here again differences between the constructs used in the case studies need to be critically mentioned. Case study 1 and 3 measured "perceived costs" by the aspects increased energy price, odor nuisance, landscape change, risk of accidents, and environmental pollution. In contrast, case study 2 used a construct consisting of the aspects increase in energy prices, negative impacts on property values, as well as personal financial loss. Thus, the effects are not directly comparable. It could further be argued that the scale used in case study 2 did not cover all relevant aspects, which might have led to the respective result. Another interesting observation is revealed by the comparison of regression coefficients of the models for socio-political and community acceptance in case study 1 and 3. In both cases, the influence of "perceived costs" is more important in the "community model" than in the "socio-political model", which again confirms the "low-cost hypothesis", addressed above in the discussion on "advocacy of renewable energies".

H9: Information and Participation

Only case study 1 revealed a weak significant effect ($B = -0.080$, $p < 0.05$) for "information and participation" on the community dimension, all other regression models did not. The revealed effect, is rather small and counter-intuitively directed. The latter is assumed to be due to the fact that the item asked for the *desired* information and participation. Hence, it is assumed that the *actual* level of information and participation is lower than the *desired* level and hence, the coefficient turned negative. Even though the empirical results of this thesis do not strongly support H9, the factor information and participation is still an often discussed issue in the literature for its indirect influence on other acceptance factors (cf. discussions on H9 in section 4.6.2).

H11: Perceived Costs of Energy Crops

Case study 1 confirmed a weak negative effect of perceived costs of energy crops ($B = -0.76$, $p < 0.01$) on public acceptance on the socio-political level whereas case study 3 did not find any effect.[18] In this context, it needs to be mentioned that the measurement scales used in case study 1 and 3 required significant adaptation to the local study context: whereas the construct used in case study 1 covers perceived costs of increased cultivation of energy crops and the food versus fuel controversy, case study 3 uses a single item referring to perceived costs of biomass from forest plantations.[19] Thus, the two

[18] Case study 2 did not test H11 as the hypothesis was developed on the basis of the gained insights during the research process of case study 2.

[19] The construct "perceived costs of energy crops" lacks internal consistency (cf. Table 4-26) and therefore a single item was used for the regression model.

constructs are hardly comparable and a further comparison of results is not reasonable.

4.6.2 Comparison to Related Work[20]

This section compares the results of the case studies with those of related studies from the literature along the thirteen hypotheses raised in section 3.2.3. Firstly the empirical studies on public acceptance of renewable energy technologies discussed in section 2.3 are analyzed regarding their findings for the hypotheses H1 to H5. Secondly, the empirical studies introduced in section 3.2.3, which focus on factors influencing the acceptance of bioenergy plants, are analyzed with respect to their findings for H6 to H12. Concerning H13, the author is not aware of any related literature that empirically examines the relationship between public acceptance, community energy, and energy autonomy. Hence, the exploration of H13 represents one of the novelties of this thesis and is therefore not discussed in this section.

Even though the literature was grouped by countries under examination, it is not suggested drawing generalized conclusions with regard to national differences. As argued in section 2.2, there is a lack of consistency in measurement instruments for public acceptance and associated constructs in the research field (Batel et al., 2013; Rand and Hoen, 2017). Therefore, comparability of results is limited, in particular as the studies pursue various research approaches ranging from case studies of rather descriptive character to quantitative surveys. Moreover, the levels of data collection (local, regional, or national), the time perspectives (prospective or retrospective), and the target populations (e.g., residents, citizens) vary among the studies. Hence, variations in findings cannot be simply attributed to differences between the countries, but might result from various study contexts and designs.

[20] Parts of this section have previously been published in Schumacher et al. (2019b) and Schumacher and Schultmann (2017).

It needs to be acknowledged that the presented literature is an illustrative selection, which corresponds to the focus of this thesis (for the selection criteria see section 2.3). In case that findings from the selected studies appear to be insufficient, further literature is discussed which provides additional evidence regarding the respective hypothesis. Substantial literature reviews on social acceptance of renewable energies are provided e.g., by Fast, 2013; Gaede and Rowlands, 2018; Sovacool, 2014; Upham et al., 2015. An overview of literature on public acceptance of biogas plants is provided by Eswarlal et al. (2014).

H1 to H5: Comparison to Related Work

This section analyzes the findings of related empirical, peer-reviewed studies on public acceptance of renewable energy technologies and associated infrastructure for H1 to H5. Table 4-35 provides an overview of those findings by country.

Table 4-35: Comparison of findings for H1 to H5 with related work by country

Author(s)	Country	H1	H2	H3	H4	H5
Betakova et al. (2015)	Czech Republic	N/A	N/A	N/A	Yes	N/A
Bertsch et al. (2016)	Germany	Yes	N/A	Yes	Yes	N/A
Kortsch et al. (2015)	Germany	Yes (for bioenergy)	No	N/A	N/A	N/A
Musall and Kuik (2011)	Germany	Yes	N/A	N/A	N/A	N/A
Sonnberger and Ruddat (2017)	Germany	N/A	N/A	Yes	Yes	N/A
Zoellner et al. (2008)	Germany	Yes	N/A	Yes	Yes	N/A
Kontogianni et al. (2014)	Greece	Yes	No	Yes	Yes	No
Wolsink (2000)	Netherlands	Yes*	N/A	Yes*	N/A	N/A
Soland et. al. (2013)	Switzerland	N/A	N/A	N/A	N/A	Yes*

Author(s)	Country	H1	H2	H3	H4	H5
Sütterlin and Siegrist (2017)	Switzerland	Yes	N/A	Yes	N/A	N/A
Upreti (2004)	United Kingdom	No (for bioenergy)	Yes	Yes	N/A	N/A
Upreti and van der Horst (2004)	United Kingdom	No* (for bioenergy)	N/A	Yes	N/A	N/A
Upham and Shackley (2006)	United Kingdom	Yes*	N/A	Yes	N/A	N/A
Upham and Shackley (2007)	United Kingdom	Yes (except for bioenergy)	N/A	Yes	N/A	N/A
Upham (2009)	United Kingdom	Yes*	N/A	Yes	N/A	N/A
Petrova (2016)	USA	Yes*	N/A	Yes	No	N/A
Jobert et al. (2007)	France and Germany	N/A	N/A	N/A	Yes (regarding visibility)	N/A
Warren et al. (2005)	Ireland & Scotland	Yes	N/A	Yes	Yes for Scotland, No for Ireland	Yes for Scotland, N/A for Ireland
Aas et al. (2014)	Norway, Sweden & UK	Yes (for high voltage power lines)	N/A	Yes	N/A	N/A

Notes:

Yes: The hypothesis has been (partly or fully) addressed and confirmed.
No: The hypothesis has been (partly or fully) addressed and rejected.
N/A: The hypothesis has not been addressed.
* The hypothesis has been addressed but not empirically tested with own data.

H1: Renewable Energies Generally Enjoy High Public Acceptance for Future Energy Generation.

H1 is confirmed by the large majority of examined studies. Most of them draw this conclusion based on their own empirical results (cf. e.g., Bertsch et al., 2016); some of them confirm H1 without testing it empirically (cf. e.g., Wolsink, 2000). Regarding the individual technologies, it is striking that solar power is always one of the most accepted technologies in all studies (cf. e.g., Sütterlin and Siegrist, 2017). Moreover, a particularity is found for bioenergy: Upreti (2004) and Upreti and van der Horst (2004) report substantial public opposition to bioenergy plants. Upham & Shackley (2007) confirm general high public acceptance for renewable energies, but mention prevailing doubts regarding bioenergy because of environmental concerns. This fits the empirical findings of this thesis. It is therefore concluded that H1 holds true for various contexts and renewable energy technologies with the exception of bioenergy, being one of the least publicly accepted renewable energy technologies (compared to small and large PV as well as wind energy).

H2: There is Public Disposition to Act Towards Renewable Energy Plants in the Neighborhood.

The findings of the literature for H2 are less conclusive. Kortsch et al. (2015) and Kontogianni et al. (2014) do not find active opposition in their study regions for wind and bioenergy, whereas Upreti (2004) reports active resistance by local residents towards nearby biogas plants in the United Kingdom. Hence, the existence of local opposition cannot be simply assumed but requires deeper analysis. It is concluded that opposition is not an inevitable fact due to unavoidable local impacts of renewable energy technologies, but depends on context related factors, such as perceived costs and benefits of a local plant as well as perceived fairness (for a comprehensive review of influencing factors see e.g., Perlaviciute and Steg, 2014). With regard to active support, Musall and Kuik (2011) reveal that active support in form of co-ownership leads to higher public acceptance towards wind energy in general as well as towards nearby installed wind turbines. Many studies, however, provide little information on supportive action by the public, which again underlines the critique of Batel et al. (2016) that former research has mostly focused on public opposition and neglected the multiple facets of support. In this thesis, a disposition for both active resistance and support was confirmed, however, the extent of public disposition to act varied strongly across countries and technologies.

H3: General Public Acceptance (Socio-Political Dimension) Exceeds Public Acceptance of Plants in the Neighborhood (Community Dimension).

H3 is unanimously confirmed by all selected studies. Even though some authors acknowledge that they find empirical evidence for NIMBY attitudes (Warren et al., 2005; Kontogianni et al., 2014; Upreti and van der Horst, 2004), it seems to be common understanding that NIMBYism is not appropriate to explain differences between acceptance on the general and the community level (cf. also section 2.1). Sütterin and Siegrist (2017) argue that the evaluation-gap might be due to an overly positive estimation of renewable energies when judging them from an abstract point of view. Several other authors share the opinion that community acceptance is usually lower as a result of inadequate implementation processes on the local level. Identified shortcomings might be lacking involvement of residents in planning and decision making (Zoellner et al., 2008), lacking common understanding of the project and missing coordinated action (Upreti, 2004), as well as a lack of perceived fairness (Sonnberger and Ruddat, 2017).

H4: Public Acceptance of Renewable Energy Plants is Influenced by the Distance of the Plant to the Respondent's Home.

The reviewed studies support H4 in so far that they unanimously confirm an influence of distance on public acceptance, however, findings regarding the direction of the proximity effect are inconsistent. Some studies find empirical evidence that acceptance increases with higher distances (cf. Bertsch et al., 2016; Upham, 2009; Upreti, 2004), others make the exact opposite observation. For example, Warren et al. (2005) report that support was highest among persons living in the innermost zone of a wind farm in Ireland. Petrova (2016) compares public acceptance of three communities in the United States and finds that those situated closest to wind turbines express the highest level of support. Petrova (2016, p. 1290) concludes that proximity cannot be "the only explanatory factor" and suggests that public acceptance depends on four larger categories of influencing factors, namely visual/ landscape, socioeconomic, environmental, and procedural aspects. Thus, the relationship between distance and public acceptance is moderated by other variables, such as the characteristics of the technology, visibility, and perceived intrusion of the landscape.

Looking for findings in the broader literature, there is again strong evidence that distance to renewable energy plants plays an important role for public acceptance. However, no clear conclusions regarding the direction of the proximity effect are found but rather variables which moderate the effect. For example, Van der Horst (2007) states that proximity to a proposed renewable energy project has a strong influence on local attitudes, even though the nature and extent of the influence varies according to the local context. Similarly, Harold et al. (2018) find that proximity preferences for various energy technologies are influenced by other factors, such as preferences regarding energy political goals, perceptions of the individual technologies, as well as socio-demographic factors, particularly the country of residence. The importance of proximity for public acceptance is also reflected by studies of practitioners, which for example consider the distance to settlements and the scenic value of a countryside for the calculation of wind potentials (e.g., Jäger et al., 2016 for Baden-Württemberg, Germany; Höltinger et al., 2016 for Austria).

A further strand of research, which deserves to be mentioned in the context of proximity, is concerned with the visual effects of renewable energy plants on the landscape, including aspects such as the "quality" of the landscape and the visibility (or not) of technologies (e.g., Molnarova et al., 2012; Wolsink, 2017a). The question of landscape quality has been explored with surveys of landscape photographs, whereby participants are required to rate these on a quantitative scale (e.g., Roser, 2011; Seresinhe et al., 2017a; Seresinhe et al., 2017b). Visibility is more closely related to the proximity of technologies and the extent to which they (are perceived to) infringe on the local landscape (e.g., Bertsch et al., 2016; van der Horst, 2007; Wolsink, 2017a). Betakova et al.

(2015) for example found differences in public acceptance of wind turbines with regard to the perceived quality of the landscape. More precisely, they identified an upper threshold, above which the negative visual impact of wind turbines disappears: 10 km for the most attractive and 5 km for the least attractive landscape. However, the concepts are distinct as Kontogianni et al. (2014) suggest that "The ensuing tension between visual intrusion and proximity is resolved in the concept of visibility." Despite these common themes, this research field is highly heterogeneous: on the one hand this encourages widening the scope of this research to consider additional perspectives, on the other hand it highlights the lack of a common theoretical framework in this area (Leibenath and Lintz, 2018).

H5: Public Acceptance of Renewable Energy Plants is Higher Among Respondents with Previous Experience with Renewable Energy Projects.

The findings of the literature for H5 are mixed, even though most of the studies support a positive influence of experience on public acceptance. Warren et al. (2005) for example report that the feared impacts of a local windfarm (in particular visual impact and noise) did not unfold as expected and hence public acceptance increased after the local wind farm was built. Similarly, van der Horst (2007) observes that opposition to wind farms is lower, the closer respondents live to a wind turbine. A similar effect but in the opposite direction is described by Fast (2013), noting a high level of protest in the UK compared to the relatively low level of installed wind capacity, also known as the "mythology of the countryside" (Toke et al., 2008). Fast (2013, p. 859) refers to this observation as "reverse distance-decay relationship", which suggests that persons without previous experiences with renewable energy plants in their vicinity tend to overestimate local impacts and therefore desire a larger distance to their homes. In contrast to those findings, Kontogianni et al. (2014, p. 176) state that "experiencing wind farms seems to affect positively public perceptions only marginally" and further add that a significant part of respondents shows lower acceptance after having experienced wind farms themselves. Hence, based on the reviewed studies, no clear conclusion regarding H5 can be drawn.

Moreover, it needs to be acknowledged that the reviewed studies (including this thesis), cannot explain the causal relationship: it is both possible that either experience positively influences public acceptance or that renewable energy projects tend to be sited in areas where public acceptance is already high, or that projects are not realized due to lacking public acceptance. To understand how experience influences public acceptance over time, longitudinal data is necessary (cf. section 6.3.4). So far only very few studies have done so. Wolsink (2007) analyzed data of 16 sample points along different phases of project planning and found that attitudes are not static but developing over time. He describes a U-shaped development with high public acceptance when people are not confronted with wind power projects in their neighborhood, a decline of public acceptance during the proposal phase, and an increase of public acceptance after project implementation (provided that environmental impacts are handled adequately). Another longitudinal study conducted by Kortsch et al. (2015) with three points of measurement in time compares between four sites in Germany. Based on a sample of 423 respondents they observe that public acceptance remains constantly high over time but the strength of the factors influencing public acceptance change, with the exception of a constantly strong influence of perceived benefits on public acceptance.

H6 to H12: Comparison to Related Work

This section analyzes related empirical, peer-reviewed studies, which investigate factors influencing the public acceptance of bioenergy plants (cf. section 3.2.3) and analyzes their findings for H6 to H12. Table 4-36 provides an overview of the results of the investigated studies by country.

Table 4-36: Comparison of findings for H6 to H12 with related work by country

Author(s)	Country	H6	H7	H8	H9	H10	H11	H12
Kortsch et al. (2015)	Germany	Yes	Yes	N/A	No	Yes	N/A	Yes
Zoellner et al. (2008)	Germany	No	Yes	Yes	Yes	Yes	Yes	N/A
Bertsch et al. (2016)	Germany	N/A	Yes	N/A	N/A	N/A	N/A	Yes
Wüste and Schmuck (2013), Wüste (2013)	Germany	N/A	Yes	Yes	N/A	N/A	Yes	Yes
Griesen (2010)	Germany	N/A	Yes	N/A	N/A	Yes	Yes	No
Soland et al. (2013)	Switzerland	N/A	Yes	Yes	Yes	Yes	N/A	Yes
Upreti (2004), Upreti and van der Horst (2004)	United Kingdom	N/A	No	Yes	Yes	Yes	N/A	Yes
Upham (2009), Upham and Shackley (2006), Upham and Shackley (2007)	United Kingdom	N/A	Yes	Yes	Yes	Yes	N/A	Yes

Notes:

Yes: The influencing factor has been (partly or fully) addressed and confirmed.
No: The influencing factor has been (partly or fully) addressed and rejected.
N/A: The influencing factor has not been addressed.

H6: Advocacy of Renewable Energies

In this thesis, regression analysis confirms a significant positive effect of general advocacy of renewable energies on public acceptance of biomass plants. Looking at the literature, Kortsch et al. (2015) back this finding by reporting the same effect for all three waves of a longitudinal study covering several bioenergy plants in Germany. Most of the investigated studies, however, do not consider general advocacy of renewable energies as a potential factor for acceptance in their analysis (cf. e.g., Bertsch et al., 2016; Griesen, 2010; Soland et al., 2013; Upham, 2009; Upham and Shackley, 2006; Upham and Shackley, 2007; Upreti, 2004; Upreti and van der Horst, 2004; Wüste, 2013; Wüste and Schmuck, 2013), which is assumed to be connected to the controversial debate around the NIMBY effect (cf. section 2.4.1). Based on the findings of this thesis, it is however recommendable to considered general advocacy of renewable energies as potential factor influencing public acceptance.

H7: Perceived Benefits

Perceived benefits of bioenergy plants turns out to be the by far the strongest predictor for public acceptance in all three case studies conducted in this thesis. This result is backed by various similar findings reported in the literature (cf. e.g., Bertsch et al., 2016; Griesen, 2010; Kortsch et al., 2015; Soland et al., 2013; Wüste, 2013; Wüste and Schmuck, 2013; Zoellner et al., 2008). The methods and scales used to measure perceived benefits, however, differ rather strongly between the studies. Whereas this thesis uses constructs covering the issues of distributive justice, climate protection, regional value creation, benefits for the community, reduction of import dependency, and environmental protection (cf. Appendix A), other studies include additional aspects, such as benefits for the bioenergy industry (Upham and Shackley, 2007), the German economy (Bertsch et al., 2016), reputation of the community, community sense, and self-efficacy (Wüste, 2013; Wüste and Schmuck, 2013). Only two of the reviewed studies do not report a significant effect of perceived benefits (Upreti, 2004; Upreti and van der Horst, 2004). Those studies, however, refer to bioenergy projects with very low public acceptance. This suggests that perceived benefits might have been simply overruled by perceived costs in these cases.

H8: Perceived Costs

For H8, the results of the three case studies of this thesis reveal mixed results: whereas case study 1 and 3 confirm H8 with regard to both the socio-political and the community dimension, case study 2 rejects the hypothesis. The latter is rather surprising, as it contradicts the findings of the investigated literature (Soland et al., 2013; Upham and Shackley, 2006; Upham and Shackley, 2007; Upreti, 2004; Upreti and van der Horst, 2004; Wüste and Schmuck, 2013; Zoellner et al., 2008), which unanimously confirm perceived costs as a significant predictor for public acceptance. Here again differences with regard to the used constructs of this theses and the literature require to be discussed. In addition to the aspects covered in this work, which are increased energy price, odor nuisance, landscape change, risk of accidents, environmental pollution, negative impacts on property values, and personal financial loss, other studies include the aspects impact on affect (Zoellner et al., 2008), health impact (Bertsch et al., 2016), and quality of life (Upham and Shackley, 2006; Upham and Shackley, 2007).

H9: Information and Participation

Surprisingly, no notable, significant effect is found in the regression models of this thesis for the construct "information and participation" on public acceptance of bioenergy plants. Looking at the literature, several authors (Rau et al., 2012; Soland et al., 2013; Upham and Shackley, 2006) suggest that the impact of participation options on acceptance might be reflected by other interconnected factors. Upham and Shackley (2006), for example, highlight in their case study of a proposed biomass gasifier, that early consultation might influence processes in a way that increases public acceptance. Hence, a lack of participation might not directly decrease acceptance, but exerts an influence on other factors, which could potentially be altered through the process, such as perceived distribution of costs and benefits as well as trust. Similarly, Soland et al. (2013) find that the provided information offers increase trust and perceived benefits and at the same time reduce perceived costs of biogas plants. This assumption is backed by the conclusion of Rau et al. (2012, p. 177) that "participation is mediated by several aspects that are relevant in the context of environmental change, including justice and trust".

H10: Trust

In this thesis, trust is only considered with regard to trust in a local plant operator and therefore only covered in case study 2. The construct is measured by the factors reliability of information, consideration of residents' concerns, and competency of the plant operator to operate the plant properly. The regression analysis in case study 2 reveals that perceived trust in the plant operator is a significant predictor for public acceptance, which is in line with all other analyzed studies on public acceptance of biogas plants. Besides the issue of trust in the plant operator, other authors address trust in other local authorities (Upreti, 2004; Upreti and van der Horst, 2004). In the free text comments of case study 2, some respondents also expressed doubts about the trustworthiness of control bodies, responsible for the compliance of the plants with legal provisions. Thus, for future studies the construct of trust could be further strengthened through the consideration of trust in authorities on the socio-political level.

H11: Perceived Costs of Energy Crops

In this thesis a significant influence of perceived costs of energy crops on public acceptance is only confirmed by case study 1 on the socio-political dimension. Looking at the literature, three of the reviewed studies support this finding. All of them were conducted in Germany, which is not surprising given the prominent public "food versus fuel" debate (Herbes et al., 2014), especially in times when the use of corn as feedstock for biogas plants was promoted through the RES Act (EEG, 2000). Wüste and Schmuck (2013) report a strong preference of respondents for the use of waste materials and state as main reasons for the rejection of energy crops the associated land use competition between food and fuel production and the negative impacts associated with monocultures. In particular, transformation of rural landscapes through increased cultivation of energy crops is discussed as a cost to society, which can lead to feelings of estrangement and evoke protective reactions (Hildebrand et al., 2012; Wüste, 2013). Griesen (2010) find a significant effect for the construct ethics/ landscape, which includes the aspects ethical concerns regarding the combustions of grains, ethical concerns regarding the use of corn for energetic purposes, and landscape changes through the cultivation of energy corn. Other studies also mention the effect of landscape changes associated with bioenergy without explicitly referring to the issue of energy crops (Bertsch et al., 2016; Zoellner et al., 2008). Because of lacking transparency and comparability with regard to the used measurement instruments, it is however difficult to conclude on the findings of the latter studies.

H12: Perceived Odor

Case study 2 of this thesis confirms a highly significant negative effect of perceived odor on public acceptance. This finding is in line with all other analyzed studies, except one (cf. Griesen, 2010). Moreover, the analysis of free text comments of case study 2 (cf. section 4.4.2) produces a rather surprising result: Several respondents stress the point that odor emissions are simply part of rural life and often not easily attributable to their source. It could therefore be assumed that persons, who are actually supporting the plant, might more easily come to terms with the odor emissions, whereas opponents perceive odor as more disturbing. A similar discussion is raised by Soland et al. (2013) regarding their finding that respondents indicating to perceive odor emissions also report lower perceived benefits and higher perceived costs. Soland et al. (2013) suggest that the perception of smell might influence the perception of costs and benefits, or that respondents who perceive smell indeed bear higher costs from the biogas plant, for example, because of reduced property values of their houses. Moreover, Soland et al. (2013) reveal that persons who report odor emissions also show lower trust in the plant operator supposedly because the odor emissions are attributed to a lack of competency of the plant operator. This discussion shows, that the link between perceived odor and other factors influencing local acceptance still requires further investigation. However, the reviewed studies provide sufficient evidence to confirm the hypothesis that perceived odor influences public acceptance of biogas plants.

5 Conclusions and Policy Recommendations

This section summarizes the findings of this thesis and offers recommendations for project developers and policy makers. Section 5.1 starts with a summary of findings of the empirical case studies and the related literature (cf. section 4). Section 5.2 translates those findings into recommendations for action to effectively inform the policy debate and create practical knowledge for developers of renewable energy projects. Section 5.3 concludes the section with a summary of the main contributions of this thesis to the research field.

5.1 Summary of Findings

This thesis adopts a cross-national, comparative research approach to go beyond the mere description of public acceptance phenomena of a specific case. The comparison across countries and technologies adds significant explanatory power to the results, which can be assessed regarding their transferability to different contexts. In the following, the most important findings are summarized and discussed with respect to their generalizability for different countries and technologies along the thirteen raised hypotheses (cf. section 3.2.3).

H1: Renewable Energies Generally Enjoy High Public Acceptance for Future Energy Generation.

The findings for H1 vary substantially depending on the energy generation technology. Whereas H1 is unanimously confirmed for solar power (including small and large-scale PV) and wind energy, the results differ for bioenergy. However, compared to non-renewable energy options, such as coal, nuclear, oil, and gas, there is a clear preference for renewable energies in all case studies. It is hence concluded that H1 can be confirmed in general, while noting differences in the evaluation of bioenergy.

H2: There is Public Disposition to Act Towards Renewable Energy Plants in the Neighborhood.

With respect to H2, all case studies find potential disposition to act towards the studied renewable energy technologies. The extent, however, varies between (i) technologies, (ii) countries, and (iii) sub-groups of the public.

(i) Regarding technologies, the reported disposition to support is pronounced for small and large-scale PV, whereas the disposition to resist is comparatively strong for wind and bioenergy.

(ii) With respect to countries, Chilean respondents showed more extreme dispositions to act, including both support and resistance towards all covered renewable energy technologies compared to respondents from the URR. It is thus concluded that disposition to act is influenced by the respondent's country of origin.

(iii) Concerning sub-groups of the public, differences of dispositions to act between the public and residents of biogas plants are observed: whereas Swiss residents indicate higher support, German residents report higher resistance to the biogas plant in their vicinity compared to the general public in the respective sub-regions. This leads to the conclusion that disposition to act depends on the quality of former experiences with the respective technology. Thus, positive experience is likely to result in higher support, and negative experience in higher resistance.

H3: General Public Acceptance (Socio-Political Dimension) Exceeds Public Acceptance of Plants in the Neighborhood (Community Dimension).

H3 is confirmed for large PV, wind, and bioenergy. For small-scale PV, the observed effect is reversed with community acceptance exceeding socio-political acceptance in all cases. The latter is assumed to be due to the different ownership structure of small PV plants, which are likely to be owned by the respondents themselves or by members of the local community. Hence, it is supposed that the willingness to accept a plant on the community level is higher if respondents expect a direct local or personal benefit.

H4: Public Acceptance of Renewable Energy Plants is Influenced by the Distance of the Plant to the Respondent's Home.

Regarding H4, the three case studies confirm an increase of public acceptance with larger distances of plants to the respondent's home. The extent varies according to the technology in question with a stronger effect for bioenergy, wind, and large-scale PV, and a weaker effect for small-scale PV. Moreover, the rank order of technologies with respect to desired distance is the same in all countries with the largest desired distance for bioenergy and the smallest for small-scale PV plants.

The results further reveal that neither is distance a remedy for lacking public acceptance, nor is proximity an exclusion criterion: on the one hand, a certain share of respondents rejects renewable energy plants (especially mid- and large-sized technologies) independently from the distance; on the other hand, respondents already living with a renewable energy plant in the neighborhood tend to accept smaller distances to their homes than respondents without previous experiences. The literature further reports some cases in which low distances go hand in hand with high public acceptance. It is thus concluded that the role of proximity is moderated by contextual factors and (expected) local impacts.

H5: Public Acceptance of Renewable Energy Plants is Higher Among Respondents with Previous Experience with Renewable Energy Projects.

H5 is confirmed for all covered renewable energy technologies based on the extended dataset (cf. section 4.6.1). In addition, it is revealed that desired distance decreases with experience and that respondents with former experience with renewable energy plants are less likely to reject a respective plant regardless of the distance. This indicates that experience leads to a more realistic assessment of local impacts and hence to smaller desired distances.

Hypotheses Regarding Influencing Factors for Public Acceptance of Bioenergy Plants.

H6: General Advocacy

General advocacy of renewable energy is confirmed as significant influencing factor for public acceptance with a stronger effect on the socio-political than on the community dimension. An explanation provides the "low-cost hypothesis" according to which attitudinal factors are more important on a general than on the concrete project level. On the community level abstract attitudes are assumed to be superposed by more concrete factors, such as perceived costs and benefits.

H7: Perceived Benefits

Perceived benefits are unanimously confirmed as the by far strongest predictor for public acceptance of bioenergy plants on both the community and the socio-political dimension.

H8: Perceived Costs

Perceived costs are affirmed as important predictor for public acceptance of bioenergy plants with a stronger effect on the community than on the socio-political dimension. The "low-cost hypothesis" again delivers a plausible explanation, as perceived costs are usually related to a specific plant and are therefore less relevant on an attitudinal level (cf. also results for H6).

H9: Information and Participation

Surprisingly, information and participation is not confirmed by the case study results as predictor for public acceptance of bioenergy plants. However, the literature and the results from the expert interviews suggest that information and participation indirectly influences public acceptance through other predictors. For example, early consultation might influence implementation processes in such a way that it increases perceived benefits and decreases perceived costs, and timely and accurate information might increase trust in local authorities. Moreover, results reveal that the desire to participate surpasses the actual possibilities offered in all covered countries.

H10: Trust in the Plant Operator

Trust in the plant operator is confirmed as important predictor for public acceptance. The literature supports this conclusion and suggests that besides trust in the plant operator, trust in other key actors needs to be considered as influencing factor for public acceptance.

H11: Perceived Costs of Energy Crops

A negative effect of perceived costs of energy crops is confirmed for Germany only. The review of other studies conducted in Germany support this result and point to strong reservations of the German public towards the use of energy crops as feedstock for biogas plants, which has been promoted by German energy policy in the past. The review of the literature further shows that landscape changes induced by the increased cultivation of energy crops is an associated aspect to be considered.

H12: Perceived Odor

Perceived odor is affirmed to strongly influence public acceptance of biogas plants. The analysis of free text comments as well as the review of the literature further suggest that perceived odor is related to other relevant predictors, such as perceived costs and benefits as well as trust in the plant operator. The exploration of this interdependence requires further investigation in future research (cf. section 6.3.2.2).

H13: Public Acceptance of Renewable Energies is Linked to Community Energy and Advocacy of Energy Autonomy.

Results point to a link between public acceptance and energy autonomy, but not necessarily to active engagement, although the expressed willingness to engage strongly exceeds the actual involvement in community energy. The correlation between public acceptance and energy autonomy seems plausible, as higher levels of energy autonomy typically require more locally installed renewable energies. Moreover, there is empirical evidence for a positive effect of (co-)ownership of local plants on public acceptance.

5.2 Recommendations for Policy Makers and Project Developers[21]

The recommendations derived from the afore summarized results of this thesis are directed towards all actors involved in the implementation process of renewable energies, e.g., regulators, policy actors, legislative authorities, local and regional decision-makers, plant operators, and associations (cf. also Table 2-1). Since the recommendations generally concern either measures at the socio-political dimension or the implementation of concrete projects at the community dimension, this section uses the simplified terms "policy makers" and "project developers" respectively to differentiate between the two dimensions. Some of the recommendations have general validity, others are aimed at specific actor groups. The following sections propose three main areas of improvement and several options for action for each of them with practical suggestions how the improvements can be achieved.

5.2.1 Development of Management Strategies

For the development of strategies to promote public acceptance, it is important to acknowledge that "the public" is not a homogenous group but consists of a variety of sub-groups and individuals with diverse attitudes and claims. Besides the four simplified acceptance groups defined by Schweizer-Ries (2008) which are approval, support, rejection, and resistance, there are many other positions and actions, manifesting in various forms, such as tolerance, apathy, indifference, uncertainty etc. (cf. Wolsink, 2018a; Wüstenhagen et al., 2007). In consequence, options for actions to promote public acceptance need to take this diversity of positions into account and develop suitable management and communication strategies as well as tailored participation options for the different target groups. Based on the empirical findings of this thesis, the following three options for action are suggested.

[21] Parts of this section have previously been published in Schumacher et al. (2019b) and Schumacher and Schultmann (2017).

5.2.1.1 Strategies for Sub-Groups of the Public

Interpretation of empirical data along the four dimensions of public acceptance (cf. Figure 2-2) reveals important information about the sub-groups of the public, which approve, support, reject, or resist renewable energy plants (cf. H2). Prioritizing on urgency, special attention should be paid to those groups, which indicate their willingness to actively support or oppose the plant. In the long term, however, it should not be neglected that there are also relatively large groups of respondents, who are still undecided regarding their assessment of renewable energy plants and a potential active involvement (cf. results for H2, section 4.6.1). As public acceptance is a dynamically unfolding process, precautions should be taken to ensure that this group of stakeholders does not develop a more negative attitude, particularly if the density of plants increases. For this reason, a careful analysis of arguments and claims of all local interest groups is essential to identify their expectations and conditions under which they are willing to accept renewable energy plants in their vicinity. Based on this information, appropriate management strategies should be developed to enhance public acceptance (Hitzeroth and Megerle, 2013). Those strategies could be derived from stakeholder theory, using for example stakeholder grids to develop strategies for sub-groups of the public as proposed by Savage et al. (1991), Olander (2007), or Johnson et al. (2005, pp. 179–188). Another interesting approach is to center the strategy on issues connected to the implementation of renewable energy plants. The idea basically consists in mapping relevant issues, such as climate change mitigation, plant safety, or minimization of local impacts, and evaluating them with regard to their relevance for different public sub-groups. From this, appropriate, target-group and issue specific management strategies can be developed (cf. Luoma-aho and Vos, 2010).

5.2.1.2 Tailored Communication Plans

The empirical results of this thesis provide some indications for the necessity to tailor communication messages to respective sub-groups of the public. An important insight of the case studies in this respect is the finding that the relevance of predictors for public acceptance varies according to the acceptance dimension. For example, "perceived costs" (H8) are more important on the community dimension, whereas “advocacy of renewable energies” (H6) has higher relevance on the socio-political dimension. Referring to the “low-cost hypothesis” (Diekmann and Preisendörfer, 2003), it is concluded that for concrete projects general attitudes, such as advocacy of renewable energies, are superposed by more concrete factors, such as perceived costs (H8), which exert a direct impact on the community level. Moreover, results show that perceived benefits (H7) are by far the most important predictor for public acceptance, on both the local and the socio-political level. Based on these results, communication should be tailored to the respective acceptance dimension and audience by carefully defining target groups and key messages. On the community level, communication should focus on informing about expected costs and benefits of renewable energy plants for local residents, whereas on the socio-political level, communication should address superordinate issues, such as the role of renewable energies for climate change mitigation and reduction of dependency on fossil fuels. On both levels, communication should provide accurate, precise, and reliable information to build the basis for a trustful relationship (H10) between decision makers and the sub-groups of the public, which is decisive for public acceptance.

5.2.1.3 Target Group Specific Participation Options

To reach the ambitious targets for the expansion of decentralized renewable energies (cf. section 4.2.2.3), active support of the population will be necessary (Rau and Zoellner, 2008; Schweizer-Ries et al., 2010). By offering appropriate participation possibilities, a perception of justice can be achieved regarding both the decision process and the distribution of costs and benefits between the involved actors and the public. The analysis of participation options for bioenergy projects in the URR (cf. results for H9, section 4.4.2) shows, that the desire to participate surpasses the actual possibilities offered (cf. H9). Hence, there is a gap between the actual and the desired participation, which compromises the potential of the public to actively contribute to the energy transition. Moreover, the analysis reveals that the respondents’ desire to participate decreases with increasing assumption of responsibility for the project. Hence, respondents generally prefer participation options on a low level of involvement over those which require higher commitment. In consequence, low level participation options, such as providing timely and accurate information and consultation processes for local interest groups, should be offered (cf. Rau et al., 2012). In addition, target group-specific offers on higher levels of involvement should be proposed to those respondents, who express the wish to assume responsibility in the planning, construction, and management of plants. The latter can create additional opportunities to increase participation, perceived benefits (cf. H7), and trust (cf. H10) at once, especially when projects are citizen-driven, such as German bioenergy villages (cf. Jenssen et al., 2014).

5.2.2 Design of Renewable Energy Projects

The results of the case studies provide several indications for designing renewable energy projects in a way which promotes high public acceptance. The following sections suggest options for action for policy makers and project developers with regard to siting, community energy, and information on local impacts of renewable energy projects.

5.2.2.1 Siting of Renewable Energy Plants

The choice of a plant location for renewable energies should be made very carefully. In addition to technology-specific requirements, such as biomass availability for bioenergy plants or solar radiation for PV, other criteria should be taken into consideration to anticipate conflicts with the public. Regarding proximity to residential areas, the results of the case studies confirm a positive link between public acceptance and increasing distance of plants to the respondents' homes (cf. H4). However, the strength of the link varied according to the technology in question, with higher relevance for bioenergy, wind, and large-scale PV, and lower relevance for small-scale PV. The latter is also accepted independently from the distance by the majority of respondents, whereas the mid- and large-sized technologies are rejected by a relatively large share of respondents independently from the distance. It is hence concluded that neither is distance a panacea nor is proximity an exclusion criterion. Instead, contextual factors and (expected) local impacts of the technology moderate the role of proximity. Still, it is recommendable that policy relating to site selection takes specific characteristics of the technologies into account to define appropriate minimal distances to residential areas for mid- and large-sized renewable energy plants. In addition to minimal distances, the case studies have revealed other factors which should be incorporated into the choice of a plant location. For example, the visual impact plays an important role for all mid- and large-sized technologies (cf. H4). Moreover, an important link between perceived odor emissions and public acceptance is detected for biogas plants (cf. H12). Therefore, siting decisions for biogas plants should take into account wind directions, access routes for feedstock delivery, and other topographic factors, which exert an impact on the diffusion of odor. In addition to those impacts, more indirect effects, such as landscape changes or effects on the local tourism sector should also be considered in the selection of a suitable site.

5.2.2.2 Community Energy and Public (Co-)Ownership

The findings and experience from Germany demonstrate a link between community energy, energy autonomy, and public acceptance (cf. H13). The data also reveals significantly more engagement in community energy in Germany and Switzerland (both around 10%) than in France (4%) (cf. results for H13, section 4.3.2), which is assumed to be due to a more favorable institutional setting in the two former countries (cf. section 4.2.3.1). Hence, removing barriers in France such as achieving priority grid access for renewable energy plants might be one way to indirectly improve public acceptance. Despite an overall engagement in community energy of about 9%, however, 43% of the respondents expressed a willingness to get involved in renewable energy projects in some form. Thus, there is a gap between the desire to be involved and the actual degree of participation in community energy. This offers opportunities for policy makers and project developers to increase public acceptance by offering respective participation possibilities to the population (cf. section 5.2.1.3). To close this gap, there might also be a need to inform individuals about the possibilities to get financially involved in renewable energy projects, e.g., through information campaigns and advertisements on the possibilities of community energy. Moreover, there is empirical evidence that (co-)ownership of local plants has a positive effect on public acceptance (cf. results for H13, section 4.3.2). It is therefore recommended to involve the population as owners and operators of renewable energy plants, especially beyond small PV-plants. Policy measures aimed at promoting renewable energy therefore need to consider this fact, for example by providing special conditions for community energy in the context of tendering processes.

5.2.2.3 Accurate Information on Local Impacts

Another finding is that respondents with experience with renewable energy plants in their direct vicinity show higher public acceptance on average (cf. H5). Moreover, the average desired distance to a renewable energy plant is significantly smaller for respondents already living with a plant in their vicinity. It is hence concluded that former experience is favorable for public acceptance as it provides a more realistic picture of the actual impacts of local renewable energy plants, which otherwise tend to be overestimated. Therefore, accurate information on the actual impacts, including costs (cf. H8) and benefits (cf. H7) of renewable energies for the community and the individual, are important for promoting public acceptance of renewable energies. In addition, a transfer of experience between countries, such as the German Bioenergy Villages or the Swiss Energy Regions seem a promising policy to enable people to get a more accurate picture of the impacts of different renewable energy technologies if implemented in a suitable manner.

5.2.3 Transfer of Research Findings into Practice

The transfer of research findings into the practice of project developers and policy makers has been limited so far (Rand and Hoen, 2017; Sovacool, 2014; Wolsink, 2018b). Therefore, an essential recommendation for both policy makers and project developers is to base their decisions on sound scientific findings. Hence, policy makers need to understand the various impacts of their decisions on public acceptance and include considerations on public acceptance into the design of policy frameworks and projects. One the one hand, researchers need to put increased efforts into developing practical guidelines and frameworks, which provide suitable decision support for the practice (Zaunbrecher and Ziefle, 2016). On the other hand, policy makers and project developers need to acknowledge the relevance of public acceptance for a successful and truly sustainable energy transition (Hauff et al., 2011). This implies that those in charge of setting the political guidelines need to participate in the change process themselves as lacking institutional change constitutes one of the main challenges to overcome in the transition to low carbon renewable energy technologies (Jacobsson and Johnson, 2000; Wolsink, 2018a). With these goals in mind, the subsequent three options for action are suggested.

5.2.3.1 Public Acceptance and Policy Frameworks

The case studies provide various indications for a direct influence of political frameworks on public acceptance. For example, a significantly smaller gap between desired and actual participation regarding locally installed biogas plants is revealed in the Swiss than in German and French part of the URR (cf. section 4.4.2). This finding is assumed to be related to the various options of direct democracy in the Swiss political system. Another example is the negative evaluation of biogas plants in Germany, which can be traced back to the incentivation of the use of energy crops by energy policy, and the related "food versus fuel" debate (cf. H12). A third example is the significantly higher engagement in community energy in Germany and Switzerland (in both around 10%) compared to France (4%) (cf. results for H13, section 4.3.2), which is supposed to be related to the more favorable institutional settings in the two former countries (cf. section 4.2.3.1). Based on this empirical evidence, it is recommended that policy makers should consider potential consequences on public acceptance when setting legal framework conditions. The exploration of the link between political frameworks and public acceptance is therefore an important field of future research (cf. sections 6.3.3.1 and 6.3.5).

5.2.3.2 Interpretation of Results of Opinion Surveys

Practitioners need to be able to correctly interpret scientific findings, including potential limitations of opinion surveys. In particular, policy makers should be aware of the difference between general attitudes towards renewable energies on the socio-political dimension and attitudes towards specific plants on the community dimension. Even though all case studies reveal a strong general support of renewable energies and the energy turnaround, the preferences regarding the individual technologies differ substantially (cf. H1). Hence, a general high public support for renewable energy should not be mistaken as a sufficient condition for public acceptance of individual technologies on the community level. Moreover, the findings of the case studies for H3 confirm that general public acceptance (socio-political dimension) exceeds public acceptance of plants in the neighborhood (community dimension) for all mid- and large-sized technologies. In addition, the case studies show that attitudinal factors are more important on the socio-political, whereas project-related factors, such as perceived benefits, costs, and trust are more relevant on the community dimension. Consequently, opinion polls on the national level cannot be used as a decision basis for local renewable energy projects as the acceptance object is different. Whereas opinion polls assess public acceptance of renewable energy technologies *as such*, the acceptance of *specific* renewable energy projects needs to be assessed on a case by case basis including the project's inherent characteristics (such as ownership structure, participation possibilities, siting etc.). Besides the difference between acceptance dimensions, there are other potential pitfalls regarding the interpretation of results of opinion surveys, which are addressed in more detail in section 6.1.4.

5.2.3.3 Application-Oriented Research

Finally, the mutual understanding between research and practice needs to be improved by conducting further application-oriented research on issues with high relevance for the practice. For example, the results of all three case studies of this thesis pointed to the fact that perceived benefits are by far the most important predictor for public acceptance of biomass plants (cf. H7). Hence, further research should be directed at exploring those benefits in detail and how they can be realized in practice, for example, through different forms of cooperation between local residents and the operator of locally installed renewable energy plants. An interesting approach to increase perceived benefits of local energy plants, was recently introduced by the Chilean government which grants a discount on the prices of electricity for residents of municipalities with high installed electric capacities (Watts Casimis and Pérez Odeh, 2018). The impact on public acceptance has not been captured by this thesis, it can however be assumed that perceived benefits would increase and hence, public acceptance would be positively influenced. The effectiveness of such approaches should be scientifically evaluated through close cooperation between research and practitioners. Finally, both parties could widen their understanding and knowledge on public acceptance and the transfer of research results into the practice would be substantially facilitated.

5.3 Main Contributions of this Work

This section recalls the claims made in the introduction (section 1.2) and the description of the state of the art (section 2.2) regarding the contributions of this thesis to the research field of public acceptance of renewable energy innovations. In the following, the main contributions with regard to the collected data, the methodology, and the results of the thesis are summarized.

A noteworthy contribution of this work is the quality and comprehensiveness of the data collected within the scope of the three case studies. The mixed-methods research design, which combines the advantages of qualitative expert interviews and quantitative questionnaire-based survey data, ensures high data quality, holistic results and thus appropriate interpretations (cf. section 3.1). In total, qualitative data from roughly 100 interviews with bioenergy experts and quantitative survey-data on public acceptance of renewable energies from more than 3,300 respondents in four countries has been gathered. The obtained data provides a comprehensive picture of current public opinion towards a set of renewable energy technologies in the four countries. Around 70 variables cover personal attitudes, beliefs, perceptions, and evaluations with respect to some of the most prominently discussed hypotheses in the area of acceptance research on renewable energy technologies. The data is representative for the study regions regarding selected socio-demographic criteria (e.g., age, sex, social status). The collected data can be considered a distinguishing achievement in the research field. To the best knowledge of the author there are no other studies so far, which have collected comparatively comprehensive data including both qualitative and quantitative information on public acceptance of renewable energies.

A central objective of this work is to explore whether public acceptance is shared across countries and institutional settings or a country or project specific phenomena. To answer this question, the research approach of this thesis was designed in such a way that it compares public acceptance across countries, technologies, and acceptance dimensions. Applying the same rigorous research design in four countries allows for comparative testing of various hypotheses from public acceptance research on renewable energies which thus leads to stronger empirical evidence. This is reflected by the discussion of the main findings (section 5.1) which include thoughts on the generalizability of results for various contexts. Another noteworthy achievement from a methodological point view is the development of various measurement scales in four languages (German, French, English, and Spanish), which can be used as basis for further cross-national research on public acceptance.

Another central contribution of this work, which is closely related to the generalizability of results, is to effectively inform the policy debate and to create practical guidance for developers of renewable energy projects. Only results which hold true for different contexts are suitable to derive general recommendations. Again, the comparative research approach applied in this work contributes substantially to achieve this goal. The comparison of public acceptance across countries reveals practices, which potentially promote or hinder the formation of public acceptance. Moreover, examining various renewable energy technologies in concert allows for discriminating between the technologies. This better reflects the reality of decision makers and thus provides more suitable insights to derive guidance for designing future energy policies than could be obtained from the analysis of single cases or single technologies. Finally, recommendations for policy makers and project developers are derived and proposed (section 5.2), which are applicable in different contexts and countries, including best practices and lessons learned which can be transferred from one country to another.

6 Critical Appraisal and Outlook[22]

This section addresses the limitations of this contribution and discusses the transferability of the presented approach and the obtained results. Finally, an outlook on future research in the field of public acceptance of renewable energies is given.

6.1 Critical Appraisal

This thesis faces some limitations regarding the study scope and the chosen theoretical concepts. Moreover, there are challenges inherent to cross-national studies and data collection from different national contexts. In addition, representativeness of the data is an issue which deserves some critical reflection. Besides the particular challenges of this thesis, there are some limitations concerning the explanatory power of opinion surveys in general, which also apply to this work. All the afore mentioned limitation and challenges are addressed and critically discussed in the following sections.

6.1.1 Study Scope and Underlying Concepts

There are some limitations resulting from the scope of this thesis as defined in section 2.1. The scope of this thesis consists in examining public acceptance in depth by conducting expert interviews and representative population surveys across renewable energy technologies and countries. Public acceptance is investigated comprehensively with regard to the socio-political and the community dimension. This is realized by requesting attitudes towards different renewable energy technologies in general and towards (potential) renewable energy plants in the neighborhood in particular. Hence, the public assumes different roles in the case studies, namely the role of the general public and the role of residents living nearby renewable energy plants. Even though

[22] Parts of this section have previously been published in Schumacher et al. (2019b) and Schumacher and Schultmann (2017).

the public has an important stake in the energy debate, it still has to be kept in mind that it only represents one of many stakeholders of the energy transition. The context, in which this thesis is embedded, is much larger, and the process of increasing the share of decentralized renewable energy innovations touches upon many more stakeholder groups including governmental and economic players, which interact and transform the current energy system through "complex, multilevel and polycentric processes" (Wolsink, 2018a, p. 287). It therefore is important to be aware that the survey data collected in this thesis on *public* acceptance should not be misinterpreted as a proxy for *social* acceptance (but only for public opinion). Hence, the collected data does not comprehensively represent the wide range of multilevel processes and polycentric actors involved in the process of social acceptance of renewable energy innovations (Wolsink, 2018a), but is limited to the view of the public.

It further needs to be acknowledged that this thesis concentrates on public acceptance with regard to the socio-political and community dimension, whereas the market dimension is omitted (cf. Wüstenhagen et al., 2007). The reason for this limitation lies in the very different point of view of the market acceptance dimension, which requires a rather distinct approach: whereas the socio-political and community dimension mainly address public attitudes towards renewable energy technologies and local renewable energy plants, the market dimension addresses questions of preferences for products related to renewable energy (e.g., green energy tariffs, renewable energy technologies on the household level). Analyzing public acceptance with respect to the market dimension requires a different approach, which is closely related to market research and uses different models, such as willingness to pay, technology diffusion models (cf. e.g., Jacobsson and Johnson, 2000), or behavioral economics (cf. e.g., Frederiks et al., 2015).

Furthermore, there is some criticism concerning the chosen acceptance concept by Schweizer-Ries (2008), which distinguishes between passive approval and active support (cf. section 2.1). Even though the concept is highly cited in the acceptance literature, one needs to be aware that the definition is limited to the psychological perspective of (static) actor positions and does not account for the multiple interactions between the actors. Also, the four levels of acceptance (approval, support, rejection, and resistance) are a simplification as public acceptance unfolds in a dynamic process with many different positions and actions, manifesting in many different forms, such as tolerance, apathy, indifference, uncertainty etc. (cf. Wolsink, 2018a; Wüstenhagen et al., 2007). The differentiation between supporters and resisters is another simplification of a complex, interlinked discourse with a variety of arguments (Aitken, 2010). Despite these limitations, the definition allows to operationalize the abstract term "acceptance" and is therefore used in this thesis to assess and compare acceptance levels across countries and technologies (cf. section 4).

6.1.2 Challenges of Cross-National Surveys

Regarding the comparability of results, it needs to be acknowledged that the measurement instruments differ slightly between the three case studies. The reason are necessary adaptations to the varying study contexts of the different case studies. In case that measurement instruments are adapted to the study context, the author decides to prioritize local context over the exact comparability of measurement instruments. All adaptations of measurement instruments are transparently documented (cf. Appendix A) and discussed in terms of their impact on the comparability of the cases (cf. e.g., sections 4.6.1 and 4.6.2). It is concluded that there is an inherent challenge of cross-national studies with regard to the tradeoff between the best possible adaptation of research designs and measurement instruments to the national context while ensuring a high comparability between studies in different countries.

Another challenge inherent in the conduction of cross-national comparative research is the objectivity of interpretation of data from different cultural contexts. Even though the researcher makes an effort to be as unbiased as possible, the western education and cultural perception of the researcher is still a limiting factor which might introduce biases to the interpretation of data.

In this thesis, this has been avoided to a large extent by

- preferring interviewers from the respective countries,
- pretesting the measurement instruments in the respective populations,
- and conducting expert workshops in the respective study regions to validate results (cf. section 3.1).

However, conducting research in several countries always bears the risk of misinterpretations due to the personal background of the researcher and cannot be fully excluded in this thesis either.

6.1.3 Challenges of Data Collection

This thesis faces some limitations with respect to the data collected. As discussed in sections 4.3.1.2, 4.4.1.3, and 4.5.1.3, there are deviations between the socio-demographic characteristics of the samples and statistical population data. Even though the deviations are rather small regarding the selected socio-demographic characteristics (income, age, home owner rate etc.), selection bias cannot be completely excluded. In case study 1 and 3, the limitations inherent in incentivized online surveys need to be addressed. Using the internet for data collection, younger persons are more likely to be reached than elderly. Similarly, internet access might be more limited for persons with lower social status which could introduce another bias, especially in less industrialized countries such as Chile. Moreover, in case study 2, the probability of a (positive and negative) selection bias is quite high considering the use of mixed modes (personal interviews and paper and pencil), various exclusion criteria, and high levels of affectedness of the respondents (cf. section 4.4.1.1). Consequently, the data representativeness in case study 2 for the whole sub-regions is limited. Caution is required regarding the choice of sample sites in case study 2. Although the plants have been chosen very carefully in order to avoid any bias from the plant characteristics, possible effects of the plant size or the technical configuration cannot be fully excluded. Moreover, the author wants to stress that the obtained data in case studies 1 and 2 provide a good picture of the public acceptance of renewable energy installations in the URR, but does not claim to be representative for the entire countries of France, Germany, and Switzerland.

6.1.4 Limitations of Opinion Surveys

Like for other opinion surveys, there are some limitations, which also apply to this thesis. Generally, it is important to be conscious that the results of opinion surveys reflect stated, momentary opinions and preferences of respondents. Especially regarding reported dispositions to act towards various renewable energy technologies, the answers refer to a hypothetical situation and thus do not represent observations of real actions. Hence, stated and realized preferences might diverge (cf. Bertsch et al., 2016). In particular, low levels of knowledge can introduce bias to the results as the level of education (which includes knowledge about renewable energies) influences the consistency of stated preferences for renewable energies (Bertsch et al., 2016). Moreover, opinions and preferences are not static, but evolve over time with the development of renewable energies and the associated increase in information and experiences. This is especially important with respect to the relatively large share of respondents evaluating local renewable energy plants as “neutral”, which might become more or less supportive over time. Therefore, further insights into the development of public acceptance over time should be gained by collecting longitudinal data (cf. section 6.3.4).

6.2 Transferability

This section discusses in how far the gained insights of this thesis are transferable to other studies and contexts. Firstly, it is argued how the presented cross-national comparative research approach can be used for other studies to deepen the knowledge in the field of public acceptance research of renewable energies. Subsequently, it is discussed in how far the developed measurement instruments can and should be used by future studies. Moreover, potential new areas of application are highlighted. Finally, it is discussed how the approach of this thesis contributes to create practical knowledge for developers of renewable energy projects and to inform the policy debate.

6.2.1 Transferability of the Research Approach

The applied cross-national, comparative research approach can be easily transferred to other technologies and contexts. Generally speaking, the investigation of several cases instead of one single case study significantly increases the quality of insights gained. The idea of conducting cross-national comparative surveys is not new but state of the art in many research fields (for more information see Gesis, 2019). Especially for rather new, dynamically developing, and interdisciplinary research topics, such as the field of public acceptance of renewable energy innovations, cross-national approaches should be applied from the beginning to test theories before they get widely cited and commonly agreed. The many critiques of key assumption of the research field raised in the last years (cf. Aitken, 2010; Batel et al., 2013, Wolsink, 2018a, 2018b) have addressed this issue and call for more comparative, cross-national research. Moreover, this thesis suggests to put more attention on the transparent reporting of measurement instruments (cf. section 6.3.2.2) and representativeness of the collected data (cf. section 6.3.2.1) to increase replicability of results and comparability between studies of various authors. Besides the comparison between countries, the results of this thesis demonstrates that additional knowledge can be gained by comparing public acceptance of different technologies and acceptance dimensions. For the impact of the research, this is of vital importance as investigating the acceptance of a single technology does not adequately represent the reality of policy makers and practitioners, which rather have to discriminate between different technologies to build up publicly accepted electricity generation portfolios (cf. section 6.3.2.1).

6.2.2 Transferability of Measurement Instruments

The reuse of the developed items and constructs of this thesis (cf. Appendix A) by future studies on public acceptance of renewable energies is possible and desirable. The application of the same or slightly adapted items and constructs in new contexts would be interesting to further increase the number of cases between which results can be compared.

Regarding the transferability of measurement instruments to other contexts one has to differentiate between several types of factors. For example, items and scales referring to general concepts and procedural aspects could easily be used to explore public acceptance of other technologies. Such items include for example those used to measure public acceptance (cf. Appendix A, items "socio-political acceptance", "community acceptance", "appraisal of local plant", "active support", and "active resistance") as well as other general concepts, such as the role of distance to a renewable energy plant (cf. Appendix A, construct "distance") and procedural justice (cf. Appendix A, construct "desired information and participation" and "actual information and participation").

In contrast, there are several items and scales, which are highly technology-specific and cannot be transferred to other technologies, which do not share the same characteristics. This applies to those scales and items developed to assess public acceptance of bioenergy (e.g., constructs "perceived odor emissions", "perceived benefits of biogas plants", "perceived costs of biogas plants", "perceived costs of energy crops").

In addition, the underlying theories applied in this thesis are also valid for other projects apart from renewable energies. For example, the concept of public acceptance by Schweizer-Ries (2008) (cf. Figure 2-1) and the participation pyramid by Rau et al. (2012) (cf. Figure 2-3), which is based on Arnstein's ladder of participation (Arnstein, 1969), may also be relevant for the assessment of public acceptance of other medium and large-sized projects with high public interest. Examples are energy related medium and large-scale infrastructure projects (e.g., high voltage power lines, waste water treatment plants) or other energy related projects with high public concern and attention (e.g., carbon capture and storage, nuclear dismantling projects, and final nuclear storage), as well as large-scale publicly funded construction projects which receive high public attention (e.g., public buildings and mobility infrastructure).

6.2.3 Transferability of Conclusions

A major contribution of this thesis is the creation of reliable, generalizable, and thus transferable conclusions which are suitable to generate practical knowledge for project developers and to effectively inform the policy debate (cf. section 5.3). This has been achieved by testing a set of hypotheses on public acceptance across acceptance objects (technologies), contexts (countries), and acceptance dimensions (socio-political and community acceptance). The comparative research approach leads to the possibility to assess the transferability of findings to other contexts and thus improves the reliability of results. In particular, the comparison between countries reveals important insights on issues, which potentially promote or hinder the formation of public acceptance. Based on these insights best practices and lessons learned can be formulated and potentially replicated or avoided respectively in other countries.

6.3 Future Research

This section proposes several avenues for future research, which have been identified during the preparation of this thesis. Some of the research topics are proposed from the need to improve existing methodological approaches, others are suggested to further develop the research field based on the gained insights of this thesis.

6.3.1 Consolidating Theoretical Frameworks

As discussed in section 2.1, there is a variety of theoretical frameworks and definitions in the field of social acceptance research, which is sometimes complementary and sometimes conflicting. Even though a range of reviews has recently been published (Busse and Siebert, 2018; Fast, 2013; Gaede and Rowlands, 2018; Sovacool, 2014; Upham et al., 2015), which contribute to a more universal understanding of the intellectual roots, concepts, and definitions of the research field, there is still a lot of dissent with respect to the conceptualization of social acceptance. As the research field is by nature interdisciplinary, including contributions from sociology, environmental-psychology, political science, geography, economics, and innovation research, the consolidation of theories and definitions requires a dynamic process through scientific discussion. Future research could advance the field by shedding some light on the communalities and differences of the used approaches, theories, and frameworks. In this context two notable articles by Sovacool and Hess (2017) and Busse and Siebert (2018) are exemplarily mentioned which provide guidance on theories and definitions of the research field. Another example for a scientific discussion is Wolsink's (2018a) reply to the review article by Gaede and Rowlands (2018), which has recently received another response by Gaede and Rowlands (2019). This type of conversation adds depth to the research field and contributes to the consolidation of theories, concepts, and definitions. Even though a complete consolidation is neither possible nor desirable, it should become common practice that scholars precisely define their understanding of acceptance and the theories they use. As demonstrated in section 2.1, scholars should at least report on (i) the acceptance dimension(s) they cover, (ii) the acceptance subject, object, and context, as well as (iii) the definition of acceptance they use as basis for their investigations.

6.3.2 Improving Comparability

6.3.2.1 Cross-National, Comparative Surveys

There is a lack of cross-national, comparative research based on representative, random samples (cf. section 2.2). Most public acceptance studies either take a descriptive case-based view on single projects, or examine public acceptance in a single country, region, or community (cf. section 2.3). Consequently, the gained knowledge is rather specific for the covered population and technology and thus not easily transferable beyond the case-studies in question. Moreover, sampling procedures and measurement instruments are in many cases insufficiently documented (cf. section 6.3.2.2) and the obtained data often lacks representativeness for the observed population (cf. section 2.3). These shortcomings result in lacking generalizability of insights and prevents the development of the research field. Therefore, future research should correspond to this need by conducting more systematic cross-national comparisons based on representative data, which results in stronger empirical evidence and broader applicability of findings. Regarding the choice of countries, it could be interesting to look at more divergent cases from Africa, Latin America, the Middle East, and Australia as the current body of research strongly focuses on Europe and North-America (Sovacool, 2014).

Besides cross-national studies, systematic comparisons of preferences for different renewable energy technologies and portfolios of technologies are lacking. In reality, there is no isolated decision for or against one single technology but rather a decision for or against different portfolios of electricity generation technologies, also including non-renewable technologies, such as fossil-based and nuclear energy. Examining technologies in concert provides more meaningful results for practitioners by allowing for discrimination between technologies. Hence, to provide guidance for designing and implementing future energy policies, it is important to gain insights into preferences for technologies in comparison with others as well as electricity generation portfolios (cf. Bertsch et al., 2016; Rand and Hoen, 2017; Scheer et al., 2013).

6.3.2.2 Measurement Instruments

A major obstacle to enhance comparability between empirical studies on public acceptance is missing information on measurement instruments. Future research should contribute to overcome limitations resulting from the current state of the art in reporting of results. Despite a growing body of literature, most studies do not publish detailed information about the items and constructs they use to measure public acceptance and associated explanatory factors. For this reason, scales differ substantially between the studies and thus measure different aspects. This decreases transparency, prevents comparability of results, and hinders the advancement of the research field.

Beyond that, further research should aim at improving and complementing the existing measurement instruments for factors influencing public acceptance. This includes the assessment of additional predictors, such as personal norms and peer effects, and the improvement of measurement scales for predictors, which have been proven to be meaningful for public acceptance. For example, regression analysis revealed for all three case studies of this thesis that perceived benefits from bioenergy plants are the strongest predictor for public acceptance. Hence, future research should aim at refining the measurement scale by examining how different benefits are perceived by the public.

Moreover, the results of this thesis provide empirical evidence for links between the identified predictors for public acceptance. For example, information and participation and perceived odor are both assumed to exert an indirect influence on perceived costs, perceived benefits, and trust. Hence, the link between the predictors is a further area of future research.

Finally, it is suggested that the exchange within the international scientific community on factors and associated measurement instruments should be intensified for a more differentiated view on the various aspects of social acceptance (cf. Batel et al., 2013).

6.3.3 Enhancing Comprehensiveness

6.3.3.1 Links between Acceptance Dimensions

Most public acceptance studies focus on only one specific dimension of social acceptance (cf. section 2.3) despite the often stated critique that social acceptance is a multilevel, multi-actor process (Wolsink, 2018a), which can only be captured by investigating several acceptance dimensions at once (Sovacool, 2014). Regarding this thesis, there are strong indications of the importance of investigating links between public acceptance and socio-political frameworks (cf. section 5.2.3.1). Thus, to develop a deeper understanding of how legal and political frameworks influence public acceptance of renewable energies, future research should be dedicated to jointly investigate socio-political and community public acceptance. Moreover, the investigation of the market dimension together with the other two dimensions is of vital importance considering the high and often neglected potential of the public to become actively involved in the energy turnaround as prosumers or investors (cf. results for H13, section 4.3.2).

6.3.3.2 Facets of Acceptance and Support

Another issue which is often neglected by existing literature is the study of the positive side of public acceptance. Many scholars still stick to the initial focus on local opposition, which risks to overlook the potential of the public to actively support the energy transition, for example as prosumers or investors. Hence, research should be stronger directed to investigate the many facets of acceptance and support (Dermont et al., 2017; Devine-Wright and Batel, 2017). This thesis contributes to the exploration of public support by investigating for the first time how public acceptance is linked with community energy and energy autonomy. The empirical results point to a link between energy autonomy and acceptance of renewable energies, which deserves further investigation in future studies. To conclude, the investigation of drivers for active public support is essential to offer suitable options to the general public and residents of renewable energy plants to contribute to the energy transition and therefore requires increased attention in future research.

6.3.4 Conducting Longitudinal Studies

Longitudinal studies would add value and depth to the research field (cf. Rand and Hoen, 2017). In particular, the exploration of causalities requires measurements at multiple points in time. One example is the link between experience with renewable energies and their public acceptance, which was explored in this thesis. Even though the results of the three case studies conducted clearly confirm the link, the collected data does not allow final conclusions on causality. For example, in case that public acceptance of residents of renewable energy plants exceeds public acceptance of the general public, it is both possible, that either public acceptance was positively influenced by the experience with the local plants, or that the plant location was chosen because public acceptance was already high before. Other questions include the development of public acceptance over time for specific projects, e.g., before, during, and after the implementation of a renewable energy plant. The latter has been investigated by Wolsink (2007) who found that attitudes are not static, but developing over time. Another example is the study by Kortsch et al. (2015) which showed that the strength of the factors influencing public acceptance differed over time. Despite these findings, which clearly point to a dynamic development of public acceptance over time, very few studies have collected longitudinal data so far, which is therefore and important task for future research.

6.3.5 Developing Concepts for the Practice

So far, the transfer of research findings into practice has been limited (Rand and Hoen, 2017; Sovacool, 2014; Wolsink, 2018b). On the one hand side, guidelines which translate research findings into specific frameworks and measures are rare (Zaunbrecher and Ziefle, 2016) and, therefore, the incorporation of those findings by project developers and policy makers has been slow (Rand and Hoen, 2017). On the other hand, previous research tends to provide rather descriptive than explanatory insights because predominantly qualitative case-based approaches are applied, which do not easily translate into generalizable recommendations for action. To effectively inform the policy debate and to create practical knowledge for project developers, it is therefore essential to develop methodologies, which allow for more universal insights into public acceptance phenomena. The aim of public acceptance research should be to anticipate conflicts with the public by increasing community engagement and decreasing perceived injustice associated with the implementation of renewable energy plants (Rand and Hoen, 2017). Future research should therefore keep this goal in mind and derive valuable guidelines for the practice from their findings. Moreover, there is the need that those institutions, which set the political guidelines for the energy transition, also participate in the change processes themselves and use the provided empirical evidence to improve their policy instruments and decisions.

Appendix

A Items and Construct Measures[23]

Table A-1: Items and constructs measures of case study 1 (translated from German)

Construct		Source	Item
Single item	Socio-political acceptance	Based on Wüste (2013)	Small-scale PV/ large-scale PV/ wind energy/ biogas plants are a suitable form of energy generation. [a]
Single item	Community acceptance	Based on Schweizer-Ries et al. (2010)	I support small-scale PV/ large-scale PV/ wind energy/ biogas plants in my neighborhood. [a]
Single item	Appraisal of local plant	Newly developed, based on Schweizer-Ries (2008)	How do you rate small-scale PV/ large-scale PV/ wind energy/ biogas plants in your neighborhood? [b]
Single item	Active support	Newly developed, based on Schweizer-Ries (2008)	Are you in principle prepared to actively support a small-scale PV/ large-scale PV/ wind energy/ biogas plant in your neighborhood? [c]
Single item	Active resistance	Newly developed, based on Schweizer-Ries (2008)	Are you in principle prepared to actively oppose a small-scale PV/ large-scale PV/ wind energy/ biogas plant in your neighborhood? [c]

[23] For the translated scales in French, Germany, and Spanish, please directly contact the author of this thesis.

Construct		Source	Item
Distance	Relevance of proximity	Newly developed	To what extent is the distance between your house/ apartment and a small-scale PV/ large-scale PV/ wind energy/ biogas plant important to you? [e]
	Desired distance	Based on Griesen (2010), Bertsch et al. (2016)	What should be the minimum distance of a small-scale PV/ large-scale PV/ wind energy/ biogas plant to your home for you to accept the plant? [f]
Advocacy of renewable energies	Future energy generation	Based on Schweizer-Ries et al. (2010), Rau & Zoellner (2008)	Renewable energies (e.g., solar, wind, bioenergy) should play an important role in future energy generation. [a]
	Local support	Schweizer-Ries et al. (2010)	All in all, I support renewable energy facilities in my neighborhood. [a]
Perceived benefits of biogas plants	Distributive justice	Based on Wüste (2013)	The ratio of costs (e.g., odors) and benefits (e.g., financial gains) of biogas plants is distributed fairly. [a]
	Climate protection	Soland et al. (2013)	Biogas plants contribute to climate protection. [a]
	Regional economic development	Schweizer-Ries et al. (2010)	Biogas plants have a positive impact on the economic development of my region. [a]
	Import dependency	Based on Soland et al. (2013)	Biogas plants help to reduce the dependency on imported energy. [a]
	Environmental protection	Musall & Kuik (2011)	Biogas is a clean energy source. [a]
Perceived costs of biogas plants	Increased energy price	Based on Zoellner et al. (2008)	The increased usage of biogas will increase the price of energy. [a]
	Odor nuisance	Soland et al. (2013)	Biogas plants cause odor nuisances for residents. [a]

Construct		Source	Item
Perceived costs of biogas plants	Landscape change	Based on Soland et al., 2013	Biogas plants spoil the natural landscape. [a]
	Risk of accidents	Wüste (2013)	The operation of a biogas plant entails an increased risk of accidents for residents e.g., through gas leakage or the leakage of a container. [a]
	Environmental pollution	Wüste (2013)	The operation of biogas plants jeopardizes groundwater or surface water. [a]
Perceived costs of energy crops	Perceived costs of energy crops	Schweizer-Ries et al. (2010)	As a result of the increased use of biogas, monocultures (such as maize) will dominate agriculture. [a]
	Food versus fuel controversy	Based on Wüste (2013)	The production of biogas competes with the production of food. [a]
Desired information and participation	Desired information	Based on Rau et al. (2012), Schweizer-Ries et al. (2010)	It's important for me to be informed in advance about planned biogas plants. [a]
	Desired consultation	Based on Rau et al. (2012), Schweizer-Ries et al. (2010)	In the realization of a biomass plant the population's opinion should be asked for. [a]
	Desired cooperation	Based on Rau et al. (2012), Schweizer-Ries et al. (2010)	The population should have a say in the implementation processes of biogas plants. [a]
	Desired assumption of responsibility	Based on Rau et al. (2012), Schweizer-Ries et al. (2010)	The population should shape the planning processes of biogas plants themselves to a large extent. [a]

Construct		Source	Item
Engagement for renewable energies	Convince others	Rau & Zoellner (2008)	I try to convince my friends during conversations about the benefits of renewable energies. [g]
	Financial participation	Rau & Zoellner (2008)	I am interested in financially participating in a renewable energy plant. [d (recoded)]
	General active support of renewable energies	Based on Schweizer-Ries et al. (2010)	Are you in principle willing to actively support a renewable energy plant in your neighborhood? (E.g., through membership in a citizens' initiative or in a cooperative) [d]
Single item	Active involvement	Newly developed	Are you already actively involved in a local renewable energy plant? [i]
Advocacy of energy autonomy	General support of energy autonomy	Newly developed	All in all, I think that approaches leading to higher local energy autonomy make sense. [a]
	Local support of energy autonomy	Newly developed	I support approaches which lead to higher energy autonomy in my neighborhood. [a]
	Appraisal of energy autonomy	Newly developed	How do you rate energy autonomy in your neighborhood? [b]
Single item	Knowledge of energy autonomy	Newly developed	How do you rate your general knowledge of renewable energies? [h]
Single items	Community energy	Newly developed	Are you already supporting local renewable energy projects? [j]

Notes to Table A-1:

[a] Five-point Likert scale with 1 = "entirely incorrect" and 5 = "completely correct" as anchors and 90 = "don't know".

[b] Five- point Likert scale with 1 = "very negative" and 5 = "very positive" as anchors and 90 = "don't know".

[b/c] 1 = "Yes", 2 = "No".

[d] 1 = "Yes", 2 = "No", 90 = "don't know".

[e] 1 = "I do not accept the plant, independent of the distance.", 2 = "The distance of the plant to my home is not relevant for me.", 3 = "The distance is not relevant but the plant should not be visible from my home.", 4 = "The plants should keep a minimal distance to my home."

[f] <1 kilometer (km), 1 km, 2 km, 3 km, 4 km, 5 km, 6 km, 7 km, 8 km, >9 km.

[g] Five-point Likert scale with 1 = "never" and 5 = "always".

[h] Five-point Likert scale with 1 = "very bad" and 5 = "very good".

[i] 1 = "No", 2 = "Plant operator", 3 = "Financial stake", 4 = "Community energy initiative", 5 = "Community energy cooperative", 6 = "Other (please state).

[j] 1 = "No, I am not supporting any local renewable energy project.", 2 = "Yes, I am running my own plant.", 3 = "Yes, I am financially involved in a renewable energy plant.", 4 = "Yes, I am a member of an energy cooperative.", 5 = "Yes, I am engaged in another form than the above (please briefly describe your commitment)."

Table A-2: Items and construct measures of case study 2 (translated from German)

Construct		Source	Item
Single item	Socio-political acceptance	Based on Wüste (2013)	Biogas plants are a suitable form of energy generation. [a]
Single item	Community acceptance	Based on Schweizer-Ries et al. (2010)	I support biogas plants in my neighborhood. [a]
Single item	Appraisal of local plant	Newly developed, based on Schweizer-Ries (2008)	How do you rate the biogas plant in your neighborhood? [b] (recoded)
Single item	Active support	Newly developed, based on Schweizer-Ries (2008)	Are you prepared in principle to actively support a biogas plant in your neighborhood? [c]

Construct		Source	Item
Single item	Active resistance	Newly developed, based on Schweizer-Ries (2008)	Are you prepared in principle to actively oppose a biogas plant in your neighborhood? [c]
Single item	Desired distance	Newly developed, based on Griesen (2010)	What should be the minimum distance of a biogas plant to your home for you to accept the plant? [d]
Advocacy of renewable energies	Future energy generation	Based on Rau and Zoellner (2008), Schweizer-Ries et al. (2010)	Renewable energies (e.g., solar, wind, bioenergy) should play an important role in future energy generation. [a]
	Local support	Schweizer-Ries et al. (2010)	All in all, I support renewable energy facilities in my neighborhood. [d]
Perceived benefits of biogas plants	Distributive justice	Based on Schweizer-Ries et al. (2010)	The ratio of costs (e.g., odors) and benefits (e.g., financial gains) of the biogas plant is distributed fairly. [a]
	Climate protection	Soland et al. (2013)	The biogas plant protects the climate. [a]
	Regional economic development	Schweizer-Ries et al. (2010)	The biogas plant has a positive effect on our municipality as a business location. [a]
	Benefits for the community	Schweizer-Ries et al. (2010)	In the end, we all benefit from the realization of the biogas plant. [a]
Perceived costs of biogas plants	Increased energy price	Based on Zoellner et al. (2008)	The increased usage of biogas will increase the price of energy. [a]
	Property values	Based on Soland et al. (2013), Wüste (2013)	The biogas plant has a negative impact on the property values in our community. [a]

Construct		Source	Item
Perceived costs of biogas plants	Personal financial loss	Soland et al. (2013)	The biogas plant hurts me financially (e.g., reduced property values, less tourists). [a]
Perceived odor	Frequency of odor	Newly developed	How often did you perceive odor from the biogas plant during the last year? [e]
	Quality of odor	Based on Soland et al. (2013)	How do you perceive the odor? [b]
	Strength of odor	Based on Soland et al. (2013)	How strong is the odor you perceive? [f]
Trust in the plant operator	Reliability of information	Based on Soland et al. (2013)	I can rely on the information provided by the plant operator. [a]
	Consideration of residents' concerns	Soland et al. (2013)	The plant operator appreciates the neighborhood's concerns. [a]
	Competency for plant operation	Soland et al. (2013)	The plant operator knows how to operate his plant. [a]
Actual information and participation	Procedural fairness	Based on Rau et al. (2012), Schweizer-Ries et al. (2010)	The planning process of the local plant was conducted fairly. [a]
	Actual information	Based on Rau et al. (2012), Schweizer-Ries et al. (2010)	During the planning process of the local plant, sufficient information was available. [a]
	Actual consultation	Based on Rau et al. (2012), Schweizer-Ries et al. (2010)	The opinion of the population regarding the local biogas plant was asked for and respected. [a]
	Actual cooperation	Based on Rau et al. (2012), Schweizer-Ries et al. (2010)	The decisions with regard to the realization of the local biogas plant were taken jointly with the population. [a]

Construct		Source	Item
	Actual assumption of responsibility	Based on Rau et al. (2012), Schweizer-Ries et al. (2010)	The population contributed decisively to the realization of the local biogas plant. [a]
Desired information and participation	Desired information	Based on Rau et al. (2012), Schweizer-Ries et al. (2010)	It's important for me to be informed in advance about planned biogas plants. [a]
	Desired consultation	Based on Rau et al. (2012), Schweizer-Ries et al. (2010)	In the realization of a biomass plant the population's opinion should be asked for. [a]
	Desired cooperation	Based on Rau et al. (2012), Schweizer-Ries et al. (2010)	The population should have a say in the implementation processes of biogas plants. [a]
	Desired assumption of responsibility	Based on Rau et al. (2012), Schweizer-Ries et al. (2010)	The population should shape of the planning processes of biogas plants themselves to a large extent. [a]

Notes to Table A-2:

[a] Five-point Likert scale with 1 = "entirely incorrect" and 5 = "completely correct" as anchors and 90 = "don't know"

[b] Five- point Likert scale with 1 = "very negative" and 5 = "very positive" as anchors and 90 = "don't know"

[c] 1 = "Yes", 2 = "No", 90 = "don't know"

[d] less than 1 kilometer (km), between 1 and 3 km, between 3.1 and 8 km, between 8.1 and 11 km, more than 11 km

[e] Five-point Likert scale with 1 = "almost daily or even more often" to 5 = "once a year or even more rarely" as anchors and 90 = "don't know"

[f] Five- point Likert scale with 1 = "very strong" to 5 = "very weak" as anchors and 90 = "don't know"

Table A-3: Items and construct measures of case study 3 (translated from Spanish)

Construct		Source	Item
Single item	Socio-political acceptance	Based on Wüste (2013)	Small-scale PV/ large-scale PV/ wind energy/ bioenergy plants are a suitable form of electricity generation. [a]
Single item	Community acceptance	Based on Schweizer-Ries et al. (2010)	I support small-scale PV/ large-scale PV/ wind energy/ bioenergy plants in my neighborhood. [a]
Single item	Appraisal of local plant	Newly developed, based on Schweizer-Ries (2008)	How do you rate small-scale PV/ large-scale PV/ wind energy/ biomass plants in your neighborhood? [b]
Single item	Active support	Newly developed, based on Schweizer-Ries (2008)	Are you in principle prepared to actively support a small-scale PV/ large-scale PV/ wind energy/ biomass plant in your neighborhood? [c]
Single item	Active resistance	Newly developed, based on Schweizer-Ries (2008)	Are you in principle prepared to actively oppose a small-scale PV/ large-scale PV/ wind energy/ biomass plant in your neighborhood? [c]
Advocacy of renewable energies	Future energy generation	Based on Schweizer-Ries et al. (2010), Rau & Zoellner (2008)	Renewable energies (e.g., solar, wind, bioenergy) should play an important role in Chile's future energy generation. [a]
	Local support	Schweizer-Ries et al. (2010)	All in all, I support renewable energy facilities in my neighborhood. [a]
Distance	Relevance of proximity	Newly developed	To what extent is the distance between your house/ apartment and a small-scale PV/ large-scale PV/ wind energy/ biomass plant important to you? [d]

Construct		Source	Item
Distance	Desired distance	Based on Griesen (2010), Bertsch et al. (2016)	What should be the minimum distance of a small-scale PV/ large-scale PV/ wind energy/ biomass plant to your home for you to accept the plant? [e]
Perceived benefits of biomass combustion plants	Distributive justice	Based on Wüste (2013)	The ratio of costs (e.g., odors) and benefits (e.g., financial gains) of biomass combustion plants is distributed fairly. [a]
	Climate protection	Soland et al. (2013)	Biomass combustion plants contribute to climate protection. [a]
	Regional economic development	Schweizer-Ries et al. (2010)	Biomass combustion plants have a positive impact on the economic development of my region. [a]
	Import dependency	Based on Soland et al. (2013)	Biomass combustion plants help to reduce the dependency on imported energy. [a]
	Environmental protection	Musall & Kuik (2011)	Bioenergy is a clean electricity source. [a]
Perceived costs of biomass combustion plants	Increased energy price	Based on Zoellner et al. (2008)	The increased usage of biomass will increase the price of energy. [a]
	Odor nuisance	Soland et al. (2013)	Biomass plants cause odor nuisances for residents. [a]
	Landscape change	Based on Soland et al., 2013	Biomass plants spoil the natural landscape. [a]
	Risk of accidents	Wüste (2013)	The operation of a biomass plant entails an increased risk of accidents for residents e.g., through gas leakage or the leakage of a container. [a]
	Environmental pollution	Wüste (2013)	The operation of biomass plants jeopardizes groundwater or surface water. [a]

Construct		Source	Item
Perceived costs of energy crops	Energy crops from forest plantations	Schweizer-Ries et al. (2010)	As a result of the increased use of bioenergy, monocultures (such as plantations of pines and eucalyptus) will increase excessively. [a]
	Energy crops from agriculture	Based on Wüste (2013)	The production of bioenergy competes with the production of food. [a]
Actual information and participation	Actual information	Based on Rau et al. (2012), Schweizer-Ries et al. (2010)	There is sufficient information available with regard to renewable energy plants. [a]
	Actual consultation	Based on Rau et al. (2012), Schweizer-Ries et al. (2010)	The opinion of the population regarding renewable energy plants is asked for. [a]
	Actual cooperation	Based on Rau et al. (2012), Schweizer-Ries et al. (2010)	The decisions with regard to the realization of renewable energy plants are taken jointly with the population. [a]
	Actual assumption of responsibility	Based on Rau et al. (2012), Schweizer-Ries et al. (2010)	The population contributes decisively to the realization of renewable energy plant. [a]
Desired information and participation	Desired information	Based on Rau et al. (2012), Schweizer-Ries et al. (2010)	It's important for me to be informed in advance about planned bioenergy plants. [a]
	Desired consultation	Based on Rau et al. (2012), Schweizer-Ries et al. (2010)	In the realization of a biomass plant the population's opinion should be asked for. [a]

Construct		Source	Item
Desired information and participation	Desired cooperation	Based on Rau et al. (2012), Schweizer-Ries et al. (2010)	The population should have a say in the implementation processes of biomass plants. [a]
	Desired assumption of responsibility	Based on Rau et al. (2012), Schweizer-Ries et al. (2010)	The population should shape the planning processes of biomass plants themselves to a large extent. [a]

Notes to Table A-3:

[a] Five-point Likert scale with 1 = "entirely incorrect" and 5 = "completely correct" as anchors and 90 = "don't know".

[b] Five-point Likert scale with 1 = "very negative" and 5 = "very positive" as anchors and 90 = "don't know".

[c] 1 = "Yes", 2 = "No".

[d] 1 = "I do not accept the plant, independent of the distance.", 2 = "The distance of the plant to my home is not relevant for me.", 3 = "The distance is not relevant but the plant should not be visible from my home.", 4 = "The plants should keep a minimal distance to my home."

[e] < 1 kilometer (km), 1 km, 2 km, 3 km, 4 km, 5 km, 6 km, 7 km, 8 km, > 9 km.

B Questionnaires

Table B-1: Likert scales of the questionnaires

Scale	German	Spanish
1	Trifft überhaupt nicht zu Trifft eher nicht zu Bin unentschieden Trifft teilweise zu Trifft voll zu	Totalmente en desacuerdo En desacuerdo Ni de acuerdo ni en desacuerdo De acuerdo Totalmente de acuerdo
2	Sehr positiv Positiv Neutral Negativ Sehr negativ	Muy positivamente Positivamente Ni positivamente ni negativamente Negativamente Muy negativamente
3	Sehr stark Stark Neutral Schwach Sehr schwach	N/A
4	Nie Selten Gelegentlich Oft Immer	N/A
5	Sehr schlecht Schlecht Mittelmäßig Gut Sehr gut	N/A

Table B-2: Questionnaire case study 1

Introduction

Liebe Teilnehmerin, lieber Teilnehmer,
vielen Dank, dass Sie an dieser Umfrage zur Akzeptanz Erneuerbarer Energien und Energieautarkie teilnehmen. Der Ausbau Erneuerbarer Energien führt unter anderem dazu, dass die Zivilgesellschaft zunehmend in ihrem direkten Umfeld von den Auswirkungen Erneuerbarer Energieanlagen betroffen ist. Dabei stoßen Erneuerbare Energieanlagen in der direkten Nachbarschaft nicht immer auf Zustimmung. Die Akzeptanz der lokalen Bevölkerung spielt somit für die Umsetzung solcher Projekte eine wichtige Rolle. Wir am Karlsruher Institut für Technologie interessieren uns daher für Ihre Einstellung zu Erneuerbaren Energien und zum Konzept der Energieautarkie.
Erneuerbare Energien sind sehr vielfältig. Es gibt viele verschiedene Energiequellen und noch mehr Technologien um diese zu verwerten. In dieser Umfrage sind mit dem Begriff "Erneuerbare Energien" hauptsächlich die Technologien Wind, Photovoltaik und Bioenergie (insbesondere Biogas) gemeint. Hier finden Sie eine kurze Erklärung der einzelnen Energietechnologien. Die Erklärungen zu den einzelnen Erneuerbaren Energien werden später im Fragebogen an geeigneter Stelle wiederholt.

Bei der Windenergie wird die Energie des Windes in Elektrizität umgewandelt. Dies geschieht üblicherweise mit Windturbinen mit einer horizontalen Achse und drei Blättern.

Bild: Windrad (Quelle: Andol, https://commons.wikimedia.org/wiki/File:N117,_Hohenahr_7.JPG, „N117, Hohenahr 7“, https://creativecommons.org/licenses/by-sa/3.0/legalcode)

Bei Photovoltaik wird Sonnenenergie in Elektrizität umgewandelt. Hier kann zwischen Klein- und Großanlagen unterschieden werden. Eine Photovoltaik-Kleinanlage wird z.B. auf dem Dach eines Einfamilienhauses, eine Photovoltaik-Großanlage z.B. auf einer Freifläche installiert.

Bild: Photovoltaik-Kleinanlage (Quelle: https://upload.wikimedia.org/wikipedia/commons/thumb/3/34/SolarFachwerkhaus.jpg/776px-SolarFachwerkhaus.jpg)

Bild: Photovoltaik-Großanlage (Quelle: Ceinturion, https://commons.wikimedia.org/wiki/File:SolarPowerPlantSerpa.jpg, „SolarPowerPlantSerpa“, https://creativecommons.org/licenses/by-sa/3.0/legalcode)

Biogasanlagen wandeln verschiedene Arten von Biomasse durch Vergärung in ein energiereiches Gas um. In landwirtschaftlichen Biogasanlagen werden meist Gülle und/oder Mist sowie Reststoffe eingesetzt. In Deutschland kommen zudem häufig Energiepflanzen (insbesondere Mais) zum Einsatz. In nicht-landwirtschaftlichen Anlagen werden Abfälle aus der Biotonne oder aus der Lebensmittelindustrie verwendet. Bei den meisten Biogasanlagen wird das entstandene Gas vor Ort zur Strom- und Wärmeerzeugung genutzt.
Alternativ gibt es einige Anlagen, die das Biogas auch in anderer Form nutzbar machen (z.B. Biomethan, Biomass to Liquid).

Bild: Biogasanlage (Aufnahme: Kira Schumacher)

Die Beantwortung des Fragebogens wird circa 20 Minuten Ihrer Zeit in Anspruch nehmen. Alle Daten werden anonym gespeichert und nur zur Erstellung wissenschaftlicher Arbeiten verwendet.

Viel Spaß beim Ausfüllen des Fragebogens!

Heading	Fragen zu Ihrer Person
Die folgenden Fragen helfen, die Ergebnisse dieser Umfrage auszuwerten. Dabei ist es wichtig, dass die Forscher/innen Ihre Antworten nach Merkmalen auswerten können, die gesellschaftliche Gruppen beschreiben. Die Forscher/innen werten die Daten nicht für Ihre Person aus, sondern für solche Gruppen, zu denen man Sie zum Beispiel entsprechend Ihrer Altersgruppe, Ihrem Geschlecht oder Ihrem Schulabschluss zuordnen kann. Ihre Daten werden vertraulich behandelt und ausschließlich zu wissenschaftlichen Zwecken ausgewertet.	
Number	1
Question	Sie sind…
Answer type	Single choice
Items	Männlich
	Weiblich
Number	2
Question	In welchem Jahr wurden Sie geboren?
Instructions	Bitte geben Sie Ihr Geburtsdatum vierstellig an (z.B. 1984)
Answer type	(Free text field)

Number	3
Question	Sind Sie Eigentümer Ihres Wohnhauses/ Ihrer Wohnung?
Answer type	Binary question (yes, no)
Number	4
Question	Wohnen in Ihrem Haushalt Kinder unter 16 Jahren?
Instructions	Die Frage bezieht sich auf Kinder, die <u>permanent</u> in Ihrem Haushalt wohnen.
Answer type	Binary question (yes, no)
Number	5
Question	Welche Erwerbssituation passt für Sie?
Instructions	Bitte kreuzen Sie die zutreffene Antwort an.
Answer type	Single choice
Items	Erwerbstätig (einschließlich: Vollzeit, Teilzeit, geringfügig erwerbstätig) Gelegentlich oder unregelmäßig beschäftigt In einer beruflichen Ausbildung/Lehre Nicht erwerbstätig (einschließlich: Schüler(n)/-innen oder Studierende, die nicht gegen Geld arbeiten, Arbeitslosen, Vorruheständler(n)/-innen, Rentner(n)/-innen ohne Nebenverdienst) Sonstiges: (free text field)
Number	6
Question	Bitte geben Sie die Postleitzahl Ihres Wohnortes an:
Instructions	Damit ist der Ort gemeint, an dem Sie Ihren Lebensmittelpunkt haben.
Answer type	(Free text field)
Number	7
Question	In welchem Land wohnen Sie?
Instructions	Damit ist das Land gemeint, in welchem Sie Ihren Lebensmittelpunkt haben.
Answer type	Single choice
Items	Deutschland Schweiz Frankreich
Filter	If *Deutschland*, then go to question 8_DE. If *Schweiz,* go to question 8_CH.
Number	8_DE
Question	Wie viele Jahre waren Sie insgesamt in Schule, Hochschule, oder anderer schulischer Ausbildung, ohne betriebliche Ausbildung?
Instructions	Sollten Sie Schuljahre wiederholt haben, zählen diese bitte NICHT mit. Wenn Sie noch Schüler(in) oder Student(in) sind, zählen Sie bitte die Jahre, die Sie bereits in Schule oder Hochschule verbracht haben (inklusive dem laufenden Jahr).
Answer type	(Free text field)

Filter	Go to question 9.
Number	8_CH
Question	Wie viele Jahre Ausbildung haben Sie seit der ersten Primarschulklasse absolviert?
Instructions	Zählen Sie bitte alle Vollzeit Aus- und Weiterbildungen dazu, nicht aber eine eventuelle Lehrzeit und immer ohne wiederholte Jahre. Wenn Sie noch Schüler(in) oder Student(in) sind, zählen Sie bitte die Jahre dazu, die Sie bereits in Schule oder Hochschule verbracht haben (inklusive dem laufen-den Jahr).
Answer type	(Free text field)
Filter	Go to question 9.

Heading	Erneuerbare Energieanlagen in Ihrer Nachbarschaft
Number	9
Question	Befinden sich im Umkreis von einem Kilometer von Ihrem Wohnhaus bzw. Ihrer Wohnung Erneuerbare Energieanlagen? (z.B. Photovoltaik, Wind- oder Bioenergieanlagen)
Instructions	Damit ist der Ort gemeint, an dem Sie Ihren Lebensmittelpunkt haben.
Answer type	Binary question (yes, no) + don't know
Filter	If *yes*, then go to question 10. Otherwise go to question 12.
Number	10
Question	Um welche Art von Erneuerbarer Energieanlage handelt es sich?
Instructions	Bitte kreuzen Sie alles an, was zutrifft.
Answer type	Multiple choice
Question items	Photovoltaik - Kleinanlage (z.B. auf dem Dach eines Einfamilienhauses) Photovoltaik - Großanlage (z.B. auf einer Freifläche) Windkraftanlage Biogasanlage Holzheizkraftwerk/Holzheizkessel (in einem Holzheizkraftwerk bzw. Holzheizkessel werden Wärme und/oder Strom durch Holzverbrennung erzeugt) Geothermie (Geothermie ist Wärmeenergie in der Erde, die verwendet werden kann, um Wärme und/oder Strom zu erzeugen) Sonstige: (free text field)
Number	11
Question	Besteht zwischen Ihnen und dem Betreiber der Erneuerbaren Energieanlagen eine direkte Beziehung
Instructions	Bitte kreuzen Sie alles an, was zutrifft
Answer type	Multiple choices
Items	Nein

	Ja, ein Beschäftigungsverhältnis Ja, eine Kunden- oder Geschäftsbeziehung Ja, ich bin selbst Betreiber der Anlage Sonstiges Verhältnis (bitte beschreiben Sie dieses kurz): (free text field)

Heading	Mitwirkung in Bezug auf Erneuerbare Energien
Number	12
Question	Ich versuche in Gesprächen, Bekannte/Freunde vom Nutzen von Erneuerbaren Energien zu überzeugen.
Instructions	Geben Sie bitte an, inwieweit diese Aussage auf Sie zutrifft.
Answer type	Likert scale 4 + don't know
Number	13
Question	Ich habe Interesse, mich an einer Erneuerbaren Energieanlage finanziell zu beteiligen.
Instructions	Geben Sie bitte an, inwieweit diese Aussage auf Sie zutrifft.
Answer type	Binary question (yes, no) + don't know
Number	14
Question	Sind Sie grundsätzlich bereit sich aktiv für Erneuerbare Energieanlagen vor Ort einzusetzen? (z.B. durch Mitgliedschaft in einer Bürgerinitiative oder in einer Genossenschaft)
Answer type	Binary question (yes, no) + don't know
Filter	If *yes*, then go to question 15
Number	15
Question	Engagieren Sie sich bereits für Erneuerbare Energieanlagen vor Ort?
Instructions	Bitte kreuzen Sie alles an, was zutrifft.
Answer type	Multiple choices
Items	Nein, ich engagiere mich nicht für Erneuerbare Energieanlagen vor Ort. Ja, ich betreibe eine eigene Anlage. Ja, ich beteilige mich finanziell an einer Erneuerbaren Energieanlage. Ja, ich bin Mitglied in einer Bürgerinitiative für Erneuerbare Energien. Ja, ich bin Mitglied in einer Energiegenossenschaft. Ja, ich engagiere mich in einer anderen als oben genannten Form (bitte beschreiben Sie kurz Ihr Engagement): (free text field)
Filter	If Nein, ich engagiere mich nicht für Erneuerbare Energieanlagen vor Ort, then go to 17. Otherwise go to 16.
Number	16
Question	Was waren die wichtigsten Gründe für Ihr Engagement?

Instructions	Bitte kreuzen Sie alles an, was zutrifft.
Answer type	Multiple choices
Items	Wirtschaftliche Gründe (z.B. Gewinn, Rendite) Ökologische Gründe (z.B. Umweltschutz, Ressourcenschonung) Unabhängigkeit von Importen fossiler Energieträger Erhöhung der Energieunabhängigkeit der Region Soziales Engagement Regionale/lokale Wertschöpfung (z.B. Schaffung von Arbeitsplätzen) Unabhängigkeit von überregionalen Energieversorgungsunternehmen Sonstige Gründe (bitte beschreiben Sie kurz): (free text field)

Heading	Bewertung von Erneuerbaren Energien
Number	17
Question	Welche Energieformen sollten Ihrer Meinung nach zukünftig bevorzugt werden?
Instructions	Bitte kreuzen Sie alles an, was zutrifft.
Answer type	Multiple choices
Items	Solarenergie (Bei Solarenergie wird Sonnenenergie in Elektrizität umgewandelt) Windenergie (Bei Windenergie wird die Energie des Windes in Elektrizität umgewandelt) Bioenergie (Als Bioenergie bezeichnet man Strom, Wärme und Kraftstoffe, die aus fester, flüssiger und gasförmiger Biomasse gewonnen werden) Geothermie (Geothermie nutzt die Wärmeenergie in der Erde um Wärme und Strom zu erzeugen) Wasserkraft (Wasserkraft wandelt die kritische Energie von fallendem Wasser in Elektrizität um) Kohle Kernenergie Erdöl Erdgas Sonstige: (free text field)
Number	18
Question	Ich finde, dass Erneurbare Energien (z.B. Solar-, Wind-, Bioenergie) eine wichtige Rolle bei der zukünftigen Stromerzeugung spielen sollten.
Instructions	Geben Sie bitte an, inwieweit diese Aussage auf Sie zutrifft.
Answer type	Likert scale 1 + don't know

Number	19
Question	Von der vermehrten Nutzung von Erneuerbaren Energien profitieren wir zum Schluss alle.
Instructions	Geben Sie bitte an, inwieweit diese Aussage Ihrer Meinung nach zutrifft.
Answer type	Likert scale 1 + don't know
Number	20
Question	Die vermehrte Nutzung von Erneuerbaren Energien leistet einen Beitrag zur wirtschaftlichen Entwicklung meiner Region.
Instructions	Geben Sie bitte an, inwieweit diese Aussage Ihrer Meinung nach zutrifft.
Answer type	Likert scale 1 + don't know
Number	21
Question	Grundsätzlich befürworte ich Erneuerbare Energieanlagen in meiner Nachbarschaft.
Instructions	Mit Nachbarschaft ist der Umkreis von einem Kilometer um Ihr Wohnhaus/Ihre Wohnung gemeint. Geben Sie bitte an, inwieweit diese Aussage auf Sie zutrifft.
Answer type	Likert scale 1 + don't know
Number	22
Question	Wie schätzen Sie Ihren allgemeinen Kenntnisstand in Bezug auf Erneuerbare Energien ein?
Answer type	Likert scale 5 + don't know

Heading	Bewertung von Photovoltaik-Kleinanlagen

Bei Photovoltaik wird Sonnenenergie in Elektrizität umgewandelt. Hier kann zwischen Klein- und Großanlagen unterschieden werden. Eine Photovoltaik-Kleinanlage wird z.B. auf dem Dach eines Einfamilienhauses installiert.

Bild: Photovoltaik-Kleinanlage (Quelle: Túrelio, 2007, Creative Commons CC-BY-SA-3.0-de, https://commons.wikimedia.org/wiki/File:SolarFachwerkhaus.jpg, „SolarFachwerkhaus“, https://creativecommons.org/licenses/by-sa/3.0/de/legalcode)

Number	23
Question	Photovoltaik-Kleinanlagen stellen eine geeignete Form der Elektrizitätserzeugung dar.
Instructions	Geben Sie bitte an, inwieweit diese Aussage Ihrer Meinung nach zutrifft.
Answer type	Likert scale 1 + don't know
Number	24
Question	Ich befürworte Photovoltaik-Kleinanlagen in meiner Nachbarschaft.
Instructions	Geben Sie bitte an, inwieweit diese Aussage auf Sie zutrifft.
Answer type	Likert scale 1 + don't know
Number	25
Question	Wie negativ oder positiv bewerten Sie Photovoltaik-Kleinanlagen in Ihrer Nachbarschaft gesamthaft?
Answer type	Likert scale 2 (reversed) + don't know
Filter	If *sehr positiv* or *positiv*, then go to question 26. If *sehr negativ* or *negativ,* then go to question 27. If *neutral* or *weiß nicht*, then go to question 28.
Number	26
Question	Sind Sie grundsätzlich bereit, sich aktiv für eine Photovoltaik-Kleinanlage vor Ort einzusetzen?
Instructions	(z.B. durch Mitgliedschaft in einer Bürgerinitiative)
Answer type	Binary question (yes, no)
Filter	Go to question 28.
Number	27
Question	Sind Sie grundsätzlich bereit, sich aktiv gegen eine Photovoltaik-Kleinanlage vor Ort einzusetzen?
Instructions	(z.B. durch Mitgliedschaft in einer Bürgerinitiative)
Answer type	Binary question (yes, no)
Number	28
Question	Als nächstes möchten wir gerne wissen, inwieweit Ihnen die Entfernung zwischen Ihrem Wohnhaus/ Ihrer Wohnung und der Photovoltaik-Kleinanlage wichtig ist.
Instructions	Bitte kreuzen Sie die zutreffende Antwort an.
Answer type	Single choice
Items	Für die Anlage(n) sollte ein Mindestabstand zu meinem Wohnhaus/ meiner Wohnung eingehalten werden. Die Entfernung der Anlage(n) zu meinem Wohnhaus/ meiner Wohnung spielt keine Rolle. Die Entfernung der Anlage(n) zu meinem Wohnhaus/ meiner Wohnung spielt keine Rolle aber die Anlage(n) sollte(n) nicht von meinem Wohnhaus/ meiner Wohnung aus sichtbar sein. Ich akzeptiere die Anlage(n) überhaupt nicht, egal in welcher Entfernung sie sich befindet.

Filter	If Für die Anlage(n) sollte ein Mindestabstand zu meinem Wohnhaus/ meiner Wohnung eingehalten werden, then go to question 29. Otherwise go to question 30.
Number	29
Question	Wie weit sollte eine Photovoltaik-Kleinanlage mindestens von Ihrem Wohnhaus/Ihrer Wohnung entfernt sein, damit Sie diese akzeptieren würden?
Instructions	Bitte klicken Sie auf den Balken, um den Abstand in Kilometern (km) zu wählen.
Answer type	Slide bar
Items	< 1 km, 1 km, 2 km, 3 km, 4 km, 5km, 6 km, 7 km, 8km, > 9 km

Heading	Bewertung von Photovolatik-Großanlagen

Bei Photovoltaik wird Sonnenenergie in Elektrizität umgewandelt. Hier kann zwischen Klein- und Großanlagen unterschieden werden. Eine Photovoltaik-Großanlage wird z.B. auf einer Freifläche oder auf dem Dach einer (großen) Scheune installiert.

Bild: Photovoltaik-Großanlage (Quelle: Ceinturion, https://commons.wikimedia.org/wiki/File:SolarPowerPlantSerpa.jpg, „SolarPowerPlantSerpa“, https://creativecommons.org/licenses/by-sa/3.0/legalcode)

Number	30
Question	Photovoltaik-Großanlagen stellen eine geeignete Form der Elektizitätserzeugung dar.
Instructions	Geben Sie bitte an, inwieweit diese Aussage Ihrer Meinung nach zutrifft.
Answer type	Likert scale 1 + don’t know
Number	31
Question	Ich befürworte Photovoltaik-Großanlagen in meiner Nachbarschaft.
Instructions	Geben Sie bitte an, inwieweit diese Aussage auf Sie zutrifft.

Answer type	Likert scale 1 + don't know
Number	32
Question	Wie negativ oder positiv bewerten Sie Photovoltaik-Großanlagen in Ihrer Nachbarschaft gesamthaft?
Answer type	Likert scale 2 (reversed) + don't know
Filter	If *sehr positiv* or *positiv,* then go to question 33. If sehr *negativ* or *negativ,* then go to question 34. If *neutral* or *weiß nicht*, then go to question 35.
Number	33
Question	Sind Sie grundsätzlich bereit, sich aktiv für eine Photovoltaik-Großanlage vor Ort einzusetzen?
Instructions	(z.B. durch Mitgliedschaft in einer Bürgerinitiative)
Answer type	Binary question (yes, no)
Filter	Go to question 35.
Number	34
Question	Sind Sie grundsätzlich bereit, sich aktiv gegen eine Photovoltaik-Großanlage vor Ort einzusetzen?
Instructions	(z.B. durch Mitgliedschaft in einer Bürgerinitiative)
Answer type	Binary question (yes, no)
Number	35
Question	Als nächstes möchten wir gerne wissen, inwieweit Ihnen die Entfernung zwischen Ihrem Wohnhaus/ Ihrer Wohnung und der Photovoltaik-Großanlage wichtig ist.
Instructions	Bitte kreuzen Sie die zutreffende Antwort an.
Answer type	Single choice
Items	Für die Anlage(n) sollte ein Mindestabstand zu meinem Wohnhaus/ meiner Wohnung eingehalten werden. Die Entfernung der Anlage(n) zu meinem Wohnhaus/ meiner Wohnung spielt keine Rolle. Die Entfernung der Anlage(n) zu meinem Wohnhaus/ meiner Wohnung spielt keine Rolle aber die Anlage(n) sollte(n) nicht von meinem Wohnhaus/ meiner Wohnung aus sichtbar sein. Ich akzeptiere die Anlage(n) überhaupt nicht, egal in welcher Entfernung sie sich befindet.
Filter	If Für die Anlage(n) sollte ein Mindestabstand zu meinem Wohnhaus/ meiner Wohnung eingehalten werden, then go to question 36. Otherwise go to question 37.
Number	36
Question	Wie weit sollte eine Photovoltaik-Großanlage mindestens von Ihrem Wohnhaus/Ihrer Wohnung entfernt sein, damit Sie diese akzeptieren würden?
Instructions	Bitte klicken Sie auf den Balken, um den Abstand in Kilometern (km) zu wählen.

Answer type	Slide bar
Items	< 1 km, 1 km, 2 km, 3 km, 4 km, 5km, 6 km, 7 km, 8km, > 9 km

Heading	Bewertung von Windkraftanlagen

Bei der Windenergie wird die Energie des Windes in Elektrizität umgewandelt, üblicherweise mit Windturbinen mit einer horizontalen Achse und drei Blättern.

Bild: Windrad (Quelle: Andol, https://commons.wikimedia.org/wiki/File:N117,_Hohenahr_7.JPG, „N117, Hohenahr 7", https://creativecommons.org/licenses/by-sa/3.0/legalcode)

Number	37
Question	Windenergie stellt eine geeignete Form der Elektizitätserzeugung dar.
Instructions	Geben Sie bitte an, inwieweit diese Aussage Ihrer Meinung nach zutrifft.
Answer type	Likert scale 1 + don't know
Number	38
Question	Ich befürworte Windkraftanlagen in meiner Nachbarschaft.
Instructions	Geben Sie bitte an, inwieweit diese Aussage auf Sie zutrifft.
Answer type	Likert scale 1 + don't know
Number	39
Question	Wie negativ oder positiv bewerten Sie Windkraftanlagen in Ihrer Nachbarschaft gesamthaft?
Answer type	Likert scale 2 (reversed) + don't know
Filter	If *sehr positiv* or *positiv,* then go to question 40. If *sehr negativ* or *negativ*, then go to question 41. If *neutral* or *weiß nicht*, then go to question 42.

Number	40
Question	Sind Sie grundsätzlich bereit, sich aktiv für eine Windkraftanlage vor Ort einzusetzen?
Instructions	(z.B. durch Mitgliedschaft in einer Bürgerinitiative)
Answer type	Binary question (yes, no)
Filter	Go to question 42.
Number	41
Question	Sind Sie grundsätzlich bereit, sich aktiv gegen eine Windkraftanlage vor Ort einzusetzen?
Instructions	(z.B. durch Mitgliedschaft in einer Bürgerinitiative)
Answer type	Binary question (yes, no)
Number	42
Question	Als nächstes möchten wir gerne wissen, inwieweit Ihnen die Entfernung zwischen Ihrem Wohnhaus/ Ihrer Wohnung und der Windkraftanlage wichtig ist.
Instructions	Bitte kreuzen Sie die zutreffende Antwort an.
Answer type	Single choice
Items	Für die Anlage(n) sollte ein Mindestabstand zu meinem Wohnhaus/ meiner Wohnung eingehalten werden. Die Entfernung der Anlage(n) zu meinem Wohnhaus/ meiner Wohnung spielt keine Rolle. Die Entfernung der Anlage(n) zu meinem Wohnhaus/ meiner Wohnung spielt keine Rolle aber die Anlage(n) sollte(n) nicht von meinem Wohnhaus/ meiner Wohnung aus sichtbar sein. Ich akzeptiere die Anlage(n) überhaupt nicht, egal in welcher Entfernung sie sich befindet.
Filter	If Für die Anlage(n) sollte ein Mindestabstand zu meinem Wohnhaus/ meiner Wohnung eingehalten werden, then go to question 43. Otherwise go to question 44.
Number	43
Question	Wie weit sollte eine Windkraftanlage mindestens von Ihrem Wohnhaus/Ihrer Wohnung entfernt sein, damit Sie diese akzeptieren würden?
Instructions	Bitte klicken Sie auf den Balken, um den Abstand in Kilometern (km) zu wählen.
Answer type	Slide bar
Items	< 1 km, 1 km, 2 km, 3 km, 4 km, 5km, 6 km, 7 km, 8km, > 9 km

Heading	Bewertung von Biogasanlagen

Biogasanlagen wandeln verschiedene Arten von Biomasse durch Vergärung in ein energiereiches Gas um. In landwirtschaftlichen Biogasanlagen werden meist Gülle und/oder Mist sowie Reststoffe eingesetzt. In Deutschland kommen zudem häufig Energiepflanzen (insbesondere Mais) zum Einsatz. In nicht-landwirtschaftlichen Anlagen werden Abfälle aus der Biotonne oder aus der Lebensmittelindustrie verwendet. Bei den meisten Biogasanlagen wird das entstandene Gas vor Ort zur Strom- und Wärmeerzeugung genutzt. Alternativ gibt es einige Anlagen, die das Biogas auch in anderer Form nutzbar machen (z.B. Biomethan, Biomass to Liquid).

Bild: Biogasanlage (Aufnahme: Kira Schumacher)

Number	44
Question	Biogasanlagen stellen eine geeignete Form der Energiegewinnung dar.
Instructions	Geben Sie bitte an, inwieweit diese Aussage Ihrer Meinung nach zutrifft.
Answer type	Likert scale 1 + don't know
Number	45
Question	Ich befürworte Biogasanlagen in meiner Nachbarschaft.
Instructions	Geben Sie bitte an, inwieweit diese Aussage auf Sie zutrifft.
Answer type	Likert scale 1 + don't know
Number	46
Question	Wie negativ oder positiv bewerten Sie Biogasanlagen in Ihrer Nachbarschaft gesamthaft?
Answer type	Likert scale 2 (reversed) + don't know
Filter	If *sehr positiv* or *positiv,* then go to question 47. If *sehr negativ* or *negativ*, then go to question 48. If *neutral* or *weiß nicht*, then go to question 49.
Number	47
Question	Sind Sie grundsätzlich bereit, sich aktiv für eine Biogasanlage vor Ort einzusetzen?

Instructions	(z.B. durch Mitgliedschaft in einer Bürgerinitiative)
Answer type	Binary question (yes, no)
Filter	Go to question 49.
Number	48
Question	Sind Sie grundsätzlich bereit, sich aktiv gegen eine Biogasanlage vor Ort einzusetzen?
Instructions	(z.B. durch Mitgliedschaft in einer Bürgerinitiative)
Answer type	Binary question (yes, no)
Number	49
Question	Als nächstes möchten wir gerne wissen, inwieweit Ihnen die Entfernung zwischen Ihrem Wohnhaus/ Ihrer Wohnung und der Biogasanlage wichtig ist.
Instructions	Bitte kreuzen Sie die zutreffende Antwort an.
Answer type	Single choice
Items	Für die Anlage(n) sollte ein Mindestabstand zu meinem Wohnhaus/ meiner Wohnung eingehalten werden. Die Entfernung der Anlage(n) zu meinem Wohnhaus/ meiner Wohnung spielt keine Rolle. Die Entfernung der Anlage(n) zu meinem Wohnhaus/ meiner Wohnung spielt keine Rolle aber die Anlage(n) sollte(n) nicht von meinem Wohnhaus/ meiner Wohnung aus sichtbar sein. Ich akzeptiere die Anlage(n) überhaupt nicht, egal in welcher Entfernung sie sich befindet.
Filter	If Für die Anlage(n) sollte ein Mindestabstand zu meinem Wohnhaus/ meiner Wohnung eingehalten werden, then go to question 50. If question 9 is answered with *yes* and if question 10 is answered with *Biogasanlage,* then go to questions 51 and 52.
Number	50
Question	Wie weit sollte eine Biogasanlage mindestens von Ihrem Wohnhaus/Ihrer Wohnung entfernt sein, damit Sie diese akzeptieren würden?
Instructions	Bitte klicken Sie auf den Balken, um den Abstand in Kilometern (km) zu wählen.
Answer type	Slide bar
Items	< 1 km, 1 km, 2 km, 3 km, 4 km, 5km, 6 km, 7 km, 8km, > 9 km
Number	51
Question	Können Sie die Biogasanlage von Ihrem Haus/ Ihrer Wohnung aus sehen?
Answer type	Binary question (yes, no)
Number	52
Question	Ich bin mit der Standortwahl für die Biogasanlage(n) in meiner Gemeinde zufrieden.
Instructions	Geben Sie bitte an, inwieweit diese Aussage auf Sie zutrifft.

Answer type	Likert scale 1 + don't know
Instruction	Geben Sie bitte an, inwieweit Sie der Meinung sind, dass die folgenden Aussagen zutreffen. Bitte beachten Sie, dass es keine richtigen und falschen Antworten gibt und es um Ihre persönliche Einschätzung zu den Aussagen geht.
Number	53
Question	Biogasanlagen helfen das Klima zu schützen.
Answer type	Likert scale 1 + don't know
Number	54
Question	Biogasanlagen tragen dazu bei, die Abhängigkeit von Energieimporten zu verringern.
Answer type	Likert scale 1 + don't know
Number	55
Question	Die Biogasproduktion ist eine saubere Form der Energieerzeugung.
Answer type	Likert scale 1 + don't know
Number	56
Question	Biogasanlagen leisten einen Beitrag zur wirtschaftlichen Entwicklung meiner Region.
Answer type	Likert scale 1 + don't know
Number	57
Question	Die vermehrte Nutzung von Biogas wird den Energiepreis in die Höhe treiben.
Answer type	Likert scale 1 + don't know
Number	58
Question	Biogasanlagen verursachen Geruchsbelästigungen für die Anwohner.
Answer type	Likert scale 1 + don't know
Number	59
Question	Biogasanlagen verschandeln das Landschaftsbild.
Answer type	Likert scale 1 + don't know
Number	60
Question	Der Betrieb einer Biogasanlage birgt ein erhöhtes Unfallrisiko für Anwohner z.B. durch Gasaustritt oder das Auslaufen eines Behälters.
Answer type	Likert scale 1 + don't know
Number	61
Question	Durch die vermehrte Biogasnutzung werden Monokulturen (wie z.B. Mais) im Ackerbau überhand nehmen.
Answer type	Likert scale 1 + don't know
Number	62
Question	Der Betrieb von Biogasanlagen gefährdet Grundwasser oder Oberflächenwasser.
Answer type	Likert scale 1 + don't know

Number	63
Question	Das Verhältnis von Kosten (z.B. Geruchsbelästigung) und Nutzen (z.B. finanzieller Gewinn) von Biogasanlagen ist fair verteilt.
Answer type	Likert scale 1 + don't know
Number	64
Question	Die Erzeugung von Biogas stellt eine Konkurrenz zur Nahrungsmittelproduktion dar.
Answer type	Likert scale 1 + don't know
Number	65
Question	Welche Biomassearten sollten Ihrer Meinung nach bevorzugt zur Biogaserzeugung genutzt werden?
Instructions	Bitte kreuzen Sie alles an, was zutrifft.
Answer type	Multiple choices
Items	Reststoffe aus der Viehhaltung (Gülle, Mist) Bioabfälle aus Haushalten und Kommunen bzw. Gemeinden Bioabfälle aus der Gastronomie und der Nahrungsmittelindustrie (z.B. Frittierfette) Rasen- und Grünschnitt (z.B. aus Gärten, Grün- und Parkanlagen und Naturschutzwiesen) Energiepflanzen (Pflanzen, die zum Zwecke der Energiegewinnung angebaut und verwendet werden, wie z.B. Mais) Klärschlamm (bei der Abwasserreinigung anfallende dickflüssige Reststoffe) Sonstige: (free text field)

Heading	Information und Mitwirkung
Number	66
Question	Mir ist es wichtig, frühzeitig über geplante Biogasanlagen informiert zu werden.
Instructions	Geben Sie bitte an, inwieweit diese Aussage auf Sie zutrifft.
Answer type	Likert scale 1 + don't know
Number	67
Question	Bei der Realisierung einer Biogasanlage sollte die Meinung der Bevölkerung eingeholt werden.
Instructions	Geben Sie bitte an, inwieweit diese Aussage Ihrer Meinung nach zutrifft.
Answer type	Likert scale 1 + don't know
Number	68
Question	Die Bevölkerung sollte bei Einführungsprozessen von Biogasanlagen mitentscheiden.
Instructions	Geben Sie bitte an, inwieweit diese Aussage Ihrer Meinung nach zutrifft.
Answer type	Likert scale 1 + don't know

Number	69
Question	Die Bevölkerung sollte große Teile von Planungsprozessen von Biogasanlagen selbst gestalten.
Instructions	Geben Sie bitte an, inwieweit diese Aussage Ihrer Meinung nach zutrifft.
Answer type	Likert scale 1 + don't know

Heading	Bewertung von Energieautarkie
Number	70
Question	Ist Ihnen der Begriff "Energieautarkie" bekannt?
Answer type	Binary question (yes, no)
Introduction	Energieautarkie Definition: Energieautarkie" bedeutet, dass die gesamte lokale Elektrizitätsnachfrage (z.B. einer Region oder einer Gemeinde) aus lokalen, teilweise Erneuerbaren Energien vor Ort gedeckt wird. Somit muss keine Elektrizität aus dem Stromnetz importiert werden. In diesem Fall spricht man von „Energieautarkie", „Energie-Selbstsuffizienz" oder „Energieunabhängigkeit". Hintergrund: Die konventionelle Energieversorgung erfolgt in der Regel zentralisiert in wenigen großen Kraftwerken, die über weite Entfernungen Elektrizität transportieren. Im Gegensatz dazu werden Erneuerbare Energieanlagen wie Wind, Photovoltaik und Biogas dezentral errichtet. Die erzeugte Elektrizität muss daher nicht weit transportiert werden und wird zumindest teilweise vor Ort direkt verwendet. Inwiefern die erzeugte Elektrizität lokal verwendet werden kann, hängt dabei von der lokalen Nachfrage ab.
Number	71
Question	Ansätze, die zu einem höheren Grad lokaler Energieautarkie führen, halte ich für generell sinnvoll.
Instructions	Geben Sie bitte an, inwieweit diese Aussage auf Sie zutrifft.
Answer type	Likert scale 1 + don't know
Number	72
Question	Auf welcher Ebene finden Sie Energieautarkie am sinnvollsten?
Answer type	Multiple choices
Items	Gebäude Wohnkomplex/ Wohneinheit Stadtteil/ Quartier Dorf/ Gemeinde/ Stadt Region Bundesland/ Kanton Land, Kontinent

Number	73
Question	Ich befürworte Ansätze in meiner Nachbarschaft, die zu einer höheren Energieautarkie führen.
Instructions	Geben Sie bitte an, inwieweit diese Aussage auf Sie zutrifft.
Answer type	Likert scale 1 + don't know
Number	74
Question	Wie negativ oder positiv bewerten Sie Ansätze zur Energieautarkie in Ihrer Nachbarschaft gesamthaft?
Answer type	Likert scale 2 (reversed) + don't know
Filter	If *sehr positiv* or *positiv*, then go to question 75. If *sehr negativ* or *negativ*, then go to question 76. If *neutral* or *weiß nicht,* then go to question 77.
Number	75
Question	Sind Sie grundsätzlich bereit, sich aktiv für mehr Energieautarkie vor Ort einzusetzen?
Instructions	(z.B. durch Mitgliedschaft in einer Bürgerinitiative)
Answer type	Binary question (yes, no)
Filter	Go to question 77.
Number	76
Question	Sind Sie grundsätzlich bereit, sich aktiv gegen mehr Energieautarkie vor Ort einzusetzen?
Instructions	(z.B. durch Mitgliedschaft in einer Bürgerinitiative)
Answer type	Binary question (yes, no)
Heading	Kommentare oder Anmerkungen
Question	Wie ging es Ihnen beim Ausfüllen des Fragebogens? Wenn Sie noch Kommentare oder Anmerkungen haben, können Sie diese hier eintragen:
Answer type	(Free text field)
Note of thanks	Die eingegebenen Daten wurden erfolgreich gespeichert. Für Ihre Unterstützung bedanken wir uns ganz herzlich!

Table B-3: Questionnaire case study 2

Introduction letter
Sehr geehrte Damen und Herren, im Auftrag des durch die Europäische Union im Rahmen des Interreg IV Programms geförderten Projektes „OUI Biomasse“ führt das Karlsruher Institut für Technologie (KIT) eine Befragung zur gesellschaftlichen Akzeptanz von Biogasanlagen in der Oberrheinregion durch. In den drei Ländern der Oberrheinregion, Deutschland, Frankreich und der Schweiz werden zu diesem Zweck die direkten Anwohner ausgewählter Biogasanlagen zu Ihrer Einstellung gegenüber der Anlage und den wahrgenommenen Auswirkungen befragt. Ihr Haushalt wurde ausgewählt, da sich Ihr Wohnort in einem Radius von 1 km zu einer Biogasanlage befindet und somit von den Auswirkungen am stärksten betroffen ist. Mit diesem Brief möchten wir Sie über die Befragung informieren und ganz herzlich darum bitten, dass Sie daran teilnehmen. Selbstverständlich ist Ihre Teilnahme freiwillig. Die Daten werden ohne Ihren Namen und Adresse erhoben und ausgewertet. Die Befragung unterliegt den Bestimmungen des Datenschutzes. Bitte beachten Sie auch die beiliegende „Erklärung zum Datenschutz“. Um die dort genannte Vorgehensweise gewährleisten zu können, möchten wir Sie bitten, **keinen Absender** auf den frankierten Rückumschlag zu schreiben. Wir hoffen, Ihr Interesse geweckt zu haben und bitten Sie ganz herzlich, uns durch Ihre Mitarbeit zu unterstützen! Sollten Sie noch weitere Fragen zu dieser Befragung, zur Studie selbst oder dem Projekt „OUI Biomasse“ haben, können Sie sich gerne schriftlich oder telefonisch mit uns in Verbindung setzen. Am KIT steht Ihnen für Rückfragen Frau Kira Schumacher (Telefon: + 49 XXX) zur Verfügung. Wir rufen Sie auch gerne zurück, damit Ihnen keine Kosten entstehen. Wir möchten uns schon heute sehr herzlich für Ihre Mitwirkung an dieser wichtigen Befragung bedanken.

Heading	Erklärung zum Datenschutz
Das Forschungsprojekt „OUI Biomasse“ wird vom Karlsruher Institut für Technologie (KIT) koordiniert. Das KIT trägt daher auch die datenschutzrechtliche Verantwortung für diese Studie. Die Befragung wird gemäß den gesetzlichen Bestimmungen Landesdatenschutzgesetzes Baden-Württemberg (LDSG-BW) durchgeführt. 1. Die Teilnahme an der Befragung ist freiwillig. Auch die Angaben zu den jeweiligen Fragen erfolgen freiwillig, so dass Sie als Teilnehmer selbst entscheiden können, ob Sie alle Fragen beantworten oder die eine oder andere Frage auslassen.	

2. Die Daten werden ohne Ihren Namen und ohne die Anschrift erhoben. Die Erhebung von Daten, wie Geschlecht, Alter, Ort usw. erfolgt ausschließlich zu dem Zweck, wissenschaftlich fundierte Aussagen zur gesellschaftlichen Akzeptanz von Biogasanlagen zu bekommen. Es werden keinerlei Versuche unternommen, aus diesen Angaben Rückschlüsse auf konkrete Personen zu ziehen.
3. Die Auswertungsergebnisse werden ausschließlich in aggregierter Form (in Tabellen und /oder Graphiken) veröffentlicht, so dass Rückschlüsse auf Einzelpersonen nicht möglich sind.

Heading	Fragen zur lokalen Biogasanlage
Number	1
Question	Ist Ihnen die Biogasanlage in Ihrer Nachbarschaft bekannt?
Answer type	Binary question (yes, no)
Number	2
Question	Besteht zwischen Ihnen und dem Biogasanlagenbetreiber ein Beschäftigungsverhältnis oder unterhalten Sie Kunden- oder Geschäftsbeziehungen zur Biogasanlage vor Ort?
Answer type	Binary question (yes, no)

Heading	Erneuerbare Energien
Number	3
Question	Ich finde, dass Erneuerbare Energien (zum Bsp. Solar-, Wind-, Bioenergie) eine wichtige Rolle bei der zukünftigen Stromerzeugung spielen sollten.
Instructions	Bitte machen Sie in jede Zeile ein Kreuz!
Answer type	Likert scale 1 + don't know
Number	4
Question	Grundsätzlich befürworte ich erneuerbare Energieanlagen in meiner Nachbarschaft.
Instructions	Bitte machen Sie in jede Zeile ein Kreuz!
Answer type	Likert scale 1 + don't know
Number	5
Question	Welche Energieformen sollten Ihrer Meinung nach zukünftig bevorzugt genutzt werden?
Instructions	Kreuzen Sie bitte alles an, was zutrifft!
Answer type	Multiple choice
Items	Solarenergie, Windenergie, Bioenergie, Geothermie Wasserkraft, Kohle, Kernenergie, Sonstige

Heading	Allgemeine Bewertung von Biogasanlagen
Number	6
Question	Die Nutzung von Biogasanlagen stellt eine geeignete Form der Energiegewinnung dar.
Instructions	Bitte machen Sie in jede Zeile ein Kreuz!
Answer type	Likert scale 1 + don't know
Number	7
Question	Ich befürworte die Biogasanlage in meiner Nachbarschaft.
Instructions	Bitte machen Sie in jede Zeile ein Kreuz!
Answer type	Likert scale 1 + don't know
Number	8
Question	Wie negativ oder positiv bewerten Sie die Biogasanlage in Ihrer Nachbarschaft gesamthaft?
Instructions	Bitte machen Sie in nur ein Kreuz!
Answer type	Linkert scale 2 + don't know
Filter	If *sehr positiv* or *positiv,* then go to question 9. If *sehr negativ* or *negativ*, then go to question 10. If *neutral* or *weiß nicht*, then go to question 11.
Number	9
Question	Sind Sie grundsätzlich bereit, sich aktiv für eine Biogasanlage vor Ort einzusetzen?
Answer type	Binary question (yes, no) + don't know
Filter	Go to question 11.
Number	10
Question	Sind Sie grundsätzlich bereit, sich aktiv gegen eine Biogasanlage vor Ort einzusetzen?
Answer type	Binary question (yes, no) + don't know

Heading	Kosten und Nutzen der Biogasanlage
Number	11
Question	Das Verhältnis von Kosten (z.B. Geruchsbelästigung) und Nutzen (z.B. finanzieller Gewinn) der Biogasanlage ist fair verteilt.
Instructions	Bitte machen Sie in jede Zeile ein Kreuz!
Answer type	Likert scale 1 + don't know
Number	12
Question	Die Biogasanlage hilft das Klima zu schützen.
Instructions	Bitte machen Sie in jede Zeile ein Kreuz!
Answer type	Likert Scale 1 + don't know
Number	13
Question	Die Biogasanlage wirkt sich positiv auf unsere Gemeinde als Wirtschaftsstandort aus.
Instructions	Bitte machen Sie in jede Zeile ein Kreuz!

Answer type	Likert scale 1 + don't know
Number	14
Question	Von der Realisierung der Biogasanlage profitieren wir alle zum Schluss.
Instructions	Bitte machen Sie in jede Zeile ein Kreuz!
Answer type	Likert scale 1 + don't know
Number	15
Question	Die vermehrte Nutzung von Biogas wird den Energiepreis in die Höhe treiben.
Instructions	Bitte machen Sie in jede Zeile ein Kreuz!
Answer type	Likert scale 1 + don't know
Number	16
Question	Die Nutzung der Biogasanlage hat einen negativen Einfluss auf die Grundstückswerte in unserer Gemeinde.
Instructions	Bitte machen Sie in jede Zeile ein Kreuz!
Answer type	Likert scale 1 + don't know
Number	17
Question	Die Biogasanlage schadet mir finanziell (zum Bsp. reduzierter Grundstückswert, Verlust von Kunden, Ausbleiben von Touristen)
Instructions	Bitte machen Sie in jede Zeile ein Kreuz!
Answer type	Likert scale 1 + don't know

Heading	Information und Beteiligung bei der Planung der Biogasanlage
Number	18
Question	Der Planungsprozess der lokalen Anlage ist fair abgelaufen.
Instructions	Bitte machen Sie in jede Zeile ein Kreuz!
Answer type	Likert scale 1 + don't know
Number	19
Question	Während des Planungsprozesses der lokalen Anlage standen ausreichend Informationen zur Verfügung
Instructions	Bitte machen Sie in jede Zeile ein Kreuz!
Answer type	Likert scale 1 + don't know
Number	20
Question	Die Meinung der Bevölkerung zur lokalen Biogasanlage wurde eingeholt.
Instructions	Bitte machen Sie in jede Zeile ein Kreuz!
Answer type	Likert scale 1 + don't know
Number	21
Question	Die Entscheidungen bei der Realisierung der lokalen Biogasanlage wurden gemeinsam mit der Bevölkerung getroffen.
Instructions	Bitte machen Sie in jede Zeile ein Kreuz!
Answer type	Likert scale 1 + don't know
Number	22

Question	Die Bevölkerung war an der Realisierung der lokalen Biogasanlage maßgeblich beteiligt
Instructions	Bitte machen Sie in jede Zeile ein Kreuz!
Answer type	Likert scale 1 + don't know
Number	23
Question	Mir ist es wichtig, frühzeitig über geplante Biogasanlagen informiert zu werden.
Instructions	Bitte machen Sie in jede Zeile ein Kreuz!
Answer type	Likert scale 1 + don't know
Number	24
Question	Bei der Realisierung einer Biogasanlage sollte die Meinung der Bevölkerung eingeholt werden.
Instructions	Bitte machen Sie in jede Zeile ein Kreuz!
Answer type	Likert scale 1 + don't know
Number	25
Question	Die Bevölkerung sollte bei Einführungsprozessen von Biogasanlagen mitentscheiden.
Instructions	Bitte machen Sie in jede Zeile ein Kreuz!
Answer type	Likert scale 1 + don't know
Number	26
Question	Die Bevölkerung sollte große Teile von Planungsprozessen von Biogasanlagen selbst gestalten.
Instructions	Bitte machen Sie in jede Zeile ein Kreuz!
Answer type	Likert scale 1 + don't know

Heading	Aussagen zum Anlagenbetreiber
Number	27
Question	Auf die Aussagen des Anlagenbetreibers kann ich mich verlassen.
Instructions	Bitte machen Sie in jede Zeile ein Kreuz!
Answer type	Likert scale 1 + don't know
Number	28
Question	Der Anlagebetreiber nimmt Rücksicht auf betroffene Anwohner und Anwohnerinnen.
Instructions	Bitte machen Sie in jede Zeile ein Kreuz!
Answer type	Likert scale 1 + don't know
Number	29
Question	Der Anlagenbetreiber weiß, wie er seine Anlage zu betreiben hat.
Instructions	Bitte machen Sie in jede Zeile ein Kreuz!
Answer type	Likert scale 1 + don't know

Heading	Geruch der von der Anlage ausgeht
Number	30
Question	Wie häufig haben Sie im vergangenen Jahr Geruch wahrgenommen?
Instructions	Bitte machen Sie nur <u>ein</u> Kreuz!
Answer type	Single choice
Items	Nahezu täglich oder öfters Mehrmals pro Woche Mehrmals pro Monat Mehrmals pro Jahr Einmal pro Jahr oder seltener Weiß nicht
Number	31
Question	Wie empfinden Sie den Geruch?
Instructions	Bitte machen Sie nur <u>ein</u> Kreuz!
Answer type	Likert scale 2 (reversed) + don't know
Number	32
Question	Wie stark ist der Geruch, welchen Sie wahrnehmen?
Instructions	Bitte machen Sie nur <u>ein</u> Kreuz!
Answer type	Likert scale 3 + don't know

Heading	Wirkung der Anlage auf Ihr Wohlbefinden
Number	33
Question	Durch die Biogasanlagen fühle ich mich in meiner Umgebung nicht mehr wohl.
Instructions	Bitte machen Sie in jede Zeile <u>ein</u> Kreuz!
Answer type	Likert scale 1 + don't know
Number	34
Question	Der Anblick der Biogasanlage stört mich.
Instructions	Bitte machen Sie in jede Zeile <u>ein</u> Kreuz!
Answer type	Likert scale 1 + don't know

Heading	Standort von Biogasanlagen
Number	35
Question	Ich bin mit der Standortwahl für die Biogasanlage in meiner Gemeinde zufrieden.
Instructions	Bitte machen Sie in jede Zeile <u>ein</u> Kreuz!
Answer type	Likert Scale 1 + don't know
Number	36
Question	Für Biogasanlagen sollte ein Mindestabstand zu Wohngebieten eingehalten werden.

Instructions	Bitte machen Sie in jede Zeile ein Kreuz!
Answer type	Likert scale 1 + don't know
Number	37
Question	Können Sie die Biogasanlage von Ihrem Haus/ Ihrer Wohnung aus sehen?
Answer type	Binary question (yes, no) + don't know
Number	38
Question	Wie weit müsste eine Biogasanlage von Ihrem Wohnort entfernt sein, damit Sie diese akzeptieren würden?
Answer type	Single choice
Items	Weniger als 1 Kilometer Zwischen 1 Kilometer und 3 Kilometern Zwischen 3,1 Kilometern und 8 Kilometern Zwischen 8,1 Kilometern und 11 Kilometern Mehr als 11 Kilometer

Heading	Fragen zu Ihrer Person
Die folgenden Fragen helfen, die Ergebnisse dieser Umfrage zu untersuchen bzw. auszuwerten. Dabei ist es wichtig, dass die Forscher/innen die Antworten auf die bisher beantworteten Fragen nach Merkmalen auswerten können, die gesellschaftliche Gruppen beschreiben. Hierfür benötigen wir detaillierte Angaben zu Ihrer Person, damit wir Sie einer entsprechenden Gruppe zuordnen können. Die Forscher/innen werten die Daten nicht für Ihre Person aus, sondern für solche Gruppen, zu denen man Sie zum Beispiel entsprechend Ihrer Altersgruppe, Ihrem Geschlecht oder Ihrem Schulabschluss zuordnen kann.	
Number	39
Question	Sind Sie
Answer type	Single choice
Items	männlich weiblich
Number	40
Question	Bitte ordnen Sie Ihr Alter in folgende Kategorien ein:
Instructions	Die Ergebnisse dieser Befragung werden auch für unterschiedliche Altersgruppen ausgewertet.
Answer type	Single choice
Items	zwischen 16 und 20 Jahren zwischen 21 und 30 Jahren zwischen 31 und 40 Jahren zwischen 41 und 50 Jahren zwischen 51 und 60 Jahren zwischen 61 und 70 Jahren zwischen 71 und 80 Jahren über 81 Jahre

Number	41
Question	In welchem Ort wohnen Sie?
Instructions	Damit ist der Wohnsitz gemeint, der in der Nähe der Biogasanlage liegt. Diese Angabe ist sehr wichtig für die spätere Auswertung des Fragebogens!
Answer type	(Free text field)
Items	Ort (ohne Angabe der Adresse): *(free text field)*
Number	42
Question	Seit wann leben Sie an diesem Ort?
Instructions	Bitte geben Sie das Jahr an.
Answer type	(Free text field)
Items	Jahr (vierstellig, zum Bsp. 1984): *(free text field)*
Number	43
Question	Sind Sie Eigentümer dieses Hauses/ dieser Wohnung?
Answer type	Binary question (yes, no)
Number	44
Question	Wohnen in Ihrem Haushalt Kinder unter 16 Jahren?
Instructions	Diese Frage bezieht sich auf Kinder, die permanent in Ihrem Haushalt wohnen
Answer type	Binary question (yes, no)
Number	45
Question	Wie viele Jahre waren Sie insgesamt in Schule, Hochschule, oder anderer schulischer Ausbildung, ohne betriebliche Ausbildung?
Instructions	Sollten Sie ein Schuljahr wiederholt haben, zählen dieses bitte NICHT mit. Wenn Sie noch Schüler(in) oder Student(in) sind, zählen Sie bitte die Jahre, die Sie bereits in Schule oder Hochschule verbracht haben (inklusive dem laufenden Jahr).
Answer type	(Free text field)
Items	Anzahl der Jahre: *(free text field)* Weiß nicht: *(check box)*
Number	46
Question	Welche Erwerbssituation passt für Sie?
Instructions	Bitte kreuzen Sie zutreffendes an:
Answer type	Single choice
Items	Erwerbstätig (einschließlich: Vollzeit, Teilzeit, geringfügig erwerbstätig) Gelegentlich oder unregelmäßig beschäftigt In einer beruflichen Ausbildung/Lehre Nicht erwerbstätig (einschließlich: Schüler(n)/-innen oder Studierende, die nicht gegen Geld arbeiten, Arbeitslosen, Vorruheständler(n)/-innen, Rentner(n)/-innen ohne Nebenverdienst)

Heading	Abschließende Fragen und Bemerkungen
Question	Wie ging es Ihnen beim Ausfüllen des Fragebogens?
Instructions	Wenn Sie noch Kommentare oder Anmerkungen haben, können Sie das hier eintragen:
Answer type	(Free text field)
Note of thanks	Für Ihre Unterstützung bedanken wir uns ganz herzlich! Bitte stecken Sie den ausgefüllten Fragebogen in den rückfrankierten Umschlag und werfen Sie ihn in einen Briefkasten oder geben Sie ihn auf einer Poststelle Ihrer Wahl ab. Bitte verzichten Sie aus Datenschutzgründen auf die Angabe eines Absenders auf dem Rückumschlag.

Table B-4: Questionnaire case study 3

Heading	Información personal
Number	1
Question	¿Eres…?
Answer type	Single choice
Items	Hombre Mujer
Number	2
Question	¿Cuántos años tienes?
Answer type	(Free text field)

Heading	Duración de la encuesta
Para completar correctamente la encuesta necesitarás entre 25 y 35 minutos. Para realizarla correctamente, te recomendamos que accedas cuando dispongas de este tiempo Te garantizamos que la recompensa que recibirás será proporcional a tu esfuerzo. Es tu derecho.	

Heading	Conocimientos acerca de las energías renovables
Number	3
Question	Según lo que sabes, has visto, leído o escuchado, ¿qué es una energía renovable?
Answer type	Single choice
Items	Es la energía que se obtiene de fuentes naturales virtualmente inagotables Es la energía que obtenemos del reciclaje

	Es la energía gratuita Es la energía que se genera en cada hogar No sé
Number	4
Question	¿Cómo calificarías tus conocimientos generales respecto a las energías renovables?
Instructions	Elige la opción que mejor describa tus conocimientos de las energías renovables.
Answer type	Likert scale 2 (reversed) + don't know

Introduction
Ahora verás unas breves explicaciones de las distintas energías renovables

Energías renovables

Las energías renovables son muy diversas. Hay muchas fuentes de energía diferentes y todavía más tecnologías para usarlas. En esta encuesta el término "Energías renovables" se refiere principalmente a la fotovoltaica, eólica y a la bioenergía. A continuación encontrarás una breve descripción de estas tecnologías. Por favor, lee atentamente estas descripciones.

Fotovoltaica

En la tecnología fotovoltaica la energía del sol se transforma en electricidad. Aquí se puede distinguir entre instalaciones de pequeña y gran escala. Una instalación fotovoltaica a pequeña escala se instala por ejemplo, en el techo de una vivienda familiar, y una instalación fotovoltaica a gran escala ,por ejemplo, en un espacio abierto o en el techo de una bodega grande.

Imagen: Instalación fotovoltaica a pequeña escala (Fuente de imagen: Georg Slickers, https://commons.wikimedia.org/wiki/File:Berlin_pv-system_block-103_20050309_p1010367.jpg, „Berlin pv-system block-103 20050309 p1010367", https://creativecommons.org/licenses/by-sa/3.0/legalcode)

Imagen: instalación fotovoltaica a gran escala (Fuente de imagen: Ceinturion, https://commons.wikimedia.org/wiki/File:SolarPowerPlantSerpa.jpg, „SolarPowerPlantSerpa“, https://creativecommons.org/licenses/by-sa/3.0/legalcode)

Energía eólica

La energía eólica transforma la energía del viento en electricidad. Esto se hace habitualmente mediante turbinas de viento con un pilar horizontal y tres aspas.

Imagen: Turbinas de viento (Fuente de imagen: Andol, https://commons.wikimedia.org/wiki/File:N117,_Hohenahr_7.JPG, „N117, Hohenahr 7“, https://creativecommons.org/licenses/by-sa/3.0/legalcode)

Central de biomasa
Las centrales de biomasa generan calor al quemar biomasa leñosa. Las centrales de biomasa de cogeneracion tambien generan energía eléctrica. En Chile se emplean principalmente los residuos de la industria forestal (por ejemplo, aserrín o residuos de plantaciones forestales) pero también se puede usar residuos de madera de producción propia. En la mayoría de las centrales, se usa el calor directo para otros procesos (por ejemplo, secar la madera) y la electricidad se alimenta a la red.

Imagen: Central de biomasa (Fuente de imagen: Sensenschmied, https://commons.wikimedia.org/wiki/File:Biomassekraftwerk_mit_Lager.jpg, „Biomassekraftwerk mit Lager", https://creativecommons.org/licenses/by-sa/3.0/legalcode)

Heading	Sistemas de energías renovables en tu barrio
Number	5
Question	¿Eres propietario/a de tu vivienda?
Answer type	Binary question (yes, no)
Number	6
Question	¿Hay alguna instalación de energía renovable ubicada en un radio de un kilómetro de tu vivienda? (Por ejemplo, instalación fotovoltaica, eólica o de bioenergía)
Instructions	Esto se refiere al lugar donde tienes tu actividad principal
Answer type	Binary question (yes, no) + don't know
Filter	If *yes,* then go to question 7. Otherwise go to question 8.
Number	7
Question	¿De qué tipo de instalación de energía renovable se trata?
Instructions	Marca todas las que correspondan.
Answer type	Multiple choices
Items	Instalación fotovoltaica a pequeña escala, Instalación fotovoltaica de gran escala, Instalación eólica, Central de biomasa, Energía geotérmica, Central hidráulica, Otras: (free text field)

Heading	Valoración de diferentes tecnologías
Number	8
Question	En tu opinión, ¿qué fuentes de energía deberían priorizarse para Chile en el futuro?
Instructions	Marca todas las que correspondan.
Answer type	Multiple choices
Items	Energía solar Energía eólica Bioenergía Energía geotérmica Energía hidráulica Carbón Energía nuclear Petróleo Gas natural Otras: (free text field)
Number	9
Question	Creo que las energías renovables (por ejemplo, la energía solar, eólica y bioenergía) deberían tener un papel importante en la futura generación de energía eléctrica de Chile.
Instructions	Indica en qué medida estás de acuerdo con la siguiente afirmación.
Answer type	Likert scale 1 + don't know
Number	10
Question	Estoy a favor de las energías renovables en mi barrio.
Instructions	El barrio se refiere al radio de un kilómetro alrededor de tu vivienda. Indica en qué medida estás de acuerdo con la siguiente afirmación.
Answer type	Likert scale 1 + don't know

Heading	Fotovoltaica a pequeña escala

En la tecnología fotovoltaica, la energía del sol se transforma en electricidad. Aquí se puede distinguir entre instalaciones de pequeña y gran escala. Una instalación fotovoltaica a pequeña escala se instala, por ejemplo, en el techo de una vivienda unifamiliar.

Imagen: Instalación fotovoltaica a pequeña escala (Fuente de imagen: Georg Slickers, https://commons.wikimedia.org/wiki/File:Berlin_pv-system_block-103_20050309_p1010367.jpg, „Berlin pv-system block-103 20050309 p1010367", https://creativecommons.org/licenses/by-sa/3.0/legalcode)

Heading	Valoración de las instalaciones fotovoltaicas a pequeña escala
Number	11
Question	Las instalaciones fotovoltaicas a pequeña escala representan una forma conveniente de generación de electricidad.
Instructions	Indica en qué medida estás de acuerdo con la siguiente afirmación.
Answer type	Likert scale 1 + don't know
Number	12
Question	Estoy a favor de las instalaciones fotovoltaicas a pequeña escala en mi barrio.
Instructions	Indica en qué medida estás de acuerdo con la siguiente afirmación.
Answer type	Likert scale 1 + don't know
Number	13
Question	¿Cómo calificarías la posibilidad de futuras instalaciones fotovoltaicas a pequeña escala en tu barrio?
Answer type	Likert scale 2
Filter	If *muy positivamente* or *positivamente*, then go to question 14. If *muy negativamente* or *negativamente*, then go to question 15. If ni positivamente ni negativamente, then go to question 16.

Number	14
Question	¿Estarías dispuesto/a, en principio, a movilizarte activamente a favor de una instalación fotovoltaica a pequeña escala en tu barrio?
Instructions	(Por ejemplo, mediante la participación en una iniciativa ciudadana)
Answer type	Binary question (yes, no)
Number	15
Question	¿Estarías dispuesto/a, en principio, a movilizarte activamente en contra de una instalación fotovoltaica a pequeña escala en tu barrio?
Instructions	(Por ejemplo, mediante la participación en una iniciativa ciudadana)
Answer type	Binary question (yes, no)
Number	16
Question	A continuación indica hasta qué punto es importante para ti la distancia entre tu vivienda y la instalación fotovoltaica a pequeña escala.
Instructions	Marca la respuesta que corresponda.
Answer type	Single choice
Items	Me opongo totalmente a las instalaciones, independientemente de a qué distancia se encuentre La distancia desde las instalaciones hasta mi casa no es importante La distancia desde las instalaciones hasta mi casa no es importante pero las instalaciones no deben verse desde mi vivienda Debe existir una distancia mínima desde las instalaciones hasta mi vivienda
Filter	If Debe existir una distancia mínima desde las instalaciones hasta mi vivienda, then go to question 17. Otherwise go to question 18.
Number	17
Question	¿Cuál es la distancia mínima que debería existir entre la instalación fotovoltaica a pequeña escala y tu vivienda, para que aceptaras su instalación?
Instructions	Haz clic en la barra para elegir la distancia en kilómetros (km).
Answer type	Slide bar
Items	menos de 1 km, 1 km, 2 km, 3 km, 4 km, 5km, 6 km, 7 km, 8km, más de 9 km

Heading	Fotovoltaica a gran escala

En la tecnología fotovoltaica la energía del sol se transforma en electricidad. Aquí se puede distinguir entre instalaciones de pequeña y gran escala. Una instalación fotovoltaica a gran escala se instala, por ejemplo, en un espacio libre o en el techo de una bodega grande.

Imagen: instalación fotovoltaica a gran escala (Fuente de imagen: Ceinturion, https://commons.wikimedia.org/wiki/File:SolarPowerPlantSerpa.jpg, „SolarPowerPlantSerpa", https://creativecommons.org/licenses/by-sa/3.0/legalcode)

Heading	Valoración de las instalaciones fotovoltaicas a gran escala
Number	18
Question	Las instalaciones fotovoltaicas a gran escala representan una forma conveniente de generación de electricidad.
Instructions	Indica en qué medida estás de acuerdo con la siguiente afirmación.
Answer type	Likert scale 1 + don't know
Number	19
Question	Estoy a favor de las instalaciones fotovoltaicas a gran escala en mi barrio.
Instructions	Indica en qué medida estás de acuerdo con la siguiente afirmación.
Answer type	Likert scale 1 + don't know
Number	20
Question	¿Cómo calificarías la posibilidad de futuras instalaciones fotovoltaicas a gran escala en tu barrio?
Answer type	Likert scale 2
Filter	If *muy positivamente* or *positivamente*, then go to question 21. If muy *negativamente* or *negativamente,* then go to question 22. If ni positivamente ni negativamente, then go to question 23.

Number	21
Question	¿Estarías dispuesto/a, en principio, a movilizarte activamente a favor de una instalación fotovoltaica a gran escala en tu barrio?
Instructions	(Por ejemplo, mediante la participación en una iniciativa ciudadana)
Answer type	Binary question (yes, no)
Filter	Go to question 23.
Number	22
Question	¿Estarías dispuesto/a, en principio, a movilizarte activamente en contra de una instalación fotovoltaica a gran escala en tu barrio?
Instructions	(Por ejemplo, mediante la participación en una iniciativa ciudadana)
Answer type	Binary question (yes, no)
Number	23
Question	A continuación indica hasta qué punto es importante la distancia entre tu vivienda y la instalación fotovoltaica a gran escala.
Instructions	Marca la respuesta que corresponda.
Answer type	Single choice
Items	Me opongo totalmente a las instalaciones, independientemente de a qué distancia se encuentre La distancia desde las instalaciones hasta mi casa no es importante La distancia desde las instalaciones hasta mi casa no es importante pero las instalaciones no deben verse desde mi vivienda Debe existir una distancia mínima desde las instalaciones hasta mi vivienda
Filter	If Debe existir una distancia mínima desde las instalaciones hasta mi vivienda, then go to question 24. Otherwise go to question 25.
Number	24
Question	¿Cuál es la distancia mínima que debería existir entre la instalación fotovoltaica a gran escala y tu vivienda, para que aceptaras la instalación?
Instructions	Haz clic en la barra para elegir la distancia en kilómetros (km).
Answer type	Slide bar
Items	menos de 1 km, 1 km, 2 km, 3 km, 4 km, 5km, 6 km, 7 km, 8km, más de 9 km

Heading	Energía eólica

En la energía eólica la energía del viento se transforma en electricidad. Esto se hace habitualmente mediante turbinas de viento con un pilar horizontal y tres aspas.

Imagen: Turbinas de viento (Fuente de imagen: Andol, https://commons.wikimedia.org/wiki/File:N117,_Hohenahr_7.JPG, „N117, Hohenahr 7“, https://creativecommons.org/licenses/by-sa/3.0/legalcode)

Heading	Valoración de las instalaciones de energía eólica
Number	25
Question	Las instalaciones de energía eólica representan una forma conveniente de generación de electricidad.
Instructions	Indica en qué medida estás de acuerdo con la siguiente afirmación.
Answer type	Likert scale 1 + don't know
Number	26
Question	Estoy a favor de las instalaciones de energía eólica en mi barrio.
Instructions	Indica en qué medida estás de acuerdo con la siguiente afirmación.
Answer type	Likert scale 1 + don't know
Number	27
Question	¿Cómo calificarías la posibilidad de futuras instalaciones de energía eólica en tu barrio?
Answer type	Likert scale 2
Filter	If *muy positivamente* or *positivamente*, then go to question 28. If *muy negativamente* or *negativamente,* then go to question 29. If ni positivamente ni negativamente, then go to question 30.

Number	28
Question	¿Estarías dispuesto/a, en principio, a movilizarte activamente a favor de una instalación de energía eólica en tu barrio?
Instructions	(Por ejemplo, mediante la participación en una iniciativa ciudadana)
Answer type	Binary question (yes, no)
Filter	Go to question 30.
Number	29
Question	¿Estarías dispuesto/a, en principio, a movilizarte activamente en contra de una instalación de energía eólica en tu barrio?
Instructions	(Por ejemplo, mediante la participación en una iniciativa ciudadana)
Answer type	Binary question (yes, no)
Number	30
Question	A continuación, indica hasta qué punto es importante la distancia entre tu vivienda y la instalación de energía eólica.
Instructions	Marca la respuesta que corresponda.
Answer type	Single choice
Items	Me opongo totalmente a las instalaciones, independientemente de a qué distancia se encuentre La distancia desde las instalaciones hasta mi casa no es importante La distancia desde las instalaciones hasta mi casa no es importante pero las instalaciones no deben verse desde mi vivienda Debe existir una distancia mínima desde las instalaciones hasta mi vivienda
Filter	If Debe existir una distancia mínima desde las instalaciones hasta mi vivienda, then go to question 31. Otherwise go to question 32.
Number	31
Question	¿Cuál es la distancia mínima que debería existir entre la instalación de energía eólica y tu vivienda, para que aceptaras su instalación?
Instructions	Haz clic en la barra para elegir la distancia en kilómetros (km).
Answer type	Slide bar
Items	menos de 1 km, 1 km, 2 km, 3 km, 4 km, 5km, 6 km, 7 km, 8km, más de 9 km

Heading	Central de biomasa

Las centrales de biomasa generan calor al quemar biomasa leñosa. Las centrales de biomasa de cogeneracion tambien generan energía eléctrica. En Chile se emplean principalmente los residuos de la industria forestal (por ejemplo, aserrín o residuos de plantaciones forestales) pero también se puede usar residuos de madera de producción propia. En la mayoría de las centrales se usa el calor directo para otros procesos (por ejemplo, secar la madera) y la electricidad se alimenta a la red

Imagen: Central de biomasa (Fuente de imagen: Sensenschmied, https://commons.wikimedia.org/wiki/File:Biomassekraftwerk_mit_Lager.jpg, „Biomassekraftwerk mit Lager", https://creativecommons.org/licenses/by-sa/3.0/legalcode)

Heading	Valoración de centrales de biomasa
Number	32
Question	Las centrales de biomasa representan una forma conveniente de generación de electricidad.
Instructions	Indica en qué medida estás de acuerdo con la siguiente afirmación.
Answer type	Likert scale 1 + don't know
Number	33
Question	Estoy a favor de las centrales de biomasa en mi barrio.
Instructions	Indica en qué medida estás de acuerdo con la siguiente afirmación.
Answer type	Likert scale 1 + don't know
Number	34
Question	¿Cómo calificarías la posibilidad de futuras instalaciones de centrales de biomasa en tu barrio?
Answer type	Likert scale 2
Filter	If *muy positivamente* or *positivamente*, then go to question 35. If *muy negativamente* or *negativamente*, then go to question 36. If ni positivamente ni negativamente, then go to question 37.

Number	35
Question	¿Estarías dispuesto/a, en principio, a movilizarte activamente a favor de una central de biomasa en tu barrio?
Instructions	(Por ejemplo, mediante la participación en una iniciativa ciudadana)
Answer type	Binary question (yes, no)
Filter	Go to question 37

Number	36
Question	¿Estarías dispuesto/a, en principio, a movilizarte activamente en contra de una central de biomasa en tu barrio?
Instructions	(Por ejemplo, mediante la participación en una iniciativa ciudadana)
Answer type	Binary question (yes, no)

Number	37
Question	A continuación, indica hasta qué punto es importante la distancia entre tu vivienda y una central de biomasa.
Instructions	Marca la respuesta que corresponda.
Answer type	Single choice
Items	Me opongo totalmente a las instalaciones, independientemente de a qué distancia se encuentre La distancia desde las instalaciones hasta mi casa no es importante La distancia desde las instalaciones hasta mi casa no es importante pero las instalaciones no deben verse desde mi vivienda Debe existir una distancia mínima desde las instalaciones hasta mi vivienda
Filter	If Debe existir una distancia mínima desde las instalaciones hasta mi vivienda, then go to question 38. Otherwise go to question 39.

Number	38
Question	¿Cuál es la distancia mínima que debería existir entre la central de biomasa y tu vivienda, para que aceptaras su instalación?
Instructions	Haz clic en la barra para elegir la distancia en kilómetros (km).
Answer type	Slide bar
Items	menos de 1 km, 1 km, 2 km, 3 km, 4 km, 5km, 6 km, 7 km, 8km, más de 9 km

Number	40
Question	Las centrales de biomasa contribuyen a proteger el clima.
Instructions	Indica en qué medida estás de acuerdo con las siguientes afirmaciones.
Answer type	Likert scale 1 + don't know
Number	41
Question	Las centrales de biomasa contribuyen a disminuir la dependencia de energías importadas (por ejemplo, gas y petróleo).
Instructions	Indica en qué medida estás de acuerdo con las siguientes afirmaciones.
Answer type	Likert scale 1 + don't know
Number	42
Question	La bioenergía es una forma limpia de generación de electricidad.
Instructions	Indica en qué medida estás de acuerdo con las siguientes afirmaciones.
Answer type	Likert scale 1 + don't know
Number	43
Question	Las centrales de biomasa pueden ser un aporte al desarrollo económico de mi región.
Instructions	Indica en qué medida estás de acuerdo con las siguientes afirmaciones.
Answer type	Likert scale 1 + don't know
Number	44
Question	El mayor uso de la bioenergía hará que aumente el precio de la energía.
Instructions	Indica en qué medida estás de acuerdo con las siguientes afirmaciones.
Answer type	Likert scale 1 + don't know
Number	45
Question	Las centrales de biomasa pueden ocasionar olores molestos para los habitantes.
Instructions	Indica en qué medida estás de acuerdo con las siguientes afirmaciones.
Answer type	Likert scale 1 + don't know
Number	46
Question	Las centrales de biomasa dañan el paisaje.
Instructions	Indica en qué medida estás de acuerdo con las siguientes afirmaciones.
Answer type	Likert scale 1 + don't know

Number	47
Question	El funcionamiento de una central de biomasa implica un mayor riesgo de accidentes, por ejemplo, incendios y explosiones.
Instructions	Indica en qué medida estás de acuerdo con las siguientes afirmaciones.
Answer type	Likert scale 1 + don't know
Number	48
Question	El mayor uso de la bioenergía haría que los monocultivos (como por ejemplo, plantación de pinos y eucaliptos) aumenten excesivamente.
Instructions	Indica en qué medida estás de acuerdo con las siguientes afirmaciones.
Answer type	Likert scale 1 + don't know
Number	49
Question	El funcionamiento de las centrales de biomasa pone en peligro las aguas subterráneas o las aguas superficiales.
Instructions	Indica en qué medida estás de acuerdo con las siguientes afirmaciones.
Answer type	Likert scale 1 + don't know
Number	50
Question	La relación de impactos negativos (por ejemplo, olores molestos) y positivos (por ejemplo, beneficio financiero) de las centrales de bioenergía se compensan equitativamente.
Instructions	Indica en qué medida estás de acuerdo con las siguientes afirmaciones.
Answer type	Likert scale 1 + don't know
Number	51
Question	La generación de bioenergía constituye una competencia para la producción de alimentos.
Instructions	Indica en qué medida estás de acuerdo con las siguientes afirmaciones.
Answer type	Likert scale 1 + don't know
Number	52
Question	Para mí es importante que me informen anticipadamente de las centrales de biomasa planificadas.
Instructions	Indica en qué medida estás de acuerdo con las siguientes afirmaciones.
Answer type	Likert scale 1 + don't know

Number	53
Question	Debería pedirse la opinión de la población antes de construir una central de biomasa.
Instructions	Indica en qué medida estás de acuerdo con las siguientes afirmaciones.
Answer type	Likert scale 1 + don't know
Number	54
Question	La población debería participar en los procesos de planification de las centrales de biomasa.
Instructions	Indica en qué medida estás de acuerdo con las siguientes afirmaciones.
Answer type	Likert scale 1 + don't know
Number	55
Question	La población debería participar en la mayor parte de los procesos de planificación de centrales de biomasa.
Instructions	Indica en qué medida estás de acuerdo con las siguientes afirmaciones.
Answer type	Likert scale 1 + don't know

Heading	Tema social y participación
Number	56
Question	Es importante que los costes de la electricidad sean una parte menor del presupuesto del hogar.
Instructions	Indica en qué medida estás de acuerdo con las siguientes afirmaciones.
Answer type	Likert scale 1 + don't know
Number	57
Question	Se debería compensar a las personas que se vean afectadas negativamente por los proyectos de generación de electricidad.
Instructions	Indica en qué medida estás de acuerdo con las siguientes afirmaciones.
Answer type	Likert scale 1 + don't know
Number	58
Question	Mi opinión sobre las centrales de energía renovable es positiva, siempre que se hagan con la participación de la comunidad local.
Instructions	Indica en qué medida estás de acuerdo con las siguientes afirmaciones.
Answer type	Likert scale 1 + don't know
Number	59
Question	Al final todos se benefician del uso de las energías renovables.
Instructions	Indica en qué medida estás de acuerdo con las siguientes afirmaciones.
Answer type	Likert scale 1 + don't know

Number	60
Question	La relación de impactos negativos (por ejemplo, alteración del paisaje, presión sobre el medio ambiente) y positivos (por ejemplo, provisión de calefacción/electricidad, beneficio económico) de las centrales de energía renovable se compensa equitativamente.
Instructions	Indica en qué medida estás de acuerdo con las siguientes afirmaciones.
Answer type	Likert scale 1 + don't know
Number	61
Question	Puedo confiar en las informaciones que entregan los responsables de proyectos de energía renovable.
Instructions	Indica en qué medida estás de acuerdo con las siguientes afirmaciones.
Answer type	Likert scale 1 + don't know
Number	62
Question	El proceso de planificación de centrales de energía renovable se desarrolla de forma transparente y justa.
Instructions	Indica en qué medida estás de acuerdo con las siguientes afirmaciones.
Answer type	Likert scale 1 + don't know
Number	63
Question	Hay información disponible suficiente sobre las centrales de energía renovable.
Instructions	Indica en qué medida estás de acuerdo con las siguientes afirmaciones.
Answer type	Likert scale 1 + don't know
Number	64
Question	Se consulta la opinión de la población sobre las centrales de energía renovable.
Instructions	Indica en qué medida estás de acuerdo con las siguientes afirmaciones.
Answer type	Likert scale 1 + don't know
Number	65
Question	La construcción de centrales de energía renovable se deciden conjuntamente con la comunidad.
Instructions	Indica en qué medida estás de acuerdo con las siguientes afirmaciones.
Answer type	Likert scale 1 + don't know
Number	66
Question	La población participa en procesos de planificación de centrales de energía renovable.
Instructions	Indica en qué medida estás de acuerdo con las siguientes afirmaciones.
Answer type	Likert scale 1 + don't know

Number	67
Question	Es importante para Chile generar electricidad a partir de fuentes renovables, para ser independiente de otros países.
Instructions	Indica en qué medida estás de acuerdo con las siguientes afirmaciones.
Answer type	Likert scale 1 + don't know
Number	68
Question	Las energías renovables son una fuente de energía confiable.
Instructions	Indica en qué medida estás de acuerdo con las siguientes afirmaciones.
Answer type	Likert scale 1 + don't know
Number	69
Question	La generación de energía renovable pueden ser un aporte al desarrollo económico de Chile.
Instructions	Indica en qué medida estás de acuerdo con las siguientes afirmaciones.
Answer type	Likert scale 1 + don't know
Number	70
Question	Las centrales de energía renovable pueden ser un aporte al desarrollo económico de mi región.
Instructions	Indica en qué medida estás de acuerdo con las siguientes afirmaciones.
Answer type	Likert scale 1 + don't know

Heading	Información personal
Number	71
Question	¿Perteneces a alguna etnia/ pueblo originario?
Answer type	Binary question (yes, no) + *prefiero no responder*
Filter	If *yes,* then go to question 82. If *no* or *prefiero no responder*, then go to question 83.
Number	72
Question	¿Qué etnia/ pueblo originario?
Answer type	(Free text field)

Heading	Tus comentarios al respecto de la encuesta
Number	73
Question	¿Qué te pareció responder al cuestionario?
Instructions	Si tienes comentarios o sugerencias, puedes ingresarlos aquí.
Answer type	(Free text field)

Number	74
Question	Por último ¿qué te ha parecido la encuesta? Selecciona de 1 a 5 estrellas para indicar si la encuesta te ha parecido muy mal hecha (1) o muy bien hecha (5)
Picture	★ ★ ★ ★ ☆
Answer type	Star ranking

Heading	Prueba de attención
Question	Por ello, te pedimos que selecciones la opción "Nunca":
Instructions	Esta pregunta nos permitirá saber si estás prestando atención y comprobar que tus respuestas se están guardando correctamente.
Answer type	Single choice
Items	Siempre A veces Nunca
Filter	If *correct*, go to next question.
Question	Por ello, te pedimos que selecciones en qué año estamos actualmente:
Instructions	Esta pregunta nos permitirá saber si estás prestando atención y comprobar que tus respuestas se están guardando correctamente.
Answer type	Single choice
Items	2016 2017 2018 2019 2020
Filter	If *correct*, go to next question.
Comment	One of these questions appears randomly to test the attention of the respondent. There are various questions. The two questions described above serve as examples.

C Screenshot of the Questionnaire (Case Study 1)

2%

Liebe Teilnehmerin, lieber Teilnehmer,

vielen Dank, dass Sie an dieser Umfrage zur Akzeptanz Erneuerbarer Energien und Energieautarkie teilnehmen. Der Ausbau Erneuerbarer Energien führt unter anderem dazu, dass die Zivilgesellschaft zunehmend in ihrem direkten Umfeld von den Auswirkungen Erneuerbarer Energieanlagen betroffen ist. Dabei stoßen Erneuerbare Energienanlagen in der direkten Nachbarschaft nicht immer auf Zustimmung. Die Akzeptanz der lokalen Bevölkerung spielt somit für die Umsetzung solcher Projekte eine wichtige Rolle. Wir am Karlsruher Institut für Technologie interessieren uns daher für Ihre Einstellung zu Erneuerbaren Energien und zum Konzept der Energieautarkie.

Erneuerbare Energien sind sehr vielfältig. Es gibt viele verschiedene Energiequellen und noch mehr Technologien um diese zu verwerten. In dieser Umfrage sind mit dem Begriff "Erneuerbare Energien" hauptsächlich die Technologien Wind, Photovoltaik und Bioenergie (insbesondere Biogas) gemeint. Hier finden Sie eine kurze Erklärung der einzelnen Energietechnologien. Die Erklärungen zu den einzelnen Erneuerbaren Energien werden später im Fragebogen an geeigneter Stelle wiederholt.

Windenergie

Bei der Windenergie wird die Energie des Windes in Elektrizität umgewandelt.
Dies geschieht üblicherweise mit Windturbinen mit einer horizontalen Achse und drei Blättern.

Bild: Windrad
(Quelle:https://upload.wikimedia.org/wikipedia/commons/f/fd/N117%2C_Hohenahr_7.JPG)

27%

Wie negativ oder positiv bewerten Sie Photovoltaik-Kleinanlagen in Ihrer Nachbarschaft gesamthaft?

sehr negativ	negativ	neutral	positiv	sehr positiv	weiß nicht
○	○	○	○	○	○

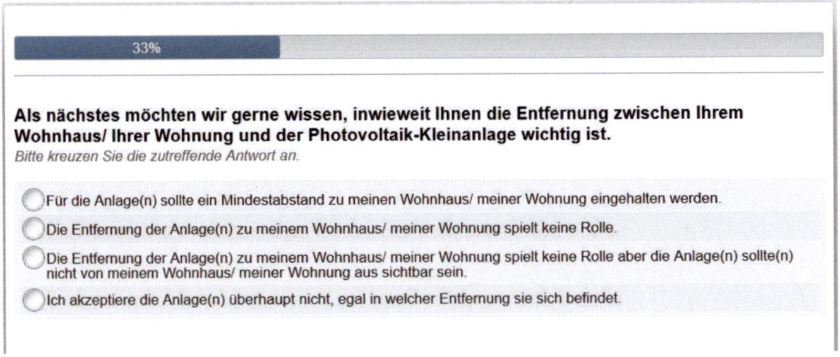

33%

Als nächstes möchten wir gerne wissen, inwieweit Ihnen die Entfernung zwischen Ihrem Wohnhaus/ Ihrer Wohnung und der Photovoltaik-Kleinanlage wichtig ist.

Bitte kreuzen Sie die zutreffende Antwort an.

- Für die Anlage(n) sollte ein Mindestabstand zu meinen Wohnhaus/ meiner Wohnung eingehalten werden.
- Die Entfernung der Anlage(n) zu meinem Wohnhaus/ meiner Wohnung spielt keine Rolle.
- Die Entfernung der Anlage(n) zu meinem Wohnhaus/ meiner Wohnung spielt keine Rolle aber die Anlage(n) sollte(n) nicht von meinem Wohnhaus/ meiner Wohnung aus sichtbar sein.
- Ich akzeptiere die Anlage(n) überhaupt nicht, egal in welcher Entfernung sie sich befindet.

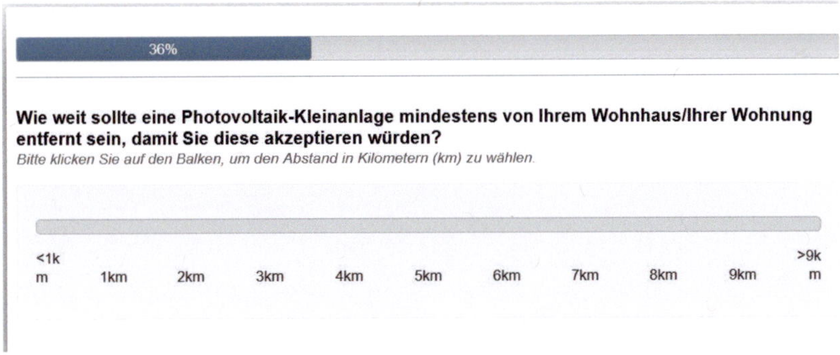

36%

Wie weit sollte eine Photovoltaik-Kleinanlage mindestens von Ihrem Wohnhaus/Ihrer Wohnung entfernt sein, damit Sie diese akzeptieren würden?

Bitte klicken Sie auf den Balken, um den Abstand in Kilometern (km) zu wählen.

<1km 1km 2km 3km 4km 5km 6km 7km 8km 9km >9km

Figure C-1: Screenshots of the questionnaire (case study 1)

References

Aas, Ø., Devine-Wright, P., Tangeland, T., Batel, S., Ruud, A., 2014. Public beliefs about high-voltage powerlines in Norway, Sweden and the United Kingdom: A comparative survey. Energy Research & Social Science 2, 30–37. 10.1016/j.erss.2014.04.012.

Adams, S., 1965. Inequity in social exchange. Academic Press, New York.

Adimark, 2017. Mapa Socioeconómico de Chile: Nivel socioeconómico de los hogares del país basado en datos del Censo. http://www.adimark.cl/medios/estudios/informe_mapa_socioeconomico_de_chile.pdf. Accessed 18 May 2018.

Agora Energiewende, 2016. Energy Transition in the Power Sector in Europe: State of Affairs in 2015. https://www.agora-energiewende.de/en/publications/energy-transition-in-the-power-sector-in-europe-state-of-affairs-in-2016-2/. Accessed 6 September 2018.

Aitken, M., 2010. Why we still don't understand the social aspects of wind power: A critique of key assumptions within the literature. Energy Policy 38, 1834–1841. 10.1016/j.enpol.2009.11.060.

Arnstein, S.R., 1969. A Ladder Of Citizen Participation. Journal of the American Institute of Planners 35, 216–224.

Avril, S., Mansilla, C., Busson, M., Lemaire, T., 2012. Photovoltaic energy policy: Financial estimation and performance comparison of the public support in five representative countries. Energy Policy 51, 244–258. 10.1016/j.enpol.2012.07.050.

Balcombe, P., Rigby, D., Azapagic, A., 2015. Energy self-sufficiency, grid demand variability and consumer costs: Integrating solar PV, Stirling engine CHP and battery storage. Applied Energy 155, 393–408. 10.1016/j.apenergy.2015.06.017.

Batel, S., Castro, P., Devine-Wright, P., Howarth, C., 2016. Developing a critical agenda to understand pro-environmental actions: Contributions from Social Representations and Social Practices Theories. WIREs Clim Change 7, 727–745. 10.1002/wcc.417.

Batel, S., Devine-Wright, P., Tangeland, T., 2013. Social acceptance of low carbon energy and associated infrastructures: A critical discussion. Energy Policy 58, 1–5. 10.1016/j.enpol.2013.03.018.

Bertsch, V., Hall, M., Weinhardt, C., Fichtner, W., 2016. Public acceptance and preferences related to renewable energy and grid expansion policy: Empirical insights for Germany. Energy 114, 465–477. 10.1016/j.energy.2016.08.022.

Betakova, V., Vojar, J., Sklenicka, P., 2015. Wind turbines location: How many and how far? Applied Energy 151, 23–31. 10.1016/j.apenergy.2015.04.060.

BFE - Bundesamt für Energie, 2014. Liste aller KEV-Bezügler im Jahr 2013. http://www.bfe.admin.ch/themen/00612/02073/index.html?dossier_id=02166&lang=de. Accessed 17 May 2017.

BFE - Bundesamt für Energie, 2016a. Schweizerische Elektrizitätsstatistik 2015 / Statistique suisse de l' électricité 2015. http://www.bfe.admin.ch/php/modules/publikationen/stream.php?extlang=de&name=de_448053209.pdf. Accessed 13 September 2018.

BFE - Bundesamt für Energie, 2016b. Erneuerbare Energien. https://www.bfe.admin.ch/bfe/de/home/versorgung/erneuerbare-energien.html. Accessed 4 March 2019.

BFS - Bundesamt für Statistik, 2014. Statistik der Bevölkerung und der Haushalte, STATPOP 2014. www.statistik.admin.ch. Accessed 17 May 2017.

BMWi - Bundesministerium für Wirtschaft und Energie, 2015. Die Energie der Zukunft: Vierter Monitoring-Bericht zur Energiewende. Ein gutes Stück Arbeit, Berlin. https://www.bmwi.de/Redaktion/DE/Publikationen/Energie/vierter-monitoring-bericht-energie-der-zukunft.pdf?__blob=publicationFile&v=24.

Busse, M., Siebert, R., 2018. Acceptance studies in the field of land use—A critical and systematic review to advance the conceptualization of acceptance and acceptability. Land Use Policy 76, 235–245. 10.1016/j.landusepol.2018.05.016.

Butler, C., Parkhill, K., Pidgeon, N., 2013. Deliberating energy transitions in the UK – Transforming the UK Energy System: Public Values, Attitudes and Acceptability. http://www.ukerc.ac.uk/publications/transforming-the-uk-energy-system-public-values-attitudes-and-acceptability-deliberating-energy-system-transitions-in-the-uk.html. Accessed 30 July 2018.

Bühner, M., 2011. Einführung in die Test- und Fragebogenkonstruktion, 3rd ed. Pearson, München.

Center for International Environmental Law, 2017. FACT SHEET: Chile's Alto Maipo Hydroelectric Project (PHAM). http://www.ciel.org/wp-content/uploads/2017/02/FactSheet_AltoMaipo_Chile.pdf. Accessed 15 May 2018.

CNE - Comisión Nacional de Energía, 2019. Capacidad installada de generación. https://www.cne.cl/estadisticas/electricidad/. Accessed 23 March 2019.

Cohen, J., 2013. Statistical Power Analysis for the Behavioral Sciences, 2nd ed. Taylor and Francis, Hoboken.

Cohen, J., Cohen, P., West, S.G., Aiken, L.S., 2003. Applied multiple regression/correlation analysis for the behavioral sciences, 3rd ed. Erlbaum, Mahwah, New Jersey.

Consejo de Defensa de la Patagonia Chilena, 2018. El Problema / Monopolio y Concentración. http://www.patagoniasinrepresas.cl/final/contenido.php?seccion=problema_monopolio. Accessed 15 May 2018.

Daniel, F.-J., Bailly, V., 2015. Socio-technical structuring of biogas in France. RA6.2 Intermediary report. UMR GESTE ENGEES-IRSTEA. http://www.oui-biomasse.info. Accessed 10 May 2017.

Dermont, C., Ingold, K., Kammermann, L., Stadelmann-Steffen, I., 2017. Bringing the policy making perspective in: A political science approach to social acceptance. Energy Policy 108, 359–368. 10.1016/j.enpol.2017.05.062.

Deshmukh, R., Bharvirkar, R., Gambhir, A., Phadke, A., 2012. Changing Sunshine: Analyzing the dynamics of solar electricity policies in the global context. Renewable and Sustainable Energy Reviews 16, 5188–5198. 10.1016/j.rser.2012.04.020.

Deuschle, J., Hauser, W., Sonnberger, M., Tomaschek, J., Brodecki, L., Fahl, U., 2015. Energie-Autarkie und Energie-Autonomie in Theorie und Praxis. Zeitschrift für Energiewirtschaft 2015.

Deutsch-Französische-Schweizerische Oberrheinkonferenz, 2015. Oberrhein / Rhin Supérieur 2014: Zahlen und Fakten / Faits et chiffres, Kehl.

Devine-Wright, P., 2003. A cross-national, comparative analysis of public understanding of, and attitudes towards nuclear, renewable and fossil-fuel energy sources, in: Crossing Boundaries - The Value of Interdisciplinary Research, In: Proceedings of the Third Conference of the EPUK (Environmental Psychology in the UK) Network, pp. 160-173.

Devine-Wright, P., 2005. Beyond NIMBYism: towards an integrated framework for understanding public perceptions of wind energy. Wind Energy 8, 125–139. 10.1002/we.124.

Devine-Wright, P., 2007. Reconsidering public attitudes and public acceptance of renewable energy technologies: a critical review. http://www.sed.manchester.ac.uk/research/beyond_nimbyism/. Accessed 28 April 2019.

Devine-Wright, P., 2009. Rethinking NIMBYism: The role of place attachment and place identity in explaining place-protective action. J. Community. Appl. Soc. Psychol. 19, 426–441. 10.1002/casp.1004.

Devine-Wright, P., Batel, S., Aas, O., Sovacool, B., Labelle, M.C., Ruud, A., 2017. A conceptual framework for understanding the social acceptance of energy infrastructure: Insights from energy storage. Energy Policy 107, 27–31. 10.1016/j.enpol.2017.04.020.

DGRV - Deutscher Genossenschafts- und Raiffeisenverband, 2014. Energiegenossenschaften: Ergebnisse der Umfrage des DGRV und seiner Mitgliedsverbände, Bundesgeschäftsstelle Energiegenossenschaften, Berlin.

Diekmann, A., Preisendörfer, P., 2003. Green and Greenback. Rationality and Society 15, 441–472. 10.1177/1043463103154002.

DigitalGlobe, 2014. DigitalGlobe. https://www.digitalglobe.com/. Accessed 11 November 2014.

Echeverria, C., Coomes, D., Salas, J., Rey-Benayas, J.M., Lara, A., Newton, A., 2006. Rapid deforestation and fragmentation of Chilean Temperate Forests. Biological Conservation 130, 481–494. 10.1016/j.biocon.2006.01.017.

EEG - Erneuerbare-Energien-Gesetz, 2000. Gesetz für den Vorrang Erneuerbarer Energien (Erneuerbare-Energien-Gesetz-EEG) sowie zur Änderung des Energiewirtschaftsgesetzes und des Mineralölsteuergesetzes. Bundesgesetzblatt.

EEG - Erneuerbare-Energien-Gesetz, 2004. Erneuerbare-Energien-Gesetz: Gesetz für den Vorrang Erneuerbarer Energien (Erneuerbare-Energien-Gesetz-EEG).

EEG - Erneuerbare-Energien-Gesetz, 2009. Erneuerbare-Energien-Gesetz: Gesetz für den Vorrang Erneuerbarer Energien.

EEG - Erneuerbare-Energien-Gesetz, 2012. Erneuerbare-Energien-Gesetz: Gesetz für den Vorrang Erneuerbarer Energien.

EEG - Erneuerbare-Energien-Gesetz, 2014. Erneuerbare-Energien-Gesetz: Gesetz für den Vorrang Erneuerbarer Energien.

EEG - Erneuerbare-Energien-Gesetz, 2017. Erneuerbare-Energien-Gesetz: Gesetz für den Vorrang Erneuerbarer Energien.

ElCom, 2018. Tarif-Rohdaten der schweizerischen Verteilnetzbetreiber. https://www.elcom.admin.ch/elcom/de/home/themen/strompreise/tarif-rohdaten-verteilnetzbetreiber.html. Accessed 5 March 2019.

Eisenhardt, K.M., Graebner, M.E., 2007. Theory building from cases: opportunities and challenges. Academy of Management Journal 50, 25–32. 10.5465/amj.2007.24160888.

Emol, 2014. Comité de Ministros rechaza proyecto Hidroaysén aunque empresa podrá apelar. http://www.emol.com/noticias/economia/2014/06/10/664572/comite-de-ministros-rechaza-proyecto-hidroaysen.html. Accessed 15 May 2018.

Engelken, M., Römer, B., Drescher, M., Welpe, I., 2016. Transforming the energy system: Why municipalities strive for energy self-sufficiency. Energy Policy 98, 365–377. 10.1016/j.enpol.2016.07.049.

Eswarlal, V.K., Vasudevan, G., Dey, P.K., Vasudevan, P., 2014. Role of community acceptance in sustainable bioenergy projects in India. Energy Policy 73, 333–343. 10.1016/j.enpol.2014.04.019.

Eurostat, 2014. Wohneigentumsquoten in ausgewählten europäischen Ländern im Jahr 2014. http://de.statista.com/statistik/daten/studie/155734/umfrage/wohneigentumsquoten-in-europa. Accessed 20 June 2015.

Eurostat, 2018. Electricity prices, Second semester of 2015-2017 (EUR per kWh). http://ec.europa.eu/eurostat/statistics-explained/index.php?title=File:Electricity_prices,_Second_semester_of_2015-2017_(EUR_per_kWh).png. Accessed 5 March 2019.

Fast, S., 2013. Social Acceptance of Renewable Energy: Trends, Concepts, and Geographies. Geography Compass 7, 853–866. 10.1111/gec3.12086.

Field, A., 2013. Discovering statistics using IBM SPSS statistics: And sex and drugs and rock 'n' roll, 4th ed. Sage, Los Angeles, London, New Delhi, Singapore, Washington DC.

Frederiks, E.R., Stenner, K., Hobman, E.V., 2015. Household energy use: Applying behavioural economics to understand consumer decision-making and behaviour. Renewable and Sustainable Energy Reviews 41, 1385–1394. 10.1016/j.rser.2014.09.026.

Gabler Wirtschaftslexikon, 2018. Erneuerbare Energien: Definition. https://wirtschaftslexikon.gabler.de/definition/erneuerbare-energien-53729/version-276797. Accessed 7 February 2019.

Gaede, J., Rowlands, I.H., 2018. Visualizing social acceptance research. Energy Research & Social Science 40, 142–158. 10.1016/j.erss.2017.12.006.

Gaede, J., Rowlands, I.H., 2019. The value of multiple perspectives. Energy Research & Social Science. 10.1016/j.erss.2018.12.007.

Gamma, K., Stauch, A., Wüstenhagen, R., 2017. 7th Consumer Barometer Renewable Energy. http://www.iwoe.unisg.ch/kundenbarometer. Accessed 29 November 2018.

GeoRhena, 2017. Kartensammlung. http://www.georhena.eu/de/Kartensammlung. Accessed 29 November 2017.

German Biogas Association, 2014. Biogas Segment Statistics 2014. Development of the number of biogas plants and the total installed electric output in megawatt [MW] in Germany (as of 11/2015). http://www.biogas.org/edcom/webfvb.nsf/id/DE_Branchenzahlen/$file/15-11-19_Biogasindustryfigures_2014-2015_english.pdf. Accessed 9 February 2016.

Gesis - Leibnitz-Institut für Sozialwissenschaften, 2019. Overview of Comparative Surveys Worldwide. www.gesis.org/ComparativeSurveyOverview. Accessed 30 March 2019.

Goedkoop, F., Devine-Wright, P., 2016. Partnership or placation?: The role of trust and justice in the shared ownership of renewable energy projects. Energy Research & Social Science 17, 135–146. 10.1016/j.erss.2016.04.021.

Gold, S., 2011. Bio-energy supply chains and stakeholders. Mitigation and Adaptation Strategies for Global Change 16, 439–462. 10.1007/s11027-010-9272-8.

Gold, S., Seuring, S., 2011. Supply chain and logistics issues of bio-energy production. Journal of Cleaner Production 19, 32–42. 10.1016/j.jclepro.2010.08.009.

Greving, B., 2009. Messen und Skalieren von Sachverhalten, in: Albers, S., Klapper, D., Konradt, U., Walter, A., Wolf, J. (Eds.), Methodik der empirischen Forschung. Gabler Verlag, Wiesbaden.

Griesen, M., 2010. Akzeptanz von Biogasanlagen. Shaker, Aachen.

Gross, C., 2007. Community perspectives of wind energy in Australia: The application of a justice and community fairness framework to increase social acceptance. Energy Policy 35, 2727–2736. 10.1016/j.enpol.2006.12.013.

Hair, J.F., Babin, B.J., Anderson, R.E., Black, W.C., 2014. Multivariate data analysis. Pearson, Harlow, Essex.

Harkness, J.A., Pennell, B.-E., Schoua-Glusberg, A., 2004. Survey Questionnaire Translation and Assessment, in: S. Presser, J. M. Rothgeb, M. P. Couper, J. T. Lessler, E. Martin, J. Martin, E. Singer (Eds.), Methods for Testing and Evaluating Survey Questionnaires. Wiley, Hoboken, N.J., pp. 453–473.

Harkness, J.A., Villar, A., Edwards, B., 2010. Translation, adaptation, and design, in: Harkness, J.A., Braun, M., Edwards, B., Johnson, T.P., Lyberg, L.E., Mohler, P.P., Pennell, B.-E., Smith, T.W. (Eds.), Survey methods in multinational, multiregional, and multicultural contexts. Wiley, Hoboken, N.J.

Harold, J., Bertsch, V., Lawrence, T., Hall, M., 2018. Drivers of people's preferences for spatial proximity to energy infrastructure technologies: a cross-country analysis. https://www.esri.ie/pubs/WP583.pdf. Accessed 21 July 2018.

Hauff, J., Heider, C., Arms, H., Gerber, J., Schilling, M., 2011. Gesellschaftliche Akzeptanz als Säule der energiepolitischen Zielsetzung 61, 85–87.

Herbes, C., Jirka, E., Braun, J.P., Pukall, K., 2014. Der gesellschaftliche Diskurs um den „Maisdeckel“ vor und nach der Novelle des Erneuerbare-Energien-Gesetzes (EEG) 2012. GAIA, 100–108.

Hildebrand, J., Rau, I., Schweizer-Ries, P., 2012. Die Bedeutung dezentraler Beteiligungsprozesse für die Akzeptanz des Ausbaus erneuerbarer Energien: Eine umweltpsychologische Betrachtung. Informationen zur Raumentwicklung, 491–501.

Hitzeroth, M., Megerle, A., 2013. Renewable Energy Projects: Acceptance Risks and Their Management. Renewable and Sustainable Energy Reviews 27, 576–584. 10.1016/j.rser.2013.07.022.

Hoffstede, U., Stelzer, M., Hahn, H., Beil, M., Krautkremer, B., Kasten, J., Beyrich, W., Holzhammer, U., 2018. Vorbereitung und Begleitung bei der Erstellung eines Erfahrungsberichts gemäß § 97 Erneuerbare-Energien-Gesetz: Teilvorhaben II a: Biomasse; Zwischenbericht. https://www.erneuerbare-energien.de/EE/Redaktion/DE/Downloads/bmwi_de/bericht-eeg-2-biomasse.pdf?__blob=publicationFile&v=8. Accessed 19 April 2019.

Höltinger, S., Salak, B., Schauppenlehner, T., Scherhaufer, P., Schmidt, J., 2016. Austria's wind energy potential – A participatory modeling approach to assess socio-political and market acceptance. Energy Policy 98, 49–61. 10.1016/j.enpol.2016.08.010.

Homburg, C., Müller, M., Klarmann, M., 2011. When Should the Customer Really Be King? On the Optimum Level of Salesperson Customer Orientation in Sales Encounters. Journal of Marketing 75, 55–74.

Hübner, G., 2012. Die Akzeptanz von erneuerbaren Energien: Einstellungen und Wirkungen, in: Felix Ekardt, Bettina Hennig, Herwig Unnerstall (Ed.), Erneuerbare Energien. Ambivalenzen, Governance, Rechtsfragen. Metropolis-Verlag, Marburg.

Hübner, G., Hahn, C., 2013. Akzeptanz des Stromnetzausbaus in Schleswig-Holstein: Abschlussbericht zum Forschungsprojekt 15.06.2015, Halle. http://www.buergerdialog-stromnetz.de/sites/default/files/mediathek/hubner_hahn_bericht_2013.pdf.

Huijts, N., Molin, E., Steg, L., 2012. Psychological factors influencing sustainable energy technology acceptance: A review-based comprehensive framework. Renewable and Sustainable Energy Reviews 16, 525–531. 10.1016/j.rser.2011.08.018.

IEA - International Energy Agency, 2016a. Energy Policies of IEA Countries: France 2016 Review: IEA. https://webstore.iea.org/energy-policies-of-iea-countries-france-2016-review. Accessed 30 July 2018.

IEA - International Energy Agency, 2016b. Non-conventional renewable energy law (Law 20.257): IEA.

IEA - International Energy Agency, 2018a. Electricity Information (2018 edition): Statistics.

IEA - International Energy Agency, 2018b. Energy policies beyond IEA countries, Chile. http://www.iea.org/publications/freepublications/publication/EnergyPoliciesBeyondIEACountriesChile2018Review.pdf. Accessed 17 May 2018.

IEA - International Energy Agency, 2019. IEA/IRENA Joint Policies and measues database: IEA. https://www.iea.org/policiesandmeasures/renewableenergy/. Accessed 27 February 2019.

InE - Instituto Nacional de Estadícas Chile, 2017a. Estadísticas Sobre Pueblos Indígenas en Chile: Población por sexo, según pertenencia a pueblos originarios o indígenas, Censo 2002. http://www.ine.cl/estadisticas/sociales/etnias. Accessed 12 December 2017.

InE - Instituto Nacional de Estadícas Chile, 2017b. País Regiones Total: Actualización Población 2002-2012 y Proyecciones 2013-2020. http://www.ine.cl/estadisticas/demograficas-y-vitales. Accessed 12 December 2017.

InE - Instituto Nacional de Estadícas Chile, 2017c. Población total de 15 años y más por situación en la Fuerza de Trabajo, nivel nacional y regional, ambos sexos. http://www.ine.cl/estadisticas/laborales/ene?categoria=Situaci%C3%B3n%20de%20Fuerza%20de%20Trabajo. Accessed 12 December 2017.

InE - Instituto Nacional de Estadícas Chile, 2017d. Primeros resultados definitivos del Censo 2017: un total de 17.574.003 personas fueron efectivamente censadas. http://www.ine.cl/prensa/detalle-prensa/2017/12/22/primeros-resultados-definitivos-del-censo-2017-un-total-de-17.574.003-personas-fueron-efectivamente-censadas. Accessed 27 May 2018.

INSEE - Institut national de la statistique et des études économiques, 2015. Résultats statistiques du recensement : POP1B - Population par sexe et âge. www.insee.fr. Accessed 18 July 2017.

IRENA - International Renewable Energy Agency, 2018. Renewable Capacity Statistics 2018, Abu Dhabi. https://www.irena.org/-/media/Files/IRENA/Agency/Publication/2018/Mar/IRENA_RE_Capacity_Statistics_2018.pdf. Accessed 4 March 2019.

Jacobsson, S., Johnson, A., 2000. The diffusion of renewable energy technology: An analytical framework and key issues for research. Energy Policy 28, 625–640. 10.1016/S0301-4215(00)00041-0.

Jäger, T., McKenna, R., Fichtner, W., 2016. The feasible onshore wind energy potential in Baden-Württemberg: A bottom-up methodology considering socio-economic constraints. Renewable Energy 96, 662–675. 10.1016/j.renene.2016.05.013.

Jenssen, T., König, A., Eltrop, L., 2014. Bioenergy villages in Germany: Bringing a low carbon energy supply for rural areas into practice. Renewable Energy 61, 74–80. 10.1016/j.renene.2012.08.014.

Jobert, A., Laborgne, P., Mimler, S., 2007. Local acceptance of wind energy: Factors of success identified in French and German case studies. Energy Policy 35, 2751–2760. 10.1016/j.enpol.2006.12.005.

Johnson, G., Scholes, K., Whittington, R., 2005. Exploring corporate strategy: [text and cases], 7th ed. Financial Times Prentice Hall, Harlow.

Klaus Novy Institut e.V. & trend: research, 2011. Marktakteure: Erneuerbare-Energien-Anlagen in der Stromerzeugung. https://sverigesradio.se/diverse/appdata/isidor/files/3345/12617.pdf. Accessed 13 November 2018.

Koirala, B.P., Koliou, E., Friege, J., Hakvoort, R.A., Herder, P.M., 2016. Energetic communities for community energy: A review of key issues and trends shaping integrated community energy systems. Renewable and Sustainable Energy Reviews 56, 722–744. 10.1016/j.rser.2015.11.080.

Konsortium OUI Biomasse, 2015. Roadmap für eine nachhaltige Biomassenutzung in der Oberrheinregion, Karlsruhe. http://www.oui-biomasse.info/fileadmin/pdf/Publikationen/Roadmap_OUI_DE.pdf.

Kontogianni, A., Tourkolias, C., Skourtos, M., Damigos, D., 2014. Planning globally, protesting locally: Patterns in community perceptions towards the installation of wind farms. Renewable Energy 66, 170–177. 10.1016/j.renene.2013.11.074.

Kortsch, T., Hildebrand, J., Schweizer-Ries, P., 2015. Acceptance of biomass plants – Results of a longitudinal study in the bioenergy-region Altmark. Renewable Energy 83, 690–697. 10.1016/j.renene.2015.04.059.

Leibenath, M., Lintz, G., 2018. Governance of energy landscapes between pathways, people and politics. Landscape Research 43, 471–475. 10.1080/01426397.2018.1444156.

Little, T. D., Lindenberger, U., Nesselroade, J. R., 1999. On Selecting Indicators for Multivariate Measurement and Modeling with Latent Variables: When ‘Good’ Indicators are Bad and ‘Bad’ Indicators are Good. Psychological Methods 4, 192–211.

Lucke, D., 1995. Akzeptanz: Legitimität in der 'Abstimmungsgesellschaft'. VS Verlag für Sozialwissenschaften; Imprint, Wiesbaden.

Luoma-aho, V., Vos, M., 2010. Towards a more dynamic stakeholder model: Acknowledging multiple issue arenas. Corporate Communications: An International Journal 15, 315–331. 10.1108/13563281011068159.

Markard, J., Stadelmann, M., Truffer, B., 2009. Prospective analysis of technological innovation systems: Identifying technological and organizational development options for biogas in Switzerland. Research Policy 38, 655–667. 10.1016/j.respol.2009.01.013.

McKenna, R., 2018. The double-edged sword of decentralized energy autonomy. Energy Policy 113, 747–750. 10.1016/j.enpol.2017.11.033.

McKenna, R., Herbes, C., Fichtner, W., 2015. Energieautarkie: Vorschlag einer Arbeitsdefinition als Grundlage für die Bewertung konkreter Projekte und Szenarien. Zeitschrift für Energiewirtschaft 39, 235–252. 10.1007/s12398-015-0164-1.

McKenna, R., Jäger, T., Fichtner, W., 2014. Energieautarkie – ausgewählte Ansätze und Praxiserfahrungen im deutschsprachigen Raum. uwf 22, 241–247. 10.1007/s00550-014-0339-y.

McKenna, R., Merkel, E., Fichtner, W., 2016. Energy autonomy in residential buildings: A techno-economic model-based analysis of the scale effects. Applied Energy. 10.1016/j.apenergy.2016.03.062.

Ministerio de Desarrollo Social, 2016. Vivienda y Etorno: Síntesis de Resultados (Casen 2015). http://observatorio.ministeriodesarrollosocial.gob.cl/casen-multidimensional/casen/docs/CASEN_2015_Resultados_vivienda_y_entorno.pdf. Accessed 12 December 2017.

Ministerio de Energía, 2016. Informe de Resultados, Encuesta Nacional de Energía. http://www.energia.gob.cl/tema-de-interes/encuesta-nacional-de-energia-2016. Accessed 23 August 2018.

Ministerio de Energía, 2018. Energy 2050-Chile's energy policy executive summary. http://www.energia2050.cl/wp-content/uploads/2016/08/Executive-summary.pdf. Accessed 19 September 2018.

Molnarova, K., Sklenicka, P., Stiborek, J., Svobodova, K., Salek, M., Brabec, E., 2012. Visual preferences for wind turbines: Location, numbers and respondent characteristics. Applied Energy 92, 269–278. 10.1016/j.apenergy.2011.11.001.

Müller, M.O., Stämpfli, A., Dold, U., Hammer, T., 2011. Energy autarky: A conceptual framework for sustainable regional development. Energy Policy 39, 5800–5810. 10.1016/j.enpol.2011.04.019.

Musall, F.D., Kuik, O., 2011. Local acceptance of renewable energy—A case study from southeast Germany. Energy Policy 39, 3252–3260. 10.1016/j.enpol.2011.03.017.

Myers, T.A., 2011. HOTDECK: An SPSS Tool for Handling Missing Data: Goodbye, Listwise Deletion: Presenting Hot Deck Imputation as an Easy and Effective Tool for Handling Missing Data. Communication Methods and Measures 5, 297–310.

Olander, S., 2007. Stakeholder impact analysis in construction project management. Construction Management and Economics 25, 277–287. 10.1080/01446190600879125.

OSM - OpenStreetMap, 2014. OpenStreetMap. http://www.openstreetmap.org. Accessed 12 November 2014.

Perlaviciute, G., Steg, L., 2014. Contextual and psychological factors shaping evaluations and acceptability of energy alternatives: Integrated review and research agenda. Renewable and Sustainable Energy Reviews 35, 361–381. 10.1016/j.rser.2014.04.003.

Petrova, M.A., 2016. From NIMBY to acceptance: Toward a novel framework — VESPA — For organizing and interpreting community concerns. Renewable Energy 86, 1280–1294. 10.1016/j.renene.2015.09.047.

PNUD - Programa de las Naciones Unidas Para el Desarrollo, 2017. Desiguales. Orígenes, cambios y desafíos de la brecha social en Chile., Santiago de Chile.

Quaschning, V., 2015. Regenerative Energiesysteme. Carl Hanser Verlag GmbH & Co. KG, München.

Rae, C., Bradley, F., 2012. Energy autonomy in sustainable communities-A review of key issues. Renewable and Sustainable Energy Reviews 16, 6497–6506. 10.1016/j.rser.2012.08.002.

Rand, J., Hoen, B., 2017. Thirty years of North American wind energy acceptance research: What have we learned? Energy Research & Social Science 29, 135–148. 10.1016/j.erss.2017.05.019.

Rau, I., Schweizer-Ries, P., Hildebrand, J., 2012. Participation: The Silver Bullet for the Acceptance of Renewable Energies?, in: Sigrun Kabisch, Anna Kunath, Petra Schweizer-Ries, Annett Steinführer (Eds.), Vulnerability, Risks, and Complexity. Impacts of Global Change. Hogrefe.

Rau, I., Zoellner, J., 2008. Akzeptanz erneuerbarer Energien und sozialwissenschaftliche Fragen: Projektabschlussbericht.

REN 21, 2017. Renewables 2017: global status report. http://www.ren21.net/wp-content/uploads/2017/06/17-8399_GSR_2017_Full_Report_0621_Opt.pdf. Accessed 13 September 2018.

REScoop, 2017. European Tour. https://rescoop.eu/european-tour. Accessed 17 August 2017.

RES-LEGAL, 2017a. Promotion in France. http://www.res-legal.eu/search-by-country/france/tools-list/c/france/s/res-e/t/promotion/sum/132/lpid/131/. Accessed 5 March 2019.

RES-LEGAL, 2017b. Promotion in Germany. http://www.res-legal.eu/search-by-country/germany/tools-list/c/germany/s/res-e/t/promotion/sum/136/lpid/135/. Accessed 5 March 2019.

RES-LEGAL, 2017c. Promotion in Switzerland. http://www.res-legal.eu/search-by-country/switzerland/single/s/res-e/t/promotion/aid/feed-in-tariff-1/lastp/396/. Accessed 5 March 2019.

Rocío Parraguez, 2014. Aprueban construcción de Central Bioenergética en Cabrero pese a rechazo de la comunidad. https://www.biobiochile.cl/noticias/2014/06/10/sea-bio-bio-aprueba-construccion-de-central-bioenergetica-en-cabrero-pese-a-rechazo-de-la-comunidad.shtml. Accessed 15 May 2018.

Rodrigo Fuentes, 2017. Celebran renuncia definitiva de Energía Austral a proyecto Hidroeléctrico Río Cuervo. http://radio.uchile.cl/2017/08/31/celebran-renuncia-definitiva-de-energia-austral-a-proyecto-hidroelectrico-rio-cuervo/. Accessed 15 May 2018.

Rodríguez-Monroy, C., Mármol-Acitores, G., Nilsson-Cifuentes, G., 2018. Electricity generation in Chile using non-conventional renewable energy sources – A focus on biomass. Renewable and Sustainable Energy Reviews 81, 937–945. 10.1016/j.rser.2017.08.059.

Roser, F., 2011. Entwicklung einer Methode zur großflächigen rechnergestützten Analyse des landschaftsästhetischen Potenzials: Ph.D. Dissertation. Department Architektur und Stadtplanung. Weißensee Verlag, Berlin, Germany.

RTE - Réseau de transport d'électricité, 2016. 2015 Annual Electricity Report. http://www.rte-france.com/sites/default/files/2015_annual_electricity_report.pdf. Accessed 29 September 2017.

RTE - Réseau de transport d'électricité, 2017. Electricity Report 2017. https://www.rte-france.com/sites/default/files/rte_elec_report_2017.pdf. Accessed 8 March 2019.

Sarstedt, M., Mooi, E., 2014. A concise guide to market research: The process, data, and methods using IBM SPSS Statistics, 2nd ed. Springer Berlin Heidelberg, Germany.

Savage, G.T., Nix, T.W., Whitehead, C.J., Blair, J.D., 1991. Strategies for assessing and managing organizational stakeholders. Academy of Management Perspectives 5, 61–75. 10.5465/ame.1991.4274682.

Scheer, D., Konrad, W., Scheel, O., 2013. Public evaluation of electricity technologies and future low-carbon portfolios in Germany and the USA. Energy, Sustainability and Society 3, 8. 10.1186/2192-0567-3-8.

Schumacher, K., Glöser-Chahoud, S., Schultmann, F., 2019a. Acceptance of Bioenergy in Chile – an Empirical Analysis of Public Opinion, in: 5th Latin American Congress on Biorefinieries - From Laboratory to Industrial Practice, Concepción, Chile. January 7-9, 2019.

Schumacher, K., Krones, F., McKenna, R., Schultmann, F., 2019b. Public acceptance of renewable energies and energy autonomy: A comparative study in the French, German and Swiss Upper Rhine region. Energy Policy 126, 315–332. 10.1016/j.enpol.2018.11.032.

Schumacher, K., Schultmann, F., 2017. Local Acceptance of Biogas Plants: A Comparative Study in the Trinational Upper Rhine Region. Waste and Biomass Valorization 8, 2393–2412. 10.1007/s12649-016-9802-z.

Schweizer-Ries, P., 2008. Energy sustainable communities: Environmental psychological investigations. Energy Policy 36, 4126–4135. 10.1016/j.enpol.2008.06.021.

Schweizer-Ries, P., Rau, I., Nolting, K., Rupp, J., Keppler, D., 2010. Aktivität und Teilhabe - Akzeptanz Erneuerbarer Energien durch Beteiligung steigern: Projektabschlussbericht. https://www.tu-berlin.de/fileadmin/f27/PDFs/Forschung/Abschlussbericht_Aktivitaet_Teilhabe_format.pdf.

Seresinhe, C.I., Moat, H.S., Preis, T., 2017a. Quantifying scenic areas using crowdsourced data. Environment and Planning B: Urban Analytics and City Science 45, 567–582. 10.1177/0265813516687302.

Seresinhe, C.I., Preis, T., Moat, H.S., 2017b. Using deep learning to quantify the beauty of outdoor places. Royal Society open science 4, 170170. 10.1098/rsos.170170.

Siems, E., Seuring, S., 2018. Stakeholder management in Chilean biomass supply chains. 25th international EurOMA, 2018, Budapest, Hungary.

Soini, K., Pouta, E., Salmiovirta, M., Uusitalo, M., Kivinen, T., 2011. Local residents' perceptions of energy landscape: The case of transmission lines. Land Use Policy 28, 294–305. 10.1016/j.landusepol.2010.06.009.

Soland, M., Steimer, N., Walter, G., 2013. Local acceptance of existing biogas plants in Switzerland. Energy Policy 61, 802–810. 10.1016/j.enpol.2013.06.111.

Sonnberger, M., Ruddat, M., 2017. Local and socio-political acceptance of wind farms in Germany. Technology in Society. 10.1016/j.techsoc.2017.07.005.

Sovacool, B.K., 2014. What are we doing here? Analyzing fifteen years of energy scholarship and proposing a social science research agenda. Energy Research & Social Science 1, 1–29. 10.1016/j.erss.2014.02.003.

Sovacool, B.K., Hess, D.J., 2017. Ordering theories: Typologies and conceptual frameworks for sociotechnical change. Social studies of science 47, 704–750. 10.1177/0306312717709363.

Sovacool, B.K., Lakshmi Ratan, P., 2012. Conceptualizing the acceptance of wind and solar electricity. Renewable and Sustainable Energy Reviews 16, 5268–5279. 10.1016/j.rser.2012.04.048.

Statista, 2014. Distribution of emissions of greenhouse gases by industry sector worldwide as of 2014. https://www.statista.com/statistics/270723/distribution-of-global-greenhouse-gas-emissions-by-sector-worldwide. Accessed 8 March 2019.

Statistisches Bundesamt, 2017. Bruttostromerzeugung in Deutschland für 2015 bis 2017. https://www.destatis.de/DE/ZahlenFakten/Wirtschaftsbereiche/Energie/Erzeugung/Tabellen/Bruttostromerzeugung.html. Accessed 4 March 2019.

Statistisches Landesamt Baden-Württemberg, 2011. Bevölkerungsfortschreibung, Basis Zensus 2011. www.statistik.baden-wuerttemberg.de. Accessed 15 April 2016.

Steiger, O., Bühler, S., Hugi, C., Schumacher, K., Daniel, F.-J., Thomson, M., 2015. OUI Biomasse Project Report: Report on biomass value chains in the URR. www.oui-biomasse.info. Accessed 11 July 2018.

Sütterlin, B., Siegrist, M., 2017. Public acceptance of renewable energy technologies from an abstract versus concrete perspective and the positive imagery of solar power. Energy Policy 106, 356–366. 10.1016/j.enpol.2017.03.061.

Swissnuclear, 2019. Gestzliche Regelung der Laufzeiten. http://www.swissnuclear.ch/de/gesetzliche-regelung-der-laufzeiten-_content---1--1056--188.html. Accessed 25 April 2019.

Thomas, W.I., Swaine Thomas, D., 1928. The child in America. Knopf, Oxford, England.

Toke, D., BREUKERS, S., Wolsink, M., 2008. Wind power deployment outcomes: How can we account for the differences? Renewable and Sustainable Energy Reviews 12, 1129–1147. 10.1016/j.rser.2006.10.021.

Torres, R., Azócar, G., Rojas, J., Montecinos, A., Paredes, P., 2015. Vulnerability and resistance to neoliberal environmental changes: An assessment of agriculture and forestry in the Biobio region of Chile (1974–2014). Geoforum 60, 107–122. 10.1016/j.geoforum.2014.12.013.

Torres-Salinas, R., García, G.A., Henríquez, N.C., Zambrano-Bigiarini, M., COSTA, T., BOLIN, B.O., 2016. Forestry development, water scarcity, and the Mapuche protest for environmental justice in Chile. Ambiente & Sociedade 19, 121–144. 10.1590/1809-4422ASOC150134R1V1912016.

U.S. Department of Commerce, 2016. 2016 Top Markets Report Renewable Energy: Country Case Study: Chile. https://www.trade.gov/topmarkets/pdf/Renewable_Energy_Chile.pdf. Accessed 22 May 2018.

UBA - Umweltbundesamt, 2015. Häufige Fragen zur Energiewende. https://www.umweltbundesamt.de/themen/klima-energie/klimaschutz-energiepolitik-in-deutschland/haeufige-fragen-zur-energiewende#textpart-1. Accessed 8 March 2019.

UNDP - United Nations Development Programme, 2018. Human Development Indices and Indicators: 2018 Statistical Update. http://hdr.undp.org/sites/all/themes/hdr_theme/country-notes/CHL.pdf. Accessed 8 March 2019.

UN - United Nations, 2019. Sustainable Development Goals: Ensure access to affordable, reliable, sustainable and modern energy. https://www.un.org/sustainabledevelopment/energy/. Accessed 15 March 2019.

Upham, P., 2009. Applying environmental-behaviour concepts to renewable energy siting controversy: Reflections on a longitudinal bioenergy case study. Energy Policy 37, 4273–4283. 10.1016/j.enpol.2009.05.027.

Upham, P., Oltra, C., Boso, À., 2015. Towards a cross-paradigmatic framework of the social acceptance of energy systems. Energy Research & Social Science 8, 100–112. 10.1016/j.erss.2015.05.003.

Upham, P., Shackley, S., 2006. The case of a proposed 21.5MWe biomass gasifier in Winkleigh, Devon: Implications for governance of renewable energy planning. Energy Policy 34, 2161–2172. 10.1016/j.enpol.2005.04.001.

Upham, P., Shackley, S., 2007. Local public opinion of a proposed 21.5MW(e) biomass gasifier in Devon: Questionnaire survey results. Biomass and Bioenergy 31, 433–441. 10.1016/j.biombioe.2007.01.017.

Upreti, B.R., 2004. Conflict over biomass energy development in the United Kingdom: some observations and lessons from England and Wales. Energy Policy 32, 785–800. 10.1016/S0301-4215(02)00342-7.

Upreti, B.R., van der Horst, D., 2004. National renewable energy policy and local opposition in the UK: the failed development of a biomass electricity plant. Biomass and Bioenergy 26, 61–69. 10.1016/S0961-9534(03)00099-0.

UVEK - Eidgenössisches Departement für Umwelt, Verkehr, Energie und Kommunikation, 2017. Ausstieg aus der Kernenergie. https://www.uvek.admin.ch/uvek/de/home/energie/energiestrategie-2050/kernenergie.html. Accessed 29 September 2017.

van der Horst, D., 2007. NIMBY or not?: Exploring the relevance of location and the politics of voiced opinions in renewable energy siting controversies. Energy Policy 35, 2705–2714. 10.1016/j.enpol.2006.12.012.

van Holt, T., Binford, M.W., Portier, K.M., Vergara, R., 2016. A stand of trees does not a forest make: Tree plantations and forest transitions. Land Use Policy 56, 147–157. 10.1016/j.landusepol.2016.04.015.

Verband Schweizerischer Elektrizitätsunternehmen, 2019. Produktion & Strommix. https://www.strom.ch/de/energiewissen/produktion-und-handel/produktion-strommix. Accessed 8 March 2019.

Walker, G., 2008. What are the barriers and incentives for community-owned means of energy production and use? Energy Policy 36, 4401–4405. 10.1016/j.enpol.2008.09.032.

Walker, G., Devine-Wright, P., Hunter, S., High, H., Evans, B., 2010. Trust and community: Exploring the meanings, contexts and dynamics of community renewable energy. Energy Policy 38, 2655–2663. 10.1016/j.enpol.2009.05.055.

Warren, C.R., Lumsden, C., O'Dowd, S., Birnie, R.V., 2005. 'Green On Green': Public perceptions of wind power in Scotland and Ireland. Journal of Environmental Planning and Management 48, 853–875. 10.1080/09640560500294376.

Watts Casimis, D., Pérez Odeh, R., 2018. Non-Conventional Renewable Energies in the Chilean Electricity Market.

Westermann, R., 1985. Empirical Tests of Scale Type for Individual Ratings. Applied Psychological Measurement 9, 265–274. 10.1177/014662168500900304.

Wolff, V., Muller, J., 2013. Etat des lieux des gisements et de la gestion de la matière organique en Alsace, perspectives de développement des installations de production de biogaz. Rapport final. http://www.energivie.info/sites/default/files/documents/rapport-final-biogaz.pdf. Accessed 15 April 2015.

Wolsink, M., 2000. Wind power and the NIMBY-myth: institutional capacity and the limited significance of public support. Renewable Energy 21, 49–64. 10.1016/S0960-1481(99)00130-5.

Wolsink, M., 2017a. Co-production in distributed generation: Renewable energy and creating space for fitting infrastructure within landscapes. Landscape Research 43, 542–561. 10.1080/01426397.2017.1358360.

Wolsink, M. (Ed.), 2017b. Framing in renewable energy policies: a glossary.

Wolsink, M., 2018a. Social acceptance revisited: Gaps, questionable trends, and an auspicious perspective. Energy Research & Social Science 46, 287–295. 10.1016/j.erss.2018.07.034.

Wolsink, M., 2018b. Social acceptance, lost objects, and obsession with the 'public'—The pressing need for enhanced conceptual and methodological rigor. Energy Research & Social Science. 10.1016/j.erss.2018.12.006.

Wüste, A., 2013. Akzeptanz verschiedener Bioenergienutzungskonzepte und Erfolgsfaktoren beim Ausbau dezentraler Bioenergieprojekte in Deutschland, 1st ed. Cuvillier, Göttingen, 156 S.

Wüste, A., Schmuck, P., 2012. Bioenergy Villages and Regions in Germany: An Interview Study with Initiators of Communal Bioenergy Projects on the Success Factors for Restructuring the Energy Supply of the Community. Sustainability 4, 244–256. 10.3390/su4020244.

Wüste, A., Schmuck, P., 2013. Social Acceptance of Bioenergy Use and the Success Factors of Communal Bioenergy Projects, in: Ruppert, H., Kappas, M., Ibendorf, J. (Eds.), Sustainable Bioenergy Production - An Integrated Approach. Springer Netherlands, Dordrecht, pp. 293–318.

Wüstenhagen, R., Wolsink, M., Bürer, M.J., 2007. Social acceptance of renewable energy innovation: An introduction to the concept. Energy Policy 35, 2683–2691. 10.1016/j.enpol.2006.12.001.

Zaunbrecher, B.S., Ziefle, M., 2016. Integrating acceptance-relevant factors into wind power planning: A discussion. Sustainable Cities and Society 27, 307–314. 10.1016/j.scs.2016.08.018.

Zoellner, J., Schweizer-Ries, P., Wemheuer, C., 2008. Public acceptance of renewable energies: Results from case studies in Germany. Energy Policy 36, 4136–4141. 10.1016/j.enpol.2008.06.026.

PRODUKTION UND ENERGIE

Karlsruher Institut für Technologie (KIT)
Institut für Industriebetriebslehre und Industrielle Produktion
Deutsch-Französisches Institut für Umweltforschung

ISSN 2194-2404

Band 1 **National Integrated Assessment Modelling zur Bewertung umweltpolitischer Instrumente.**
Entwicklung des otello-Modellsystems und dessen Anwendung auf die Bundesrepublik Deutschland. 2012
ISBN 978-3-86644-853-7

Band 2 **Erhöhung der Energie- und Ressourceneffizienz und Reduzierung der Treibhausgasemissionen in der Eisen-, Stahl- und Zinkindustrie (ERESTRE).** 2013
ISBN 978-3-86644-857-5

Band 3 Frederik Trippe
Techno-ökonomische Bewertung alternativer Verfahrenskonfigurationen zur Herstellung von Biomass-to-Liquid (BtL) Kraftstoffen und Chemikalien. 2013
ISBN 978-3-7315-0031-5

Band 4 Dogan Keles
Uncertainties in energy markets and their consideration in energy storage evaluation. 2013
ISBN 978-3-7315-0046-9

Band 5 Heidi Ursula Heinrichs
Analyse der langfristigen Auswirkungen von Elektromobilität auf das deutsche Energiesystem im europäisschen Energieverbund. 2013
ISBN 978-3-7315-0131-2

Die Bände sind unter www.ksp.kit.edu als PDF frei verfügbar oder als Druckausgabe zu bestellen.

Band 6 Julian Stengel
Akteursbasierte Simulation der energetischen Modernisierung des Wohngebäudebestands in Deutschland. 2014
ISBN 978-3-7315-0236-4

Band 7 Sonja Babrowski
Bedarf und Verteilung elektrischer Tagesspeicher im zukünftigen deutschen Energiesystem. 2015
ISBN 978-3-7315-0306-4

Band 8 Marius Wunder
Integration neuer Technologien der Bitumenkalthandhabung in die Versorgungskette. 2015
ISBN 978-3-7315-0319-4

Band 9 Felix Teufel
Speicherbedarf und dessen Auswirkungen auf die Energiewirtschaft bei Umsetzung der politischen Ziele zur Energiewende. 2015
ISBN 978-3-7315-0341-5

Band 10 D. Keles, L. Renz, A. Bublitz, F. Zimmermann, M. Genoese, W. Fichtner, H. Höfling, F. Sensfuß, J. Winkler
Zukunftsfähige Designoptionen für den deutschen Strommarkt: Ein Vergleich des Energy-only-Marktes mit Kapazitätsmärkten. 2016
ISBN 978-3-7315-0453-5

Band 11 Patrick Breun
Ein Ansatz zur Bewertung klimapolitischer Instrumente am Beispiel der Metallerzeugung und -verarbeitung. 2016
ISBN 978-3-7315-0494-8

Band 12 P. Ringler, H. Schermeyer, M. Ruppert, M. Hayn, V. Bertsch, D. Keles, W. Fichtner
Decentralized Energy Systems, Market Integration, Optimization. 2016
ISBN 978-3-7315-0505-1

Band 13 Marian Hayn
Modellgestützte Analyse neuer Stromtarife für Haushalte unter Berücksichtigung bedarfsorientierter Versorgungssicherheitsniveaus. 2016
ISBN 978-3-7315-0499-3

Band 14 Frank Schätter
Decision support system for a reactive management of disaster-caused supply chain disturbances. 2016
ISBN 978-3-7315-0530-3

Band 15 Robert Kunze
Techno-ökonomische Planung energetischer Wohngebäudemodernisierungen: Ein gemischt-ganzzahliges lineares Optimierungsmodell auf Basis einer vollständigen Finanzplanung. 2016
ISBN 978-3-7315-0531-0

Band 16 A. Kühlen, J. Stengel, R. Volk, F. Schultmann, M. Reinhardt, H. Schlick, S. Haghsheno, A. Mettke, S. Asmus, S. Schmidt, J. Harzheim
ISA: Immissionsschutz beim Abbruch - Minimierung von Umweltbelastungen (Lärm, Staub, Erschütterungen) beim Abbruch von Hoch-/Tiefbauten und Schaffung hochwertiger Recyclingmöglichkeiten für Materialien aus Gebäudeabbruch. 2018
ISBN 978-3-7315-0534-1

Band 17 Konrad Zimmer
Entscheidungsunterstützung zur Auswahl und Steuerung von Lieferanten und Lieferketten unter Berücksichtigung von Nachhaltigkeitsaspekten. 2016
ISBN 978-3-7315-0537-2

Band 18 Kira Schumacher, Wolf Fichtner and Frank Schultmann (Eds.)
Innovations for sustainable biomass utilisation in the Upper Rhine Region. 2017
ISBN 978-3-7315-0423-8

Band 19 Sophia Radloff
Modellgestützte Bewertung der Nutzung von Biokohle als Bodenzusatz in der Landwirtschaft. 2017
ISBN 978-3-7315-0559-4

Band 20 Rebekka Volk
Proactive-reactive, robust scheduling and capacity planning of deconstruction projects under uncertainty. 2017
ISBN 978-3-7315-0592-1

Band 21 Erik Merkel
Analyse und Bewertung des Elektrizitätssystems und des Wärmesystems der Wohngebäude in Deutschland. 2017
ISBN 978-3-7315-0636-2

Band 22 Rebekka Volk (Hrsg.)
Entwicklung eines mobilen Systems zur Erfassung und Erschließung von Ressourceneffizienzpotenzialen beim Rückbau von Infrastruktur und Produkten („ResourceApp"): Schlussbericht des Forschungsvorhabens. 2017
ISBN 978-3-7315-0653-9

Band 23 Thomas Kaschub
Batteriespeicher in Haushalten unter Berücksichtigung von Photovoltaik, Elektrofahrzeugen und Nachfragesteuerung. 2017
ISBN 978-3-7315-0688-1

Band 24 Felix Hübner, Rebekka Volk, Oktay Secer, Daniel Kühn, Peter Sahre, Reinhard Knappik, Frank Schultmann, Sascha Gentes, Petra von Both
Modellentwicklung eines ganzheitlichen Projektmanagementsystems für kerntechnische Rückbauprojekte (MogaMaR): Schlussbericht des Forschungsvorhabens. 2018
ISBN 978-3-7315-0762-8

Band 25 Karoline Fath
Technical and economic potential for photovoltaic systems on buildings. 2018
ISBN 978-3-7315-0787-1

Band 26 Ann-Kathrin Müller
Decision Support for Biomass Value Chains for the Production of Biochemicals Considering Uncertainties. 2018
ISBN 978-3-7315-0820-5

Band 27 Jonatan J. Gómez Vilchez
The Impact of Electric Cars on Oil Demand and Greenhouse Gas Emissions in Key Markets. 2019
ISBN 978-3-7315-0914-1

Band 28 Carmen Schiel
Real Option Based Appraisal of Environmental Investments – An Assessment of NO_x Emission Control Techniques in Large Combustion Plants. 2019
ISBN 978-3-7315-0925-7

Band 29 Hannes Schwarz
Optimierung der Investitions- und Einsatzplanung dezentraler Energiesysteme unter Unsicherheit. 2019
ISBN 978-3-7315-0919-6

Band 30 Kai Mainzer
Analyse und Optimierung urbaner Energiesysteme – Entwicklung und Anwendung eines übertragbaren Modellierungswerkzeugs zur nachhaltigen Systemgestaltung. 2019
ISBN 978-3-7315-0882-3

Band 31 Rupert Hartel, Viktor Slednev, Hasan Ümitcan Yilmaz, Armin Ardone, Dogan Keles, Wolf Fichtner, Anke Eßer, Marian Klobasa, Matthias Kühnbach, Pia Manz, Joachim Globisch, Rainer Elsland, Martin Wietschel (Hrsg.)
Dekarbonisierung des Energiesystems durch verstärkten Einsatz erneuerbaren Stroms im Wärme-, Verkehrs- und Industriesektor bei gleichzeitigen Stilllegungen von Kraftwerken – Auswirkungen auf die Versorgungssicherheit in Süddeutschland. 2019
ISBN 978-3-7315-0879-3

Band 32 Rebekka Volk, Richard Müller, Frank Schultmann, Jérémy Rimbon, Thomas Lützkendorf, Joachim Reinhardt, Florian Knappe
Stofffluss- und Akteursmodell als Grundlage für ein aktives Ressourcenmanagement im Bauwesen von Baden-Württemberg „StAR-Bau" – Schlussbericht des Forschungsvorhabens. 2019
ISBN 978-3-7315-0858-8

Band 33 Felix Hübner
Planung und Modellierung des Rückbaus kerntechnischer Anlagen unter der Berücksichtigung von Unsicherheiten – Ein Beispiel zur Planung von Großprojekten. 2019
ISBN 978-3-7315-0911-0

Band 34 Kira Schumacher
Public acceptance of renewable energies – an empirical investigation across countries and technologies. 2019
ISBN 978-3-7315-0948-6